THE PRESS EFFECT

THE PRESS EFFECT

Politicians, Journalists, and the Stories That Shape the Political World

KATHLEEN HALL JAMIESON
&
PAUL WALDMAN

OXFORD
UNIVERSITY PRESS

2003

OXFORD

UNIVERSITY PRESS

Oxford   New York
Auckland   Bangkok   Buenos Aires   Cape Town   Chennai
Dar es Salaam   Delhi   Hong Kong   Istanbul   Karachi   Kolkata
Kuala Lumpur   Madrid   Melbourne   Mexico City   Mumbai   Nairobi
São Paulo   Shanghai   Taipei   Tokyo   Toronto

Copyright © 2003 by Kathleen Hall Jamieson and Paul Waldman.

Published by Oxford University Press, Inc.
198 Madison Avenue, New York, New York 10016

www.oup.com

Oxford is a registered trademark of Oxford University Press

Library of Congress Cataloging-in-Publication Data

Jamieson, Kathleen Hall.
The press effect : politicians, journalists,
and the stories that shape the political world /
Kathleen Hall Jamieson and Paul Waldman.
p. cm.   Includes index.
ISBN 0-19-515277-8
1. Journalism—Objectivity—United States.
2. United States—Politics and government—1993–2001.
I. Waldman, Paul. II. Title.
PN4888.O25 J36 2002   071'.3—dc21   2002009845

1 3 5 7 9 8 6 4 2
Printed in the United States of America
on acid-free paper

To Robert,
who keeps ships afloat.

To Al Bennett,
who opened the mind
of every student he taught.

Contents

Acknowledgments

We wish to thank Annenberg School for Communication staff members Sharon Black, Nikki Dooner, Joshua Gesell, Deborah Porter, Deborah Stinnett, and Debra Williams for their help. The Annenberg 2000 Survey, on which much of our analysis of public opinion is based, was designed, executed, and analyzed with Richard Johnston, Michael Hagen, Kate Kenski, Princeton Survey Research staff members Christopher Adasiewicz and Mary McIntosh, and the folks at Schulman, Ronca & Bucuvalas. We are grateful to our editor Tim Bartlett for fine-tuning ideas, suggesting new directions, tempering our more extravagant academic impulses, and keeping the manuscript on course; and to Oxford stalwart Laura Brown, who has kept Kathleen sane through seven Oxford books.

Introduction

In early December 2001, journalists were told by Bush administration officials that an about-to-be-released videotape of Osama Bin Laden not only provided evidence that Bin Laden planned the September 11 attacks, but included a detail worthy of a James Bond villain: Even some of those about to die in service to his cause were unaware that the plan called for their deaths. As CNN's John King reported, administration officials said the video showed Bin Laden "talking about how, and one official says laughing when he does so, that many of those hijackers did not know, when they were planning those attacks, that they indeed would die in what ultimately became suicide hijackings."

From the tape itself, however, reporters learned that what they had been told was incorrect. On the tape, Bin Laden actually said that the hijackers hadn't known the details of the operation until just before it occurred but did know that they were participating in a "martyrdom operation," a subtle but important nuance. Yet the news reports did not charge that administration officials had misled them about the details of the tape.

Why did reporters not call the officials to account? Because the "main story" of the tape—that Bin Laden admitted planning the attacks—was so significant, the press may have decided that the incidental falsehood was not noteworthy. We suspect that it was dismissed as well because the larger story of the time, a story embraced by Republicans, Democrats, citizens of small towns and large cities, and reporters alike, focused on the terrible crime that Bin Laden had engineered and his identity, in the words of President Bush, as "the Evil One." Thus even if he hadn't actually uttered the words, it was plausible that he might have, and there was comfort in believing that all but the ringleaders had been deceived by the Devil incarnate. If some of the hijacking terrorists who boarded the planes on September 11 didn't realize that they were about to end the lives of hundreds along with their own, then the fact that they boarded at all was somehow more comprehensible. Even after the tape was broadcast and transcribed, some later news reports repeated the original erroneous claim. For instance, on March 13, 2002, NBC reporter John Hockenberry said on *Dateline*, "There is this famous video of Osama Bin Laden talking about how some people on the airplanes in New York and Washington did not even know that they were going to die, had no idea that this was a suicide mission." Because it was not corrected, the inaccuracy had become part of the historical memory of some journalists, and could thus be repeated.

This is one small case in which an inaccuracy was passed from political actors to reporters and on to the public. Because it was not corrected, the inaccuracy persisted in public memory. Officials were able to control the frame because they held a temporary monopoly on relevant information; when that monopoly disappeared, other facts were deemed to be of greater consequence and a continuing, compelling narrative overwhelmed any impulse reporters might have had to address the question of whether they and the public had been misled.

In a complex world, what the public knows and understands is a collection of facts both small and large, and stories both fleeting and persistent. In describing the process by which real-world events are translated into public knowledge through journalism, we use two primary metaphors, one novel and one common in the study of communication and public opinion. In order for an event to reach the public, it must first be viewed by reporters, then related in stories. To describe reporters' views of the world they are asked to explain (we use the metaphor of *lenses*) the shifting perspectives that color what reporters see of the world at a given moment. To describe the news coverage that results from those views, we use the metaphor of *frames*, the structures underlying the depictions that the public reads, hears, and watches.

Because they determine the content of news, those lenses and frames continuously shape what citizens know, understand, and believe about the world. In *The Press Effect*, we make sense of moments such as the Bin Laden tape and their effects on public knowledge by examining the various lenses through which reporters saw events and the frames they deployed as they told us stories about the meaning of politics in a year of presidential recounts and terrorist attacks. In order to do so, we will concentrate on the way truth and falsehood pass through news frames and the identifiable patterns of coverage that make certain interpretations more likely. Just as there are countless events reporters could write about each day, there are many more pieces of information than could possibly fit into a single story. The metaphor of a frame—a fixed border that includes some things and excludes others—describes the way information is arranged and packaged in news stories. The story's frame determines what information is included and what is ignored.

As scholar Robert Entman defined them, frames "*define problems*—determine what a causal agent is doing with what costs and benefits, usually measured in terms of common cultural values; *diagnose causes*—identify the forces creating the problem; *make moral judgments*—evaluate causal agents and their effects; and *suggest remedies*—offer and justify treatments for the problems and predict their likely effects."[1] Frames tell us what is important, what the range of acceptable debate on a topic is, and when an issue has been resolved. By choosing a common frame to describe an event, condition, or political personage, journalists shape public opinion. As communication scholar Oscar Gandy wrote, frames "are used purposefully to direct attention and then to guide the processing of information so that a preferred reading of the facts comes to dominate public understanding."[2] As scholars studying framing have argued, the fact that news frames help determine what the public knows and believes opens opportunities for interested parties to exert influence by advancing some frames and downplaying others.[3] Because reporters are dependent on those same actors to provide them with information and quotes, they can at times be susceptible to manipulation.[4] Political actors understand which frames are more amenable to their position; the greater the power an actor holds and the more central her comments are to a story, the more success she may have in getting her preferred frame adopted. In the case of the Bin Laden tape, the operative frame concerned the certainty and details of his guilt; questions of the administration's truthfulness were set aside for another day.

Journalists help mold public understanding and opinion by deciding what is important and what may be ignored, what is subject to debate and what is beyond question, and what is true and false. In order to make those judgments, they have to navigate an often confusing thicket of information and assertions. "Facts" can be difficult to discern and relate to the public, particularly in a context in which the news is driven by politicians and other interested parties who selectively offer some pieces of information while suppressing others.

Just as politicians sometimes succeed in deceiving the public, journalists sometimes fail in their task of discovering and describing the knowable, relevant information at play in public discourse. Our goal in this book is to examine those negotiations and battles over what will be accepted as fact, investigate where journalists succeed and fail, and offer some recommendations for improvements in reporting that we believe would result in a better-informed citizenry and a closer tie between campaigning and governing.

We would not go as far as some postmodernists who assert that all we know is socially constructed and thus "truth" does not exist in any meaningful way. Nor would we argue that the truth is out there, if only journalists would find it. In public discourse, when different stories compete for primacy each may embody some version of the truth. But this does not mean that some stories are not more true than others, and that there are not some facts on which most can agree. The critical variable is usually not the facts themselves but the manner in which they are arranged and interpreted in order to construct narratives describing the political world. Between these two extreme positions—that there is no such thing as truth, and that there is but a single truth that simply waits to be found—lies the terrain journalists attempt to chart every day.

As critic Kenneth Burke noted, language does our thinking for us. Language choices not only reflect individual disposition but influence the course of policy as well. Tax cuts or tax relief? Religious or faith-based? Death penalty or execution? Estate tax or death tax? Civilian deaths or collateral damage? In the early stages of almost any policy debate, one can find a battle over which terms will be chosen. Because the terms we use to describe the world determine the ways we see it, those who control the language control the argument, and those who control the argument are more likely to successfully translate belief into policy.

When competing politicians or groups adopt the same language, the press usually transmits the agreed-upon words to us. But when competing sides feud over language, the vocabulary chosen and legitimized by reporters and editors is likely to both frame debates and ultimately to embody unchallenged assumptions that facilitate some arguments and undercut others. For example, in the mid-1990s anti-abortion activists made an issue out of a procedure known to medical professionals as "intact dilation and extraction." By naming it "partial birth abortion," they attempted to move it both out of the medical realm and into the policy realm and out of impersonal technical technology into emotionally evocative language. Early in the feud over the description, the press used the words "so-called" before one or the other of the labels to characterize each as a contested phrase. Ultimately, the descriptive power of "partial birth abortion" took hold and became the phrase used more often than alternatives by reporters, an important linguistic victory for the "pro-life" forces. The U.S. Congress and legislatures in twenty-nine states passed laws banning or restricting "partial birth abortion."[5]

The language, stories, and images in which politics is cast by those in power, those seeking power, and by the press become filters through which we make sense of the political world. Citizens expect that the press will approach the competing frames offered by interested parties with skepticism. As we shall see, this is not always the case.

The frames that journalists adopt are in part a function of the lenses through which reporters view the world and their conception of their roles in the political process at a given moment. For example, during election campaigns reporters see themselves in part as unmaskers of the hypocrisy of those who seek office. That perspective carries with it a frame that is ironic and often cynical, focusing on strategic intent, motives, and appearance. A candidate's missteps are featured as signs of a defective character or questionable competence. By contrast, on September 11 and in the days that followed, reporters viewed events through a patriotic lens. Where in the campaign of 2000 the motive and strategic intent behind the message were a matter of focus, in the wake of the attacks reporters took U.S. leaders at their word, assumed that their motives were honorable, and overlooked, indeed compensated for, their missteps.

This book will explain the way these lenses, frames, and stories shape how we translate political data into presumed fact. It will also illustrate how assumptions about those who lead come into being and change, and how evidence is interpreted by journalists to support or challenge an ascendant view. To build our case, we will range across the political landscape, and press responses to it, over one of the more interesting years of modern presidential history, from the summer of 2000 through the beginning of 2002, a period encompassing the closest election in modern memory, a controversial decision by the Supreme Court, and the transitions in governance occasioned by the terrorist attacks of September 11, 2001.

In the process we will try to make sense of moments in which different versions of reality and different sets of facts competed for purchase in public consciousness. Among the questions we will ask are the following:

- In the 2000 presidential primaries, when Al Gore distorted his opponent's record, the press took little public notice. Sixth months later, reporters pounced on trivial misstatements to launch an indictment of the Democrat's character. Since the reports failed to draw on earlier, more credible evidence, Democratic partisans concluded that the press was out to get their party's nominee. But was it?

- Would Republican nominee George W. Bush's tax plan disproportionately help those in the upper 1% of income earners? Which Americans wouldn't receive a penny of benefits from Democratic nominee Al Gore's proposed education tax deduction? Many reporters didn't appear to think these were questions worth asking. When they did raise them, their answers were often confusing and occasionally inaccurate. Why were those who see themselves as custodians of fact so hesitant to help the public sort all of this out?

- In the 2000 presidential debates, reporters interpreted Gore's mistaken claim that he had visited fires in Texas with the head of FEMA as a sign of a defective character. Reporters also noted that contrary to his claim, Bush had not championed a patient's bill of rights in Texas, but in contrast to their evaluation of Gore, did not then go on to draw inferences about the Texan's character or competence. Were they applying different standards to the candidates, or was something else going on?

- Although they pride themselves on their investigative instincts, reporters were oblivious to the maneuvering of the Bush campaign that led to different standards of vote counting in Florida—a lenient standard in counting likely Bush overseas absentee ballots and a strict one in counting Gore's. Did reporters' susceptibility to the Bush spin increase the likelihood that the Supreme Court would take the case of *Bush v. Gore* and decide the election for Bush?

- When in late 2001 analyses by news organizations showed that Gore was as likely as Bush to have won the needed ballots in Florida, headlines proclaimed that Bush had indeed won and the system worked. Was this simply Bush boosting or something else?

- When Bush mangled sentences during the campaign, it was said to "raise questions" about his intellect. After September 11 the same sorts of stumbles were overlooked. Was the press wrong when it singled those cues out for comment in the campaign? Or was the president given a pass because the country was under threat?

When reporters transform the raw stuff of experience into presumed fact and arrange facts into coherent stories, they create a way of seeing individuals and events as well as a way of making sense of politics writ large. Because the success of our democracy depends so heavily on journalists' exercise of their constitutionally protected mission, it is important to understand the ways shifting journalistic perspectives alter the facts that are deemed important, the ways in which fact is framed and frames come to be assumed, and the ways that journalism's facts and frames become the stories we tell each other and our children about the meaning of our times.

THE PRESS EFFECT

CHAPTER 1

The Press as Storyteller

The reports that journalists offer their readers, listeners, and viewers are not called "stories" by accident. By arranging information into structures with antagonists, central conflicts, and narrative progression, journalists deliver the world to citizens in a comprehensible form. But the stories that journalists tell and the lenses that color their interpretation of events can sometimes dull their fact-finding and investigative instincts.

In the illustrations that follow, we describe instances in which reporters failed to investigate and locate the facts that would have undercut the coherence of a story being told because the lens they adopted made fact-finding seem unnecessary or irrelevant. In the first set of cases, while replaying coherent, compelling stories, reporters missed facts that would have disrupted the story line even though the story line itself was being disputed. In the second set, involving events in times of crisis or war, government-blessed versions of fact were uncritically embraced and deceptions tacitly forgiven.

Of course politicians cast the world in stories, too. Political actors argue through the use of narrative for a number of reasons. First, they understand that narrative has persuasive power; when arguments are arranged into stories, they are more readily recalled and more easily believed. Second, they understand the reporter's preference for good stories around which news can be built. If a story is compelling enough, it can increase the chances that coherent but inaccurate information will pass through to the public, as is the case in our first example from the 1988 presidential campaign.

The Horton Menace

The 1988 presidential election produced a telling case in which the press failed to challenge facts that sounded plausible because they completed a dramatic narrative. Seeing the story through the lens of strategy and tactics, reporters neglected their role as custodian of fact. What were the facts? William Horton, who had been convicted as an accessory to a felony murder for his part in a robbery in which a young man was murdered, was released from a Massachusetts prison on a furlough. He jumped furlough and traveled to Maryland, where he held a couple hostage, stabbed the man and raped his fiancée. The Bush campaign used the story to paint the Democratic nominee, Massachusetts governor Michael Dukakis, as soft on crime.

Whether or not the Horton story accurately symbolized Dukakis's record on crime, George H. W. Bush's embellishment of it and the press's failure to challenge the untruths the vice president told as he repeated the story provide an excellent example of the power of narrative to overwhelm concern about fact. On the stump, for example, Bush alleged that "Willie Horton was in jail, found guilty by a jury of his peers for murdering a seventeen-year-old kid after torturing him."[1] There is no direct evidence that Horton killed Joseph Fournier, and nothing on which to base a charge of torture. The untrue claim that Horton had cut off Fournier's genitals and stuffed them in the victim's mouth was whispered to reporters by Bush campaign operatives. There is some evidence that Horton may have been in the getaway car shooting heroin while his associates robbed and killed Fournier. A court official indicated that one of Horton's accomplices confessed to killing Fournier but the confession was disallowed because it had been secured without the reading of Miranda rights. Horton was convicted as an *accomplice* to a felony murder. In other words, there is no evidence that he killed Fournier and reason to believe that he did not.

Bush next alleged that Horton had murdered again when he jumped furlough. As he described it in an Ohio speech in September, "You remember the case of Willie Horton in the *Reader's Digest*, the guy was furloughed, murderer, hadn't even served enough time for parole, goes down to Maryland, and murders again, and Maryland wouldn't even let him out to go back to Massachusetts, because they didn't want him to kill again. I don't believe in that kind of approach to criminals."[2] Bush's claim that Horton had committed murder while on parole was untrue. The Republican candidate's story, then, had three flaws: It increased

Horton's role in the crime for which he was originally in jail, it embellished the details of the crime, and it magnified the horror of Horton's post-furlough activities. There is symmetry in the notion that a killer has killed again; thus Bush's exaggerated version of the story cohered thematically with the undisputed facts, and that coherence increased its plausibility. When Dukakis failed to challenge the Bush claims on the assumption that they were unbelievable, the press, taking its cue in part from the Democrat, gave Bush a pass. While reporters discussing the story usually correctly stated its facts, they did not charge Bush with deception for making the story more awful than it actually was.

The Bush campaign also falsely asserted that the furlough program was Dukakis's invention (he had inherited it from his Republican predecessor), that Horton was a first-degree murderer not eligible for parole at the time of his furlough (he was in a category that made him eligible for parole), that there were hundreds of others who escaped from Massachusetts furloughs and committed violent crimes (none committed murder, and Horton was the only one who committed rape), and that Horton's name was not William but "Willie." In fact, until June of 1988 Horton was referred to as William in all court documents and newspaper stories, including those of the *Lawrence Eagle-Tribune*, the Massachusetts newspaper that won a Pulitzer Prize for its exposé of the furlough program. The advertisement featuring Horton, which was paid for by the National Security PAC,[3] referred to him as "Willie," and Bush, who mentioned him in speeches in the summer of 1988 as well as in his debate with Dukakis on September 25, referred to him as "Willie." An examination of newspaper stories reveals that once the Bush campaign began referring to him as Willie, most newspapers began calling him that as well. Only the *Washington Post* and *New York Times* continued to call him William—although they shifted back and forth between the two names. Given the controversy, one would assume that reporters would have gone back to look at the documents surrounding the Horton case, including the *Eagle-Tribune* series. Had they done so, they would have noticed that Horton hadn't been called Willie until Bush began talking about the case. One explanation for the lack of correction is that the name Willie sounded more lower class, more criminal, and indeed more "black" to reporters, and thus cohered with the narrative concerning Horton's crimes.

The question of Horton's name demonstrates that the stories on which political arguments are built have embedded within them a variety of facts both large and small, any of which may be subject to distortion. The fact that reporters failed to call Bush on his claim that Horton had killed again while on furlough suggests the extent to which reporters, like the rest of us, often fail to check facts that seem compatible with compelling narratives. This is particularly true when the lens through which reporters are seeing is a strategic one, evaluating candidates' words and actions for their tactical intentions and electoral effects.

The Supreme Court and Election 2000

In the case of William Horton, the press permitted a compelling story—and the absence of clear rebuttal from Dukakis—to overwhelm the facts, allowing inaccuracy to pass uncorrected to the public. The denouement to the 2000 election showed how an existing narrative can drive interpretation in cases where the press is called to make sense of a finite set of facts. When the tightly fought 2000 race came down to a disputed state decided by a margin of less than one one-hundredth of one percent, the dominant narrative portrayed partisan division and a country equally divided between the "red states" supporting one candidate and the "blue states" supporting the other, as they were portrayed on the networks' electoral maps. Reporters had forecast two possible story lines about the basis for the Supreme Court decision. In the first, the conservative majority's disposition to minimize federal authority and reserve power to the states forecast a decision that would return the case to the Florida Supreme Court. A second story line suggested that the "conservatives" would find a way to hand the election to the individual most likely to strengthen their hold on the Court. Either of these was compatible with a 5–4 vote on the Court; neither was compatible with a 7–2 ruling. The ruling contained both a 7–2 decision and a 5–4 decision. Which would reporters feature?

Democrats and Republicans were divided over whether the court had decided 7–2 or 5–4. In fact, it had done both. "Seven justices of the court [Justices Stevens and Ginsburg disagreed] agree that there are constitutional problems with the recount ordered by the Florida Supreme court that demand a remedy," said the Court. "The only disagreement [among the seven] is as to the remedy." On the issue of whether there was a remedy available before a hard-and-fast deadline, two of the seven (Justices Souter and Breyer) held open the option to give it a try. In short, four of nine believed that there might be a remedy that would permit continuation of the count; five concluded that the election was over and for practical purposes a president elected.

Republicans would argue that the recount requested by Gore had been unconstitutional. But that is not actually what the Court said. "Because it is evident that *any recount seeking to meet the December 12 date* will be unconstitutional for the reasons we have discussed," the justices wrote, "we reverse the judgment of the Supreme Court of Florida ordering a recount to proceed" (emphasis added). One can parse the opinion into three questions: Was the recount to that point acceptable? Seven said no. Were the recount problems remediable? Seven said yes. ("It is obvious that the recount cannot be conducted in compliance with the requirements of equal protection and due process without substantial additional work.") Were they remediable in the time remaining? Five said no.

If *Bush v. Gore* was a 7–2 ruling then the court acted decisively; if the ruling was 5–4, the court was instead closely divided. Republicans favored the first construction; Democrats the second. Just before midnight December 12, the Gore campaign issued a statement saying that Gore and Lieberman were "reviewing the 5–4 decision issued tonight by the Supreme Court of the United States . . ." The next evening he seemed to lay fights over the size of the majority behind the ruling to rest with the words "The U.S. Supreme Court has spoken. Let there be no doubt. While I strongly disagree with the court's decision, I accept it. I accept the finality of this outcome." The Bush camp, on the other hand, characterized the ruling differently. James Baker, appearing before Gore's concession, said that the Texas governor was "very pleased and gratified that seven justices of the United States Supreme Court agreed that there were constitutional problems with the recount ordered by the Florida Supreme Court."[4]

More than six months after the Supreme Court ruling, the person who led the Bush team in the thirty-six days was still working to cast the decision as a 7–2 vote. In a letter to the editor of the *New York Times,* James Baker protested the fact that "you have once again described *Bush v. Gore* as a 5-to-4 decision . . . a point that is accurate but also incomplete . . . The court's holding that the lack of uniform standards for the recount violated the 14th Amendment guarantee of equal protection was decided on a 7-to-2 vote, with one of two Democrats joining six of seven Republicans."[5] The statement by Baker says more than he may have intended. Presumably in their role as justices of the Supreme Court, individuals do not consider themselves members of a party, although one could appropriately characterize them as nominated by presidents who were either Republicans or Democrats. In his eagerness to establish that the important decision was rendered 7–2, Baker reopened a far more damaging charge—that the justices acted politically.

Overwhelmingly, press accounts focused on the 5–4 ruling. The *New York Times* headline read: "Bush Prevails; By Single Vote, Justices End Recount." "The Supreme Court effectively handed the presidential election to George W. Bush tonight," wrote Linda Greenhouse, "overturning the Florida Supreme Court and ruling by a vote of 5 to 4 that there could be no further counting of Florida's disputed presidential votes." "Supreme Court Rules for Bush," read the headline in the *Milwaukee Journal Sentinel*, "5–4 Decision Clears Path to the Presidency." "A deeply divided U.S. Supreme Court on Tuesday night effectively handed the presidential election to Texas Governor George W. Bush," said the first sentence. "A sharply divided U.S. Supreme Court last night handed Texas governor George W. Bush what may be a presidential victory," wrote the *Cleveland Plain Dealer*. In the *San Diego Union-Tribune* the headline announced "5–4 Ruling Puts Bush on Threshold of Victory." The Court was "sharply split," said the accompanying article.

Although reporters might have spent more time discussing the elements of the Supreme Court's ruling with which seven members agreed, the 5–4 split—conservatives on one side, liberals on the other—fit so well with the larger story line of a divided country and a neck-and-neck election that it almost inevitably became the central point in describing the Court's decision. This is not to say there was anything inaccurate about that characterization; on many of the key issues of substance, the Court was indeed divided 5–4. But this provides another example of the way frames highlight some facts and interpretations instead of others.

The decision by the Gore team to concede the day after the Supreme Court ruling was, in part, a reflection of its reaction to the way the media had played the story. The staff writers for the *Washington Post* note:

> Could they fight on? Sure, Boies said. Should they? "It is not just making a decision of whether this is viable or sensible," he said later. "It is whether the viability of it or the sensibility of it [is] great enough to consider it. It is not just a legal question." It was a question about a divided country, and about the future of Al Gore.
>
> All this was hashed and rehashed in early morning conference calls. At about 8:30, Daley and Gore spoke again. "The spin on the morning news was 'It's over,'" Daley noted. Even if they wanted to keep fighting, there was scant running room and vanishing support.[6]

A process that had begun when the vice president believed the media reports and called to concede ended when the vice president heard from an aide that the news interpretation precluded any further legal challenge. The frame through which the Supreme Court decision was discussed provided a coda to the contested 2000 election. The reliance on the 5–4 frame opened a story line suggesting that a single Supreme Court justice had in fact selected the president of the United States. As we will argue later, when the so-called media recounts were complete, the press itself dismissed that story line.

Who had Political Relations with that Company?

When an assumption is widely shared within the press, an allegation consistent with the assumption is more likely than it otherwise would be to travel uncorrected into news. The campaign finance scandals of the Clinton administration were telegraphed in one often repeated claim: those who gave money were invited to spend the night in the Lincoln Bedroom.

The Lincoln Bedroom first emerged as a symbol of selling access when it was revealed that the Clinton administration had rewarded large contributors by allowing them to spend a night in the White House, some in the Lincoln Bedroom. The story became a powerful symbol because it told of wealthy contributors in effect being able to purchase the right to temporarily occupy what is in the American civil religion a kind of sacred space by virtue of its association with a revered president. The proximity of the Lincoln Bedroom to both the Oval Office and the President's bedroom translates readily into a symbol of intimate access and proximity to power.

As the Enron scandal developed at the beginning of 2002, one of the key points of contention was, first, whether it was a business scandal or a political one, and, second, if it was a political scandal, who was implicated in it. Democrats argued that Enron in general and its chairman, Kenneth Lay, in particular were much closer to the GOP than to them. Observing that three quarters of Enron's contributions went to Republicans, Democratic consultant James Carville said to Tim Russert on *Meet the Press* on February 17, 2002, "This ludicrous idea, 'Oh, they both got it,' no, it was 73 to 27. If you lose the game 73 to 27, that is not a tie." Republicans attempted to tell the story as one in which Enron spread its wealth to both parties. Supporting that view was a claim repeated in numerous media outlets: Ken Lay had spent a night in the Lincoln Bedroom during the Clinton administration. The Lincoln Bedroom story turned out to be false; although Lay had played golf with President

Clinton, he had spent the night in the White House only at the invitation of George H. W. Bush.

Because it was known that Clinton had rewarded contributors with nights in the Lincoln Bedroom, and it was also known that Ken Lay had given large amounts of money to many politicians, it was plausible that Ken Lay had rested in Lincoln's bed at Clinton's invitation. The claim originated on the *Drudge Report*, and was then picked up by the *Chicago Tribune* and *USA Today*. Subsequently, it appeared in, among other places, a news story in the *Washington Times*; editorials in the *Cleveland Plain Dealer*, *Portland Oregonian*, and *Augusta Chronicle*; and in a Newhouse News Service column by James Lileks distributed to multiple newspapers. It reached overseas, appearing in the *Times* of London, the *Sunday Age* of Melbourne, and the *Korea Herald*. Fred Barnes wrote it in the *Weekly Standard* and made the claim on Fox News's *Special Report with Brit Hume*. On the same network, Republican activist David Bossie said the same thing on Greta Van Susteren's *On the Record*. Republican media consultant Alex Castellanos made the claim on CNN's *Crossfire* on February 14, then again on ABC's *This Week* on February 17. That appearance was the only time anyone directly challenged the assertion. The exchange on *This Week* offers a good example of the way in which such claims survive untethered to fact.

> **Castellanos:** Paul forgot—Paul forgot to mention that Ken Lay slept in the Lincoln Bedroom in the Clinton administration, not Bush.
> **Begala:** No, that's not true, actually.
> **Castellanos:** But anyway—yes, it is.
> **Begala:** That's false. It's false.
> **Castellanos:** But anyway . . .
> **Begala:** Maybe Bush One, but no, not Clinton.
> **Castellanos:** Anyway, what the Democrats are doing here . . .

Moderator George Stephanopoulos probably did not attempt to settle the factual dispute because he did not know whether the story was true or not. Instead, after Castellanos and Begala went back and forth, Stephanapoulos said, "Alex, let me talk a little bit more about the Republican strategy . . ." Had Stephanopoulos stepped in to side with Begala, he would have been accurate, but might have risked the perception that his past work as a Clinton aide was compromising his role as a moderator. Would audiences have believed a former Clinton aide turned journalist in this kind of factual dispute? Ultimately the Lay-in-the-Lincoln-Bedroom story was debunked by Gene Lyons of the *Arkansas Democrat-Gazette* and

Brendan Nyhan in the on-line magazine *Salon*, but the correction did not diffuse into the national media. Mistaken information given plausibility by the past actions of Clinton and Lay and by its coherence with an existing narrative was thus able to help Republicans widen the sphere of responsibility for Enron to include Democrats. With each subsequent retelling, the story became less and less likely to be checked for accuracy. When a contested piece of information such as this arises, reporters have a responsibility to discover the truth, then sanction anyone who repeats a falsehood.

Tobacco, Taxes, and Canadian Mounties

When two sides are projecting competing outcomes from a piece of legislation, reports are likely to simply set their claims against each other and probe for tactical advantage. If the facts are checked, reporters are more likely to scrutinize the claims of those who have demonstrated a capacity to deceive the public in the past. If the contest is between the tobacco companies on one hand and groups such as the American Cancer Society and the Campaign for Tobacco-Free Kids on the other, the fact that internal documents had confirmed that the tobacco industry had lied about marketing to kids meant that the media were more likely to explore the accuracy of its arguments than those of the other side.

There was not a week in a three-and-a-half-month period in 1998 in which tobacco industry ads addressing an antitobacco bill sponsored by John McCain were not being aired. The McCain bill would have settled the states' suits against the tobacco industry by providing protection for the industry from class-action lawsuits in return for an increased tobacco tax and assurances that the industry would no longer advertise to the young through billboards near schools and the like. The industry's ad campaign was significant in part because it was the first time a large-scale, long-running nationwide broadcast ad campaign on a piece of pending legislation had run with negligible response from those on the other side. The only television ad by proponents of a "tough bill" against "Big Tobacco" was aired by the American Cancer Society for a single week in May in five states and nationally on CNN. By contrast, the tobacco industry's ads aired widely (in from thirty to fifty markets) on both cable and local spot broadcast. Much of the industry budget was spent on CNN, which did not air a single news piece evaluating the accuracy of the ads' claims.

One of the industry ads featured Ron Martelle, identified as a former Canadian Mountie, who said, "The criminals that showed up in Cornwall threatened my life and the lives of my family. All because a tax that was supposed to protect our teenagers from smoking ended up hurting all of us, and as a result, teens purchased black market cigarettes."

Illustrating the role the press should play in providing context for facts offered by those engaged in political debate, *New York Times* reporter Anthony DePalma noted that "many of the 47,000 people who live in Cornwall say Mr. Martelle is exaggerating, just as, in their view, he had tended to blow things out of proportion during the more than five years he was mayor." The same article reported the attack of his opponents: "They point out that although he calls himself a former Mountie, he was in the force for only eight months . . . They also delight in pointing out that the company Mr. Martelle now works for, Forensic Investigative Associates of Toronto, represents the National Coalition Against Crime and Tobacco Contraband, a lobbying group for tobacco wholesalers, retailers and the major cigarette producers in the United States."[7]

What else should reporters have told viewers? The tobacco industry ads implied a legitimacy that their claims lacked by providing on-screen citations to supposed forms of documentation. A number of the ads argued that the McCain bill would "create 17 new government bureaucracies . . . Washington wants to raise the price of cigarettes so high, there would be a black market in cigarettes with unregulated access to kids."

By any reasonable definition of "bureaucracy," this claim was false. The ads for the five tobacco companies source the "seventeen new government bureaucracies" assertion to an April 9, 1998 research note by David Adelman of Morgan Stanley. However, Adelman's "Industry Overview" was not an independent finding that there would be seventeen new government bureaucracies. Instead Adelman was quoting tobacco company CEO Steve Goldstone's April 8 speech at the National Press Club. And Goldstone did not use the word bureaucracies but "17 separate tobacco committees and boards." Adelman's document also contained the following information: "Within the last three years, Morgan Stanley and Co. Inc., Dean Witter Reynolds Inc. and/or their affiliates managed or co-managed a public offering of the securities of RJR Nabisco."

The statement "Lots of money for new government bureaucracy" is sourced to an article in the *Washington Post*. However, there is no backup for the assertion in the cited article. Instead it said, "President Clinton's new budget calls for spending nearly $10 billion from the proposed national tobacco settlement on a wide variety of new initiatives . . ."[8] The cited article referred not to the McCain bill but to a request in President Clinton's budget. On-screen citations for information, which have become commonplace in both candidate and advocacy ads in recent years, are a welcome development. As this case illustrates, the fact that someone offers citations does not mean that they are necessarily telling the truth.

And what of Martelle's claim that teens simply got their cigarettes on the black market created by the tax increase? In a May 19 adwatch on ABC, Aaron Brown evaluated both the industry ad claim that the McCain bill would produce a black market and the implication that kids would buy cigarettes there:

> **Narrator in ad:** There will be a black market in cigarettes with unregulated access to kids.
> **Brown:** The industry cites Canada as proof. In the early '80s when Canada increased cigarette prices, a black market did emerge. But something else happened in Canada the tobacco industry doesn't mention.
> **David Sweanor:** Non-Smokers Rights Canada: The price went up in Canada, consumption among teenagers plummeted.
> **Brown:** The number of kids who smoked every day dropped by 60% in little more than a decade. The tobacco companies know this. The evidence of their knowledge is contained in their own files. This Philip Morris strategic planning document from the early '90s states it simply.
> **Voice-over reading from Philip Morris document:** "There is no question that increasing taxes will cause a decrease in smoking. This point is best illustrated by the present situation in Canada." Five years earlier, a Philip Morris analysis of price increases concluded, "Price increases prevented 600,000 teenagers from starting to smoke. We don't need to have that happen again."

As in the case of Brown's report, the press is more likely to deconstruct and critique the narrative provided by those it perceives to be powerful and manipulative. But one other element was missing from the context reporters should have offered: when Canada increased its taxes on cigarettes, the source for a black market—that is, a place where black marketeers could purchase cigarettes Canadians wanted to buy—was just over the border in the United States. With cigarettes in Canada subject to high taxes, would similar taxes in the United States give rise to a huge black market for Mexican cigarettes? From where would the black market come?

Why should we be concerned about the small amount of fact-checking of these ads? Survey data show that the deceptive claims of the ads were believed in markets with high airing, little adwatching, and little rebuttal.[9] So the deception succeeded. Anthony DePalma's *New York Times* piece and Aaron Brown's adwatch are examples of journalists upholding their responsibility as custodians of fact, evaluating claims, and investigating to determine accuracy. Unfortunately, many more people saw the tobacco industry's inaccurate advertising than saw these isolated corrections.

When one side in a policy debate makes a prediction about the effects of legislation, reporters have a responsibility to make judgments about the likelihood that those consequences will actually occur. This is particularly true of those opposed to a legislative change, who usually predict a dire outcome should a proposed bill become law. These campaigns conduct survey and focus group research to determine the arguments against the legislation that resonate most strongly with the citizenry; sometimes these arguments are reasonable and sometimes they are not. For instance, when automobile manufacturers and business groups argue against proposals to increase fuel efficiency standards for cars, they contend that higher fuel efficiency would result in lower safety, because when a small car collides with a large sport utility vehicle, the people in the small car are more likely to be killed; more small cars would equal more people being crushed by SUVs. Indeed some ads have shown an SUV at the point of impact with a small car. But if higher fuel efficiency meant smaller cars, the same logic would dictate higher safety, since fewer SUVs would be on the road to crush those in small cars. The questionable logic of the argument presented in the advertisements is seldom pointed out by journalists.

Although predicting the effects of legislation can require a measure of speculation, reporters can evaluate the factual and logical basis of forecasts without making categorical predictions about the future. Often, reporters avoid such evaluations because of the risk of seeming biased should they determine that one side is being less than accurate. But when the press fails to critically examine these predictions, it makes it difficult for the public to assess the case for and against proposed change.

The Press as Patriot: Four War Stories

On August 3, 1964, President Lyndon Johnson ordered the Navy to take retaliatory action in the Gulf of Tonkin after, he stated, the U.S. destroyer *Maddox* had been attacked by communist PT boats. The next day, in a nationally televised speech, Johnson defined the enemy action in the

Tonkin Gulf as "open aggression on the high seas against the United States of America." He asked Congress to pass "a resolution making it clear that our government is united in its determination to take all necessary measures in support of freedom and in defense of peace in southeast Asia."[10] On August 10, Congress passed the Tonkin Gulf Resolution.

The narrative that initiated the United States's formal entry into the war in Vietnam was simple in its construction. The United States had been attacked. The attack constituted aggression on the high seas. The United States responded at once on the order Johnson gave "after the initial act of aggression." The response of the military was heroic "in the highest tradition of the U.S. Navy." The U.S. response was "limited and fitting." The cause was just; the goal, peace. "Firmness in the right is indispensable today for peace," said Johnson.

There was only one problem with the narrative. The U.S. destroyer *Maddox* had, in all likelihood, not been attacked. In 1995, Johnson's defense secretary, Robert McNamara, said that he was convinced the attack that prompted the U.S. retaliation had never actually occurred. As was later revealed in his secretly recorded audiotapes, President Johnson himself doubted whether the attack took place.[11] McNamara also said that had it not been for the Tonkin Gulf incident, the war resolution (which had been drafted months before) would have been sent to Congress later and would have been subject to a more extensive debate.[12]

The Tonkin Gulf case illustrates a number of important features of political discourse. First, what we believe is in part a function of what we are told by those entrusted with information we lack. Congress believed Johnson at a time when skepticism would have better served the country's interests. In turn, the country believed Johnson, for it had little reason to expect that a president would lie about such a consequential matter. Second, this example shows that facts matter. Policies are built on arguments describing the past, present, and future; if those arguments contain untruth, the consequences can be enormous. Third, it demonstrates that the impulse to bend the truth in order to maintain support for one's goals is a powerful one.

This is not to say that politicians persuade mostly by lying. Instead, they tell the public stories, selecting facts and arguments that support their interpretation of reality. In the context of events occurring in war zones overseas, the press is constrained by its often limited ability to confirm the factual assertions made by the government. As the next example shows, in times of crisis the press often refrains from punishing the government for deception, even when it learns the truth.

Deception Excused: Air Force One

After word of the attacks on the World Trade Center and the Pentagon reached President George W. Bush's staff at a school in Florida where Bush was making an appearance, Air Force One flew the president from Miami to a military base in Louisiana and from there to the Strategic Air Command headquarters in Nebraska before returning to Washington. Members of the press wondered why he had done this. Hoping to blunt a narrative in which Bush appeared to be the object of forces beyond his control rather than a decisive leader guiding the country through the crisis, Bush aides told reporters that there had been a "credible threat" against Air Force One. If that was true, then the moves across the country were the reasonable response of a vigilant Secret Service and a national security process to protect the commander in chief. If it was not true, then the Bush aides were deceiving reporters to create a false image of a President's behavior. "Credible evidence" that Air Force One was at risk was quickly disseminated. Bush adviser Karl Rove told journalists that the Secret Service had received a telephoned threat that "contained language that was evidence that the terrorists had knowledge of his procedures and whereabouts. In light of the specific and credible threat, it was decided to get airborne with a fighter escort."[13]

Reporters later learned that Rove and administration spokesperson Ari Fleischer had misled them. Administration officials had no record of any such call, and were unable to explain why Air Force One was less vulnerable in one location than another even if there had been such a message.[14] Had such an act occurred in a political campaign, headlines would have reported the deception. Instead, the facts were largely buried. The country needed to believe in a decisive, commanding president in the anxious days after September 11, and the press was not disposed to feature evidence incompatible with that narrative.

People generally assume that the press plays an adversarial role to those in power and is quick to unmask, debunk, and challenge. In fact, reporters play this role selectively. If they assume that the country supports the person telling the story (in this case the president) and opposing narratives are not being offered by competing players, the tendency to challenge is dramatically curtailed. At the time of the Tonkin Gulf speech, Johnson was on his way to a landslide victory against Barry Goldwater. After assuming the presidency at the death of John Kennedy, LBJ had driven much of the Kennedy legislative agenda through Congress. His was a formidable presence. At the same time, the Tonkin Gulf

Resolution was passed overwhelmingly by Democrats as well as Republicans. Only two dissenters opposed the Resolution. Faced with the allegation of an attack on the country and two parties united behind the president, reporters are disinclined to buck the tide.

Reporters sometimes say that their job is to tell the public "what it needs to know." The perceived need can shift depending on how the public feels. In a time of crisis, do citizens "need" to know if the president's representatives have misled them? As these cases indicate, in times of national crisis, when reporters learn that they have been deceived they downplay the implications. Implying that Bush was not up to the job that first day seemed unpatriotic.

While campaigns and policy debates are characterized by competing narratives, in wartime the country is often presented with a single, uncontested story line. In both cases, the successful construction and use of narrative often determines the outcome of events. We illustrate this claim with a particularly gruesome tale from the Gulf War.

Did Saddam's Soldiers Throw Babies From Their Incubators in Kuwait?

With hundreds of thousands of soldiers massing in the Persian Gulf in the fall of 1990, America was on the brink of an undeclared war against Iraq over its invasion of Kuwait. The Bush administration needed not only to provide a principled justification for action, but to demonize Saddam Hussein and those who served him. To that end, Bush focused attention on a compelling narrative—albeit one built on a fabrication.

On October 10, 1990, a fifteen-year-old using the assumed name "Nayirah" appeared before the Congressional Human Rights Caucus. "I just came out of Kuwait," she said. "While I was there, I saw the Iraqi soldiers come into the hospital with guns. They took the babies out of the incubators, took the incubators and left the children to die on the cold floor. It was horrifying. I could not help but think of my nephew, who was born premature and might have died that day as well." At the end of her testimony, Congressman John Porter said, "We've passed eight years in the existence of the Congressional Human Rights Caucus. We've had scores of hearings about human rights abuses throughout the world ... we have never heard, in all this time, in all circumstances, a record of inhumanity and brutality and sadism as the ones that the witnesses have given us today. I don't know how the people of the civilized countries of this world can fail to do everything within their power to remove this scourge from the face of our earth . . . [A]ll the countries of the world . . . must join together and take whatever action may be necessary to free the people of Kuwait." The audience for the account included the president, who told Porter that "he had seen it on CNN and that he was shocked at some of the things that he had heard."[15]

It is unclear why President Bush should have been shocked, since the day before Nayirah's testimony, identifying the Emir of Kuwait as the source, he had alluded to babies taken from incubators. In that first telling, however, he added that the stories may not have been authenticated. Specifically, at a press conference October 9, he said "babies in incubators [were] heaved out of the incubators and the incubators themselves sent to Baghdad. Now I don't know how many of these tales can be authenticated but I do know that when the Emir was here he was speaking from the heart." "Speaking from the heart" uses perceived sincerity as a test of reliability. This is one unusual instance in which the elder Bush used a technique similar to one employed often by his son, using good intentions—the contents of the Emir's heart—as a counterweight to potential criticism or factual refutation.

There was at the time another source that confirmed the incubator story. After the young woman testified, her observations were corroborated by Amnesty International, which concluded that 312 infants had died after Iraqi soldiers removed them from their incubators.

After the first reference, in which Bush qualified the story by expressing uncertainty about its authenticity, the incident moved from an undocumented tale to a statement of presumed fact. Rallying troops en route to Iraq on October 28, Bush said that twenty-two babies had died and "the hospital employees were shot and the plundered machines were shipped off to Baghdad."

The story then became a staple of the Bush drive to mobilize public support for the impending war. In a speech in Mashpee, Massachusetts on November 1, Bush said of Saddam Hussein and his forces, "They've tried to silence Kuwaiti dissent and courage with firing squads, much as Hitler did when he invaded Poland. They have committed outrageous acts of barbarism. In one hospital, they pulled twenty-two premature babies from their incubators, sent the machines back to Baghdad, and all those little ones died." Speaking to the allied forces near Dhahran, Saudi Arabia, Bush said on November 22, "It turns your stomach when you listen to the tales of those that have escaped the brutality of Saddam, the invader. Mass hangings. Babies pulled from their incubators and scattered like firewood across the floor."

The story served two purposes: legitimizing the analogy between Hitler and Hussein, and rebutting the charge that the conflict was actually about retaining U.S. access to Middle East oil. The analogy to Hitler set justification for the war not on the pragmatic claim that the United States needed access to the region's oil but on the moral claim that Saddam's acts were an affront to humanity. So, for example, on October 28 at a rally in Manchester, New Hampshire, Bush said, "I read the other night about how Hitler, unchallenged—the U.S. locked in its isolation in those days, the late thirties—marched into Poland. Behind him . . . came the Death's Head regiments of the SS. Their role was to go in and disassemble the country. Just as it happened in the past, the other day in Kuwait, two young kids were passing out leaflets in opposition. They were taken, their families made to watch, and they were shot to death— a fifteen- and sixteen-year-old. Other people on dialysis machines taken off the machines and the machines shipped to Baghdad. Kids in incubators thrown out so that the machinery, the incubators themselves, could be shipped to Baghdad." On October 15, Bush closed his litany of atrocities by saying "Hitler revisited." It was only when Bush attempted to argue that Hussein was not simply the German dictator's equal but *worse* than Hitler that the analogy was criticized.[16]

The use of the story of the babies to dismiss the pragmatic claim and justify the moral one—making the war about human rights, not oil—was clear on October 23 when Bush told a fund-raiser in Burlington, Vermont, "They had kids in incubators, and they were thrown out of the incubators so that Kuwait could be systematically dismantled. So, it isn't oil that we're concerned about. It is aggression. And this aggression is not going to stand." Speaking to the troops at Pearl Harbor on October 28, Bush said, "What we are looking at is good and evil, right and wrong. And day after day, shocking new horrors reveal the true nature of terror in Kuwait." In his list of horrors was the story of the incubators.

On *Larry King Live* on October 16, Kuwait's ambassador to the United States, Sheik Saud Nasir al-Sabah, cited the young woman's testimony and the Amnesty International report as proof of atrocities in Kuwait. Eyewitnesses, he said, "came out and described all the brutalities of the Iraqis against my people . . . and they are also being corroborated by Amnesty International." Unnoted during any of this was the fact uncovered by *Harper's* publisher John R. MacArthur long after the war was over: "Nayirah" was the Kuwaiti ambassador's daughter and a member of the royal family of Kuwait.[17] After its own investigations concluded that no babies had been removed from incubators, Amnesty International retracted its report.

On March 15, 1991, not long after the fighting had ended, ABC reporter John Martin revealed that the incubator story was a fiction when
he interviewed employees at the hospital where the incident allegedly
took place. In a *60 Minutes* exposé in January 1992, Morley Safer talked
with Andrew Whitley, executive director of Middle East Watch, who reported that a colleague went to the Adon Hospital after the liberation of
Kuwait "and interviewed the doctors, and he was able to speak to people
who said they had been on duty at that time, and that this incident didn't
happen." Asked by Safer to explain, a representative of Hill & Knowlton,
the powerhouse Washington lobbying and public relations firm that
choreographed the campaign, said, "I'm sure there will always be two
sides to a story. I believe Nayirah. I have no reason not to believe her.
The veracity of her story was indelibly marked on my mind when I saw
her and when I talked to her."[18] In this telling, truth is relative and the
perceived authenticity of the speaker is the test of veracity. But there
either were or were not Iraqi soldiers in the hospital in Kuwait. If there
were, they either did or did not remove babies from incubators and put
them on the floor; they either did or did not kill hospital personnel; they
either did or did not then ship the empty incubators to Baghdad; the
babies either did or did not die. President Bush either did or did not
have a warranted reason for outrage.

While the Gulf War may have been justified on any number of
grounds, the incubator story was offered repeatedly by the war's proponents as primary evidence of the moral righteousness of the cause. In
the Senate, where a resolution supporting the use of force was passed by
five votes, the incubator story was cited six times during debate on the
resolution. The incident was mentioned in floor debates about the war a
total of twenty-two times.

In the President's rhetoric the synoptic statement justifying the war—
"This aggression is not going to stand"—was built in part on a deception
about babies and incubators. More important for our purposes here, the
narrative was used to rebut the charge that the purpose of going to war
was securing access to oil, as opponents of the war alleged ("No blood for
oil" was the chant heard at protests of the war). Bush used the dramatic,
heartrending story to reframe the conflict as a moral one in which no
compromise was possible and the United States's actions, in the past or
present, would not be subject to debate given the evil of the enemy.

The Nayirah tale is instructive for other reasons that speak to our
need for public wariness and press vigilance when public discourse veers
into emotional anecdote. MacArthur's book and Safer's exposé both

appeared in 1992, nearly a year after the war was over; the ABC News story was the first attempt to disprove the incubator story, but it appeared after the war ended as well. The incubator story raises a number of important questions: First, was the president deceived? What efforts were made to verify the facts used to justify consequential action? Did the president believe the account because he heard it from the Emir, saw Nayirah's testimony on CNN, and read Amnesty International's seeming corroboration? Was the analogy comparing Saddam Hussein to Adolf Hitler—which was made from the day Iraq invaded Kuwait—given more legitimacy by the incubator story? These questions are important because 200,000 troops were already on the ground when the incubator story emerged.

Why did it take so long for reporters to check the facts? Of course, journalists would have had trouble getting into Kuwait to talk with the medical personnel in the hospital. Nonetheless, why was there no skepticism about a story from a young woman speaking under an assumed name? Why no tests of her credibility? Didn't any reporter in Washington know enough about the family of the ambassador to recognize his daughter? Why didn't any reporter ask for a copy of her passport to verify that she was in Kuwait at the reported time? John MacArthur reported that Congressman Tom Lantos, the cochair of the Human Rights Caucus, knew before the hearing that "Nayirah" was in fact the ambassador's daughter. Although Congressman Porter denies knowing, the Kuwaiti ambassador himself claimed that both congressmen were aware of her identity. Why did no reporters ask Lantos or Porter if they had any information that would substantiate her claims?

Why didn't someone test the claim of Amnesty International by asking U.S. doctors who had visited Kuwait how many incubators a single hospital would be expected to have in use at a given time? Does Kuwait have an unusually large number of premature births? Why didn't reporters spot the contradictions in Bush's accounts? For example, in a speech in Des Moines on October 16, Bush said, "In a hospital Iraqi soldiers unplugged the oxygen to incubators supporting twenty-two premature babies. They all died. And then they shot the hospital employees." Did the soldiers unplug the oxygen or throw the babies to the ground? The story changed in various tellings. As C. Wright Mills observed in *The Sociological Imagination*, "The problem of empirical verification is 'how to get down to the facts' . . . The problem is first *what* to verify and second *how* to verify it."[19]

The reporter who uncovered Nayirah's identity did so while writing a book about propaganda and the Gulf War. John R. MacArthur told

60 Minutes, "I set out to find out, like any reporter does. And I started asking questions. And I finally heard a rumor that Nayirah was the daughter of the Kuwaiti ambassador, so I used an old reporter's trick. I called up the embassy, and I said, 'Nayirah did a terrific job at the Human Rights Caucus, and I think her father must be very proud of her. And doesn't she deserve her place in history?' And the ambassador's secretary said to me, 'You're not supposed to know that. No one's supposed to know she's the ambassador's daughter.' "

The conditions of war made the press both more willing to accept the incubator story and less able to determine whether it was true. But in other cases, assertions that would have been quite simple to investigate have been accepted at face value because they cohered to form a powerful, coherent narrative.

Did the Patriots Intercept and Destroy the Scuds?

As Congress and the president once again debate the feasibility of deploying a missile defense shield, the ability of what Dwight Eisenhower called the "military industrial complex" to produce technology that shoots down incoming weapons should be open to question. We all remember watching the Patriot missiles blasting Scuds out of the sky, rendering Saddam Hussein's malevolence impotent in the face of our technological prowess. During the Gulf War, we were told that the Patriots worked nearly perfectly.

The rhetoric at the time reduced the Scuds vs. the Patriots to a tale of U.S. superiority, a rebuke to those who had doubted the Patriot. On February 15, 1991, President Bush visited the Raytheon plant that constructed the Patriot missiles. "The critics said that this system was plagued with problems, that results from the test range wouldn't stand up under battlefield conditions," he told the workers. "You knew they were wrong, those critics, all along. And now the world knows it too. Beginning with the first Scud launched in Saudi Arabia, right into Saudi Arabia and the Patriot that struck it down and with the arrival of Patriot battalions in Israel, all told, Patriot is 41 for 42: 42 Scuds engaged, 41 intercepted . . . Not every intercept results in total destruction. But Patriot is proof positive that missile defense works. I've said many times that missile defense threatens no one, that there is no purer defensive weapon than one that targets and destroys missiles launched against us. Thank God for the

Patriot missile." Note that the President is actually claiming interception, not destruction. Hence the qualification "not every intercept results in total destruction." But what the audience is supposed to hear is clear in the sentences that follow: The Patriot worked. Did it?

Later evidence indicated that the answer was no. Testifying before a congressional hearing in 1992, Secretary of Defense William J. Perry said that "I believe that the Patriot cannot deal with countermeasures,"[20] meaning that it could be easily fooled into missing its targets. The General Accounting Office indicated in 1994 that "the Patriot's success rate may have been no better than 9 percent: four Scuds downed or disabled out of 44 targeted."[21] When a 1992 congressional hearing produced a report critical of the Patriot's performance in the Gulf War, Raytheon lobbied successfully to prevent the report from being approved. The unapproved draft included the statement that "the public and the Congress were misled by definitive statements of success issued by administration and Raytheon representatives during and after the war."[22]

The Pentagon's impulse to overstate the success of missile defense systems emerged again in 2001. On July 14, the system successfully intercepted a missile in a test conducted over the Pacific. "Bush's Hopes for Missile System Get Boost With Successful Test," said the *Wall Street Journal*. "Interceptor Scores a Direct Hit on Missile; Successful Test a Boost to Bush's Shield Plan," said the *Washington Post*. But ten days later, an article in the magazine *Defense Week* revealed that the test had been rigged—the missile was outfitted with a homing beacon that guided the interceptor toward it (and away from the "decoy" the system was supposed to avoid).[23] The revelation that the test had been rigged was the subject of few stories in major newspapers, all of which were buried on inside pages. Once again, the story of technological success was trumpeted prominently, while the subsequent correction, revealing that the performance was not quite as advertised, would have been noticed by far fewer people.

In sum, the stories we tell and that are told matter as do the stories that are never spun. Skillfully deployed stories are important because they persuade. A young woman tells a harrowing tale of murdered babies, and the story becomes an exhibit in rallying a nation to war. Past fact can bear directly on present-day decisions, as well. If, as generals and the President told us, the Patriot missiles reliably destroyed Scuds, then that fact might bolster our confidence that their manufacturer might produce a workable missile defense shield. But if the missiles were easily confused by countermeasures, just as the missiles in the missile defense shield appear now to be, we might be more skeptical about claims that a workable technology is in the offing.

What these examples and the others we have cited have in common is that those who utilized them were able to present a dramatic narrative that played an outsized role in the debate of the moment, driving out relevant facts. As psychologists have known for many years, people don't evaluate situations and make decisions by conducting an inventory of all the information to which they have been exposed about a subject. Instead, both the press and the public use heuristics, often referred to as "information shortcuts," to make evaluation easier. One of the most commonly employed is the availability heuristic; we rely on what is most easily available in our memories. Because evocative images are more available in memory, they carry a greater importance in evaluations.[24] Dramatic, repeated, visually evocative materials can be tools of terror or vehicles that reassure. By repeatedly showing the hijacked planes hitting the World Trade Center towers, news increased our sense that such attacks were likely to occur. By repeatedly showing the towers collapsing, news magnified our fear that we would be trapped in a tall building as it collapsed. By repeatedly airing stories about anthrax, news increased the likelihood that we would be fearful as we opened our mail.

The dramatic narrative can thus drive out relevant facts. Ordinary Americans, the vast majority of whom would not be targets of an attack, feared opening their mail because of the stories of the few letters that contained anthrax, despite the billions of letters delivered spore-free. In 1991, Americans remembered the incubator and the success of the Patriot missile, understanding the war as a battle against evil in which victory was obtained in large part through the triumph of American technology. When voters in 1988 evaluated Michael Dukakis's crime record, the fact that the furlough program was begun by his Republican predecessor and that serious crime was down in Massachusetts were forgotten by most (although he mentioned them often), while the dramatic story of "Willie" Horton was remembered. In a contest between data and dramatic narrative, the narrative is likely to be stored and recalled.

The political narratives on which we have focused underscore the insight underlying Aristotle's observation that pity and fear are powerful drivers of stories, and Kenneth Burke's realization that identification is at the core of the powerful rhetoric. We respond by identifying with Nayirah and with the babies who have died because Saddam's soldiers have thrown them from their incubators; we fear criminals who, if released by well-intentioned but naive liberals, might prey on us. We fear those who might harm the young while thinking that they are helping them. The story that unmasks the well-intentioned but harmful act is powerful because it serves to warn—Dukakis's furloughs, the black markets produced by taxation of tobacco in Canada.

As custodians of fact, journalists need to help viewers and readers make sense of statements about fact while not losing sight of those facts political actors are reluctant to acknowledge. We make no claim that this is a simple task, but it is at the core of the journalist's responsibility to the public. The task becomes particularly difficult when the relevant facts are embedded in a compelling narrative.

CHAPTER 2

The Press as Amateur Psychologist, Part I

The notion that reporters should hold the powerful accountable is at the core of contemporary journalism. "Anyone tempted to abuse power looks over his or her shoulder to see if someone else is watching. Ideally, there should be a reporter in the rearview mirror," write the *Washington Post*'s Leonard Downie and Robert Kaiser.[1] When it acts as a watchdog, the press keeps an eye trained on government in order to expose—and thus prevent—abuse. In campaigns, reporters extend this perspective to vetting candidates, examining individuals instead of institutions to reveal corrupting influences and impulses. But in so doing, they sometimes distort the watchdog role to the point where it becomes disconnected from the end it is intended to serve. While the watchdog exposes corruption to ensure the honest and effective functioning of government, in campaigns reporters too often become amateur psychologists, probing the psyches of the candidates but largely failing to describe how what they find there relates to the job one of their outpatients will assume.

The human disposition to probe the difference between the public and private person is long-lived. "The chasm between the public majesty of the leader and the old coot's tawdry reality has been memorialized through the ages," noted the *Washington Post*'s Meg Greenfield. "What is different about our time is that most of the protective veils have been ripped off while the performers are still on stage."[2]

The veil-ripping process focuses not only on private words and behaviors but also on psychological profiling that seeks patterns in these private and public moments and from them draws inferences with a broad brush. Of President Bill Clinton, for example, Lewis Lapham of *Harper's* wrote, "He defines himself as a man desperately eager to please, and the voraciousness of his appetite—for more friends, more speeches, more food and drink, more time onstage, more hands to shake, more hugs—suggests the emptiness of a soul that knows itself only by the names of what it seizes or consumes."[3] About an April 2002 speech by 2000 Democratic nominee Al Gore, the *Philadelphia Inquirer's* Dick Polman noted, "He gave the strongest signal thus far that his lifelong thirst for the highest office remains unquenched."[4]

When the Voter News Service exit poll asked, "Will Gore say anything to become president?" 74% of all voters surveyed answered yes, compared to 58% who held that opinion of Bush. When the same survey asked, "Does Gore know enough to be president?" 67% agreed that he did; 54% thought that was true of Bush. How did voters come to see Gore as untrustworthy and Bush as somewhat less prepared than Gore for the presidency? One answer is that these were the two candidate qualifications stressed by the press and the campaigns in 2000.

The extent to which those characteristics are featured is colored by each candidate's fortunes in the polls. When a candidate is leading, the press seeks to answer the question why, naturally focusing on what is appealing about the man and effective about his campaign. When he falls behind, the same question leads to a focus on his personal failings and his campaign's missteps. *New York Times* reporter Frank Bruni recognized the extent to which the story reporters are telling about a candidate dictates the facts which they feature and the ones they dispatch. George W. Bush, he wrote, "often seemed content to get by on as little as possible, and we perhaps focused less on this than we might have in the fall of 1999 because his failings on the stump didn't fit the narrative in place at the time."[5]

Reporters covering the campaign create simple frames, based on one or two characteristics of personality, and channel their coverage through those frames. In so doing they simplify the task set for them in James David Barber's influential book *The Presidential Character,* which argued:

> To understand what actual Presidents do and what potential Presidents might do, the first need is to know the whole person—not as some abstract embodiment of civic virtue, some scorecard of issue stands, or some reflection of a faction, but as a human being like the rest of us, a person trying to cope with a difficult environment. To that task a candidate brings an individual character, worldview, and political style.[6]

"Over the last thirty years . . . [j]ournalists began to examine the personal histories of candidates for president, looking for clues that might bear on what kind of presidents they could turn out to be," write Downie and Kaiser. "One stimulus to this kind of reporting was a 1972 book by professor James David Barber of Duke . . . which urged journalists and academics to do more to explore the personalities of presidential candidates before they got elected." While Downie and Kaiser make the connection between the exploration of character and presidential conduct, this connection is precisely what is missing in much campaign reporting.

The struggle reporters face in linking campaigning to governance and the personal to the political was at play in the Dole–Clinton election. In 1996 the *Post* applied the relevance standard when its editors decided not to write that Republican nominee Bob Dole had had an extramarital affair two and a half decades before. Downie argued that "the revelation of a love affair from a quarter century earlier had to be justified by its relevance to the candidate's suitability for the presidency or his past conduct in public life. In this case he didn't see the relevance."[7] In deciding whether to publish, the reporters and editors at the *Post* weighed such questions as the following: Was it fair to explore Clinton's sex life but not Dole's? Was Dole's campaign arguing that he was morally superior to Clinton and hence engaged in hypocrisy? Was an almost three-decade-old event worthy of revelation without evidence that the behavior persisted?

We suspect that the relevance test used by the *Post* in 1996 was in part a function of the subject matter—sexual behavior—and in part a function of how dated the information was. In 2000, the press seemed less concerned about making the tie between the personality traits on which it focused and their relevance to conduct in office.

Following Barber's advice, campaign reporters have become amateur psychologists, probing the candidates for fatal flaws and trying to discover the "real" person behind the speeches, position papers, and staffers. This process creates a pair of portraits, neither complimentary, that determines the shape of coverage. But the press has largely failed to make the link that Barber urged: that between a candidate's character and presidential performance. Reporters have attempted to discover who the candidate really is, but have spent far less time explaining how this character—or, more specifically, these character flaws—relate to governance. If citizens are told that a candidate is dishonest or inexperienced, they should also be told in detail how this flaw would affect the job the candidate would do as president. How would it affect the policies he would propose? His success in getting legislation passed? His management of the executive branch? His ability to deal with crises? These are the types of questions that would give meaning to the exploration of character.

Performance and Authenticity

In 2000, one of the primary questions asked by reporters—and the one the Bush campaign stressed—was whether each candidate was an honest man. The question of the candidates' honesty and the press's treatment of it raises a difficult issue: how do we evaluate honesty within an enterprise—politics—that is in large part about performance, presentations intended to shape perceptions of reality? Sociologist Erving Goffman argued that all of our human interactions involve some degree of performance, presenting a persona to those whom we meet. The persona we offer "backstage," in more relaxed settings, differs from the one we present when we are "frontstage," where a more formal performance is required.[8] To illustrate, Goffman offers the example of schoolteachers acting one way in front of their students and another way in the teachers' lounge. While much of the time we pay only marginal attention to the authenticity of the personae presented by the ordinary people we know, contemporary politicians, particularly presidential candidates, have their personae and performances scrutinized to an extraordinary degree.

Even if a politician's performance accurately represents reality, it remains a performance and thus in some sense artificial. When Al Gore gave his wife Tipper a passionate kiss before ascending to the podium to deliver his acceptance speech at the 2000 Democratic convention, some commentators complained that the moment must have been planned in order to humanize Gore's image—after all, he knew that the cameras were on him. While no one questioned that the Gores have a strong and loving marriage, the genuineness of "The Kiss" was hotly debated. The question of whether the kiss was "real" or whether it was a performance could be raised because Gore's authenticity was itself in question. Bush could freely wear different types of clothing at different times without notice, but sartorial alterations on Gore's part became part of an ongoing discussion on his degree of authenticity. Just as Bush's intellect was subject to continual examination and reevaluation, the question asked of Gore's performance was usually some form of "Was it real?"

Goffman's description of "backstage" behavior describes fairly well the interactions between George W. Bush and the reporters who accompanied him. It also provides a vivid contrast to reporters' complaints

about Gore—that he was inaccessible, and that when he did make himself available he came across as scripted and careful:

> The backstage language consists of reciprocal first-naming, co-
> operative decision-making, profanity, open sexual remarks, elaborate
> griping, smoking, rough informal dress, "sloppy" sitting and standing
> posture, use of dialect or sub-standard speech, mumbling and shout-
> ing, playful aggressivity and "kidding," inconsiderateness for the
> other in minor but potentially symbolic acts, minor physical self-
> involvements such as humming, whistling, chewing, nibbling, belch-
> ing, and flatulence.[9]

With this description in mind, consider what Seth Mnookin, in an
article for *Brill's Content* about Bush's relationship with the press, said
about the future president:

> Within five minutes of meeting me for the first time, Bush developed
> some shorthand to signify our intimate connection. Since the press
> was writing about Bush, and I was writing about the press, he and I
> were joined together in a kind of enemies-of-my-enemies equation.
> Now—I've spent a total of about five days traveling with the Bush
> press corps—whenever Bush sees me, he sticks out his right hand,
> wrapping his middle finger around his index finger. And then, as he's
> waving his hand back and forth, he shouts out, "Me and you, right?"[10]

New York Times reporter Frank Bruni relates that on the campaign
trail, Bush "touched those of us around him a lot . . . He pinched our
cheeks or gently slapped them, in an almost grandmotherly, aren't-you-
adorable way."[11] Where Bush succeeded was not simply in making the
press like him better than Gore (although that was certainly the case as
well). By participating with reporters in typically backstage interactions,
he convinced them first that they had access to the "real" person, and
second that his frontstage persona was not substantially different from
the backstage persona. Because Gore did not offer reporters a convincing backstage persona, his frontstage performance was assumed to mask
an unknown and necessarily different reality.

Thus the fact that Gore wore too much makeup in the first debate
was noticed and discussed by journalists and ridiculed on late-night television. Jay Leno said Gore "had so much makeup on that if he went to
the White House looking like that, Clinton would have hit on him." Frank
Bruni later wrote that Gore "was a pumpkin-headed sigh master, ill served
by both his cosmetologist and his petulance."[12] The symbolism is hard
to miss: Makeup serves to conceal and alter the appearance, presenting a
varnished version of the true self.

The idea of performance assumes an audience. In politics there are two relevant audiences. The larger is, of course, the voting public. The other—the press—is both an audience and a participant in the performance. They simultaneously enact their own role, edit the politicians' roles, and instruct the public on how the performance should be interpreted and judged. In this context, authenticity—defined in part as a minimal difference between the frontstage persona presented to the public and the backstage persona presented to intimates—becomes one of the primary measures of value journalists assign to candidates. The search for the "real" candidate is an effort to drag the backstage persona to the front.

It was not always thus; before the latter half of the twentieth century, the question of whether a candidate was "authentic" was rarely raised. The increased value placed on authenticity occurred not only in politics but in other realms as well. A simultaneous transformation took place in the entertainment world, with a new definition of what constituted skilled acting. Until the 1950s, actors tended to perform in a broad, melodramatic, almost bombastic style rooted in the necessities of theater, that is, the requirement to have one's performance reach the last row in the house. In the early years of the medium, film performances were similarly theatrical. The transformation to a more "realistic" style of acting, with delivery mirroring everyday speech patterns, occurred over time but with some notable markers, including Marlon Brando's performance in *A Streetcar Named Desire* in 1951. The result was an alteration of the standard by which acting was judged, with a premium put on realism.

Political speech was transformed in a parallel way by a series of technological changes. The invention of the microphone allowed those without loud voices, particularly women, to become political speakers. Radio altered the relationship between speaker and listener, taking the political speech out of the town square and into the living room. Finally, television brought political speakers to an intimate distance from citizens. As a consequence, political speech became more personal, more self-disclosive, and more conversational in style.[13]

Along with the change in speaking style came a change in the way political speakers were judged by the press. While the ability to rouse a crowd to cheers is still admired, the ability to connect to individuals through the televised medium, much in evidence in figures such as Ronald Reagan and Bill Clinton, is put at a premium. Unlike the grand nineteenth-century rhetoric, this form of political communication demands

"sincerity" and "authenticity." Candidates whose performance is stilted
or uncomfortable—Michael Dukakis, George H. W. Bush, Al Gore—are
punished for appearing insincere, while those who enact the rituals of
politics with ease and comfort are judged successful. Such comfort is taken
as proof that the persona the politician represents is real and true, while
the persona presented by the awkward politician is false and contrived.

Journalists' portrait of Gore was so damaging in part because it fit-
ted him in a mold their over-arching storyline assigns to politicians in
general: Politicians are assumed to be dishonest schemers who present a
false image to the public in order to advance their quest for power. Writing this story about Gore was easy for reporters, since they had written it
so many times before.

On the Lookout for Decisive Moments

Ask an American who was politically aware at the time what she remem-
bers of the three debates between Gerald Ford and Jimmy Carter in 1976,
and she will likely answer that Ford said that Eastern Europe was not under Soviet domination. The 1980 Reagan-Carter debate? "There you go
again." The 1988 vice-presidential debate between Lloyd Bentsen and Dan
Quayle? "You're no Jack Kennedy." We recall these exchanges not because
they were so compelling that they implanted themselves forever in our
memory, but because in the wake of each debate they were played on television and quoted in newspapers again and again. Journalists at the time
told us that from the debate we had just witnessed—and especially if we
had happened to miss it—these moments were the important ones.

As a consequence, opinion about debates is often shaped more by the
post-debate interpretation than by the exchanges between the candidates.
The prototypical case is that of Ford's ill-considered remark in 1976. Few
Americans took particular note of it immediately during the debate; or if
they did, they did not see the remark as disqualifying Ford from the office
he held. *New York Times* editor Max Frankel, who asked Ford the question, signaled the journalistic perspective by asking Ford incredulously,
"Did I understand you to say, sir, that the Russians are not using Eastern
Europe as their own sphere of influence . . . ?" Frankel's colleagues deemed
the remark a "gaffe" of epic proportions, and told their audiences so in
subsequent days. The result was striking: a poll taken the night of the debate showed that people picked Carter as the winner of the debate by a
close margin, but after a wave of press discussion of the Eastern Europe

remark, that margin increased by nearly twenty points.[14] As time passes, these "decisive moments" become what we remember of debates, and to a certain extent presidential campaigns as a whole. As the most important events in every presidential campaign, debates help define the candidates and the presidents presented to the American people.

The power of the press's interpretation of debates takes on greater importance as audiences for debates decline. The first televised debates between John F. Kennedy and Richard Nixon in 1960 were revolutionary events that captivated the nation despite the fact that they were extraordinarily serious affairs with detailed policy discussion and little in the way of fireworks. Approximately 60% of American televisions were tuned to each of the Kennedy-Nixon debates. By contrast, the final debate between Bush and Gore—in an election as close as that of 1960—was watched in fewer than 26% of American homes.

Of the twenty debates for which Nielsen Media Research has data (the exception being the 1980 debate between Ronald Reagan and independent candidate John Anderson), the five with the lowest ratings were those held during the 1996 and 2000 campaigns. At a rating of 25.9 (each rating point represents 1% of homes with televisions), the final debate between Bush and Gore was the lowest-rated ever. The most watched debate, with a combined rating of 61, was the second Kennedy-Nixon exchange. The second encounter between Bill Clinton and Bob Dole had the smallest total audience (25.3 million homes); the second-lowest was the final Bush-Gore debate (26.3 million homes). These two debates were also seen in fewer homes than even those of 1960, when there were nearly 100 million fewer Americans and many homes did not have televisions.

Although in the 2000 election the debates drew an audience only slightly larger than that for a typical episode of *E.R.*, the press still considers them a major story and frames them not as an opportunity for citizens to learn but as a sporting contest—asking who the victor is, and as a test of character, asking what of each candidate is revealed by the debate. Consequently, if either candidate does or says something in a debate that reinforces a conclusion reporters have *already* reached, that moment is far more likely to be the subject of post-debate discussion. This is the common thread running through the "decisive moments" on which reporters choose to focus: They provide vivid illustrations of these pre-existing judgments. Debate coverage presents in miniature the press's approach to the campaign and the candidates.

As an illustration, let us examine two of the best-known decisive moments from recent elections. In 1988, CNN anchor Bernard Shaw opened the final debate between George Bush and Michael Dukakis by asking Dukakis, "Governor, if Kitty Dukakis were raped and murdered, would you favor an irrevocable death penalty for the killer?" Instead of pounding his lectern or reddening with anger at the thought of his wife being raped and murdered, Dukakis responded by citing the reasons for his opposition to the death penalty and touting his record in reducing crime in Massachusetts. The hint of weariness in his voice—he began his answer with "No, I don't, Bernard. And I think you know that I've opposed the death penalty during all of my life . . ."—may have been due to the fact that there was little question of where he stood; his stance on the death penalty had been the subject of multiple Republican television ads and had been criticized repeatedly by his opponent. To emphasize the preconception, later in the debate panelist Margaret Warner told Dukakis he had "won the first debate on intellect, and yet you lost it on heart."

The conclusion of journalists was nearly unanimous: Despite covering well-traveled ground, Dukakis's answer to Shaw's question revealed that—just as they had been saying for months—the Massachusetts governor was at best too careful and at worst a cold, heartless technocrat. On the next evening's *MacNeil-Lehrer Newshour*, conservative David Gergen opined that Dukakis "seemed to lack fire in the belly," while liberal Mark Shields criticized Dukakis' answer to Shaw's question for being "an impersonal abstraction." The *San Diego Union-Tribune* wrote, "Although Dukakis appeared momentarily shaken by the severity of the question, he failed in answering it to address the human tragedy and personal loss that was at the core of the inquiry."[15] Syndicated columnist Charles Krauthammer described Dukakis's answer as "stunningly mechanical."[16] David Broder agreed, saying, "A man who shows not the flicker of shock or anger at a truly brutal question about the hypothetical rape and murder of his wife is not a man who can convey the feelings he undoubtedly has about flag, country or creator."[17] Dukakis was taken to task by journalists for not displaying what they felt to be the appropriate emotional response to Shaw's question.

The moment did not reveal anything new; in fact, it was precisely because it accorded with a conclusion the press had reached months before that it was characterized as so critical. The exchange offered journalists a fresh opportunity to rewrite a familiar story.

The second illustration is that of President George H. W. Bush's performance in the "town hall" debate that took place on October 15, 1992. A citizen questioner asked the candidates, "How has the national debt personally affected each of your lives? And if it hasn't, how can you honestly find a cure for the economic problems of the common people if you have no experience in what's ailing them?" Trying to answer the question literally, President Bush displayed some understandable confusion—"I'm not sure I get it. Help me with the question and I'll try to answer it"—until moderator Carole Simpson clarified that the woman probably meant "the recession, the economic problems today the country faces rather than the deficit."[18] Bush then took issue with the implication that because he was wealthy he could not understand ordinary people's economic woes. At two other points in the debate while Clinton or Perot was talking, Bush glanced down at his watch.

Bush's trouble grappling with this question and the fact that he checked his watch were taken as evidence that he was indeed—as reporters had concluded—out of touch, with one foot out the door of the White House. Columnist Jim Hoagland wrote, "George Bush has joined pollsters and pundits in concluding that he has lost this election . . . Bush kept glancing at his watch, obviously wishing the debate thing would end. In his worst moment, he lectured the evening's most earnest and appealing questioner—a woman who asked about the impact of the long recession on him personally—about the effect of interest payments on the national debt."[19] On the *CBS Evening News*, reporter Randall Pinkston noted, "The President kept looking at his watch. Campaign aides said he was merely concerned that his opponents were getting too much time. But it made him look impatient and disinterested. Meanwhile, top campaign officials are dismissing published reports quoting sources close to the president that Mr. Bush has given up."[20] On NPR, Daniel Schorr opined that Bush "exhibited an air of almost disengagement, as though he were waging a battle that he himself believes he has lost."[21] The night after the debate, ABC News reporter John McWethy's story included an interview with a job placement consultant, discussing what Republicans in the Bush administration might do after the election.[22]

Debate coverage offers a condensed version of the campaign and the relationship between candidates and the reporters who cover them. As they watch debates, reporters are on the lookout for moments that cohere with the story lines they have already established about the candidates. As was the case with Ford, a point of which viewers take little note can thus be amplified and over time become all that is remembered of a debate, altering citizens' perceptions of the event. In 2000, we saw a similar effect of Al Gore's performance in the first debate. As they had in previous years, debates became a vehicle for reporters to reiterate their conclusions and illustrate their impressions. But for the most part, citizens are unaware of the origin of these conclusions and impressions.

Searching for the Candidate

In constructing pictures of the candidates, reporters assemble statements and actions in an attempt to describe the "real" candidate. As election day approaches, each word and deed is analyzed for what it can tell us about the man himself. Consequently, a factual mistake in a statement by Gore is explained by the fact that he is too quick to please, or eager to win at any cost. The implication: Gore is dishonest. The same mistake by Bush is explained by the fact that he is inexperienced or unfamiliar with the subject matter, with the inference being that he is a C+ intellect. Other possibilities—for instance that in either case it was simply a verbal miscue of the kind each of us makes every day—are not considered. This is an example of what psychologists call the "fundamental attribution error," the tendency to overestimate the influence of dispositional factors and underestimate the influence of situational factors when evaluating the behavior of others (but not ourselves). For example, if I had a car accident it was because the road was wet and another driver cut me off; if you had an accident it is because you are a bad driver. Voters are eager customers of these kinds of evaluations. As political scientist Samuel Popkin put it, "Because we tend to overestimate the reasonableness of our own actions, we also overestimate the probability that others would do what we would do. For this reason, we tend to believe that people who make mistakes or blunders are revealing their true character."[23]

Even if attempts to define an opponent by a single character flaw are equally successful, the consequences of that definition may vary. People will compare the candidate both to his opponent and to themselves, a comparison that probably worked to Bush's advantage in 2000. Most people do not view themselves as policy wonks or intellectuals; the argument that Al Gore was more of both than George Bush had limited persuasive power. However, most people regard themselves as honest. Reporters and citizens were willing to entertain the possibility that a high I.Q. and experience were not necessary qualities in a president, but no one was willing to suggest it was acceptable to be less than totally trustworthy and honest. In raising the question, reporters pointed to FDR and Reagan as successful presidents who were not intellectuals. "Bush lacks Washington experience," said the *Milwaukee Journal-Sentinel*, "but governors with little background in Beltway politics have thrived as presidents: Think of Franklin Roosevelt and Ronald Reagan."[24] After the candidates secured their parties' nominations, Richard Reeves wrote an article for the *Los Angeles Times* on the lack of correlation between intellect and success as a president. The caption under the four photographs accompanying the article read, "George W. Bush, above, shows iffy smarts but strong charisma, as did Ronald Reagan, right; Bill Clinton, above right, may be the smartest chief executive of recent times; FDR was credited with 'a second-class intellect but a first-class temperament.'"[25] The quote about FDR, spoken by Oliver Wendell Holmes, was often cited in support of the notion that Bush could be a good president.

In contrast to analogies linking Bush to previous presidents of average intelligence, the analogies that one might draw to past presidents who were dishonest or untrustworthy were indictments: Johnson prosecuting a war he had promised to let others fight; Nixon covering up the crimes of Watergate. Advisers can compensate for inexperience, goes the logic. Nothing can compensate for a lack of integrity. In both Bush's and Gore's cases, however, few analyses linked the assumed trait to the challenges and opportunities the next president would face, and how he would meet them.

Each day's news is a product of choices made by reporters in which certain pieces of information are deemed important and relevant and others ignored. A somewhat simplified explanation of who the candidates are is a nearly inevitable product of this process. But does all the effort to discover the candidates' "true" selves result in an electorate informed and able to predict what a candidate might do and who he might be in office? The answer may depend on which feature of the candidate's personality is in focus. When the Watergate tapes revealed Richard Nixon to have a penchant for off-color language (not to mention bigotry), many Americans were shocked by an aspect of their president of which they had been unaware. In contrast, few were truly surprised to learn that Bill Clinton had been unfaithful to his wife, behavior he had acknowledged, albeit obliquely, in a *60 Minutes* interview during the 1992 primaries.[26] The revelation of Nixon's dark side—vulgar, paranoid, and anti-Semitic, among other things—lent weight to the charges of criminal behavior. Because his frontstage persona was revealed as inauthentic, the idea that he was in fact a crook became more plausible.

Yet the anti-Semitic remarks did not translate in Nixon into a Middle East policy hostile to Israel, and the vulgarity did not translate into the sorts of personal moral failings that characterized the Kennedy, Clinton, and Roosevelt presidencies. What, then, did these pieces of evidence mean? Perhaps their strongest signal was one of hypocrisy. It was, after all, Nixon who in the famous debates with Kennedy in 1960 chided Harry Truman for his salty language while making the point that mothers should be able to point to the president as a model for their children.

Had reporters known of the anti-Semitic and vulgar streaks in Nixon, would they have drawn the wrong inferences about his personal disposition and policy preference?

Unlike the statements "Gore told a lie" or "Bush said something dumb," the claim "Gore is untrustworthy," like the claim "Bush is not too bright," is a statement about past, present, and future. By discovering the individual's essential character, we predict his future actions. When they vote, citizens are in effect making predictions about the future; "character," however defined, is thus certainly relevant, but the prediction may or may not be a good one.

The quality of the predictions citizens make rests in part on whether reporters have offered them the information required to place candidates' characters in the context of the office they seek. Unfortunately, the process that leads to the conclusions reporters make is often invisible to their readers and viewers. An incident from the 1972 presidential campaign illustrates the way reporters accumulate impressions and conclusions, then wait for events to offer the opportunity to present them to the public. Before the New Hampshire primary, Maine senator Ed Muskie was the target of dirty tricks from the Nixon campaign and strident attacks from the state's staunchly conservative newspaper, the *Manchester Union-Leader*. After a *Union-Leader* editorial attacked his wife, Muskie held a news conference outside the paper's offices. During his emotional statement, Muskie appeared to be teary-eyed. Reporters, including David Broder of the *Washington Post*—the most influential political reporter in America—wrote stories highlighting Muskie's emotional breakdown. Broder's lead began, "With tears streaming down his face and his voice choked with emotion . . ." Muskie claimed that he had merely been wiping the snow from his face, not crying. What reporters did not know at the time was that a letter supposedly written by Muskie insulting French-Canadians, which had prompted the editorials in the *Union-Leader*, was actually a fabrication concocted by the Nixon campaign.

Muskie's supposed tears—and the emotional instability they were thought to represent—became the focus of discussion in the ensuing weeks. Although he won the New Hampshire primary, Muskie did so by a smaller margin than many had expected, and the subsequent unraveling of his campaign was blamed alternatively on his performance at the press conference outside the *Union-Leader* or on press interpretation of it.

Why was Muskie's emotional response to an attack on his wife given such attention and an unflattering and cautionary interpretation? David Broder later explained: "All of us suspected that under the calm, placid

reflective face that Muskie liked to show the world, there was a volcano waiting to erupt. And so we treated Manchester as a political Mt. St. Helens explosion, and, in our perception, an event that would permanently alter the shape of 'Mt. Muskie.'" In his book *Behind the Front Page*, Broder quoted reporter Lou Cannon, relating how after playing poker with Ed Muskie he concluded that the Senator was "a little temperamental to be President of the United States." "What does a political reporter do with this kind of insight?" asked Cannon. "As in this instance, it is rarely written as a hard news story the first time the thought arises . . . What we reporters tend to do is to store away in our minds such incidents and then use them to interpret—to set a context—for major incidents when they occur."[27]

Just as many reporters felt that Al Gore was dishonest before he claimed to have taken "the lead in creating the Internet," they suspected that George W. Bush was no genius long before an enterprising local reporter quizzed him on the identities of foreign leaders. These incidents offered an opportunity to write stories fleshing out the portrayal that had been germinating among reporters over time.

Since the press rarely discloses the antecedent evidence that reporters have amassed, the play given to the contemporary event may seem—particularly to partisans—to be unfair or wildly out of proportion. This raises a number of questions for us. First, what constitutes evidence that a problematic personality tendency or disposition actually exists? Second, what does the evidence that the reporter has accumulated—for instance, a candidate's behavior in a poker game—actually indicate about the candidate? Third, what are the obligations of the reporter to disclose the evidence that led to the inference? And finally, what are the obligations of the reporter to tie the evidence to a plausible impact on the candidate's ability to lead and govern? By 1972, Muskie had served three terms in the House of Representatives, two terms as governor of Maine, and thirteen years in the U.S. Senate. Had his temperament compromised his performance in those positions? If so, how? If not, is there some reason to believe that this presumed flaw would undercut his capacity to serve as president? Instead of answering these questions, reports at the time posited the flaw, invited the inference that it was disabling, and moved on.

The same process was at work in 2000. In the primary campaign, there were reports that signaled the inference on the part of reporters that Gore was untrustworthy or dishonest. In a story reviewing factual disputes between Gore and Bill Bradley just before the New Hampshire primary, Lisa

Myers of NBC telegraphed the reporters' concern by attributing it to political insiders: "But privately, some top Democrats fear Gore is wounded, vulnerable to attack from his truthfulness long after this primary is history."[28] There may, of course, have been Democrats, most likely those who favored Bradley, voicing this concern. But Myers would not have closed her report with their view if it did not resonate with her.

Was there a pattern? And if so, did it forecast problems for Gore as president? A *New York Times* piece titled "Questions of Veracity Have Long Dogged Gore" in February reviewed Gore's misstatements going back to the 1970s.[29] Two weeks later, the *Boston Globe* also cited "long-standing concerns" that Gore "has a predilection for embellishing facts to burnish his personal resume or professional accomplishments."[30]

Just as with Muskie, reporters had built up a catalogue of evidence to support their conclusions about Gore and Bush's weaknesses. At critical times (e.g., a debate) the reporters focus on things that support the psychological profile. At the time, these choices can seem unfair. In the case of the first debate in 2000, both candidates said things that weren't true, and one could make the case that Bush's falsehoods were more consequential for governance than Gore's; similarly, whether Bush happened to know the names of the foreign leaders listed in a quiz tells us little about the quality of his mind. But the incident in focus serves more as a current example for a conclusion that is based on a buildup of incidents from the past.

Was Gore more disposed to dissemble than Bush or than most in public or private life? Was Bush a lesser light intellectually, lesser than Gore, lesser than presidents past? The more important question is whether the press connected these supposed flaws to governance, explaining to the citizenry what the potential consequences of a tendency to exaggerate or a lack of experience might be in a president. By 2000 Al Gore had served as a congressman, senator, and vice president. Had the fact that he embellished stories impaired his performance in those positions? In Bush's case, had his lack of experience or circumscribed cognitive complexity diminished his capacity to lead as governor of Texas? The press should have asked how the kind of self-promoting exaggerations to which it believed Gore was prone would affect his performance in office, and whether this tendency affected the Republican nominee as well. The same comparative inquiry should have been undertaken about Bush's supposed inexperience, intellect, and infelicitous use of language. Such discussion was largely absent, however.

While reporters freely speculate on candidates' personal traits, they are much more circumspect when it comes to their records and biographies. For example, the national press was extraordinarily careful in handling rumors that George W. Bush had used cocaine; when hard evidence could not be found, the question was dropped with little mention in major news outlets. The same was true of allegations that Bush had skipped out on part of his National Guard service.

Inferences about traits, as opposed to whether a candidate did or did not do drugs or dodge the draft, are not statements about what did or did not happen but matters of interpretation. As such, they are less subject to the corrective structures in place to ensure accuracy. When one enters the world of personality profiling, the question asked is not did the event happen, but rather, is there a pattern, and, if so, what does it mean. The accuracy of the account of the event or statement that provides evidence for the trait is assumed. In the case of Muskie's supposed tears or Gore's presumed statements about Love Canal and the Internet, that presumption may in its own right be faulty. But once reporters lock in a conclusion about a fatal flaw, and construct a coherent story about the candidate's identity with it as part of the plot, facts are more likely than in other circumstances to fall from focus and the linkage between fact and the psychological meaning to come to the fore.

When the evidence is clear, the meaning-making process is even more subjective. For example, if a candidate makes a statement that is untrue, the effect resides in the interpretation. Was the candidate given incorrect information? Was he intentionally attempting to mislead? Or was he too dumb to remember or to know what the truth was? The inference reporters draw about the statement will be influenced by the conclusions they have made about the candidate to that point, though any of the three interpretations or some other alternative may be plausible.

When reduced to one or two traits, these personality profiles may be true or false, but the story they tell is always an incomplete one. The portrait can also shortchange the electorate both by what it brings into focus and what it excludes, particularly when it devolves into the caricatures presented on late-night television. All caricatures fail on the second point—important information is necessarily excluded—and most fail on the first point as well. By casting disproportionate attention on otherwise trivial events and statements, they distort reality in the service of a unified portrait. Just as candidates repeat the same lines over and over again to ensure their penetration into the public psyche, reporters return to the same story, piling on more evidence consistent with the portrayal. By the end of the 2000 campaign, voters could not be blamed for believing that Al Gore was a pathological liar or that George W. Bush could barely tie his own shoes. The speed with which reporters later discarded the image of Bush they had constructed suggests that it had outlived its usefulness—or that it was not particularly useful in the first place.

The vetting process through which reporters describe candidates is an extension of their watchdog role—by exposing what is wrong with candidates, as they do with government, they seek to prevent demagogues and dolts from assuming the highest office in the land. But by focusing on a single character flaw, reporters place a lens over their eyes that can distort the public's view.

CHAPTER 3

The Press as Amateur
Psychologist, Part II

The day-to-day reporting of the 2000 campaign seldom attempted to relate evaluations of each candidate's psyche to what he might or might not do in office, or had done in office to that point. Instead, each candidate's character was explored for its own sake. Ultimately, the dominant press frame in the 2000 election hurt Gore more than Bush.

A *Los Angeles Times* article from the day before the election encapsulates press coverage of the 2000 campaign:

> To a great extent, the descriptions that *voters* [emphasis added] hung on the candidates at the beginning of the campaign have held until its end. Bush is seen as the more likable, adept at discussing education policy yet lacking experience in a wide range of presidential demands. Gore is the experienced issues expert, versed in the intricacies of children's health insurance but saddled with questions about his trustworthiness . . . Victory is likely to hinge less on tax proposals and Social Security platforms than which element voters are best able to live with: questions of Bush's inexperience or Gore's truthfulness.[1]

Gore's flaw was reduced to trustworthiness, while Bush's was reduced to lack of knowledge, translated ultimately as inexperience. Inexperience can be remedied by experience or by marshaling a cabinet and selecting a vice president with experience. A lack of trust, on the other hand, is much harder to remedy. In addition, surveys of journalists have shown that honesty is the most important quality reporters believe a

41

presidential candidate should have; while experience is also rated as important, it lags behind trustworthiness.[2] Unfortunately for Gore, an allegation of untrustworthiness cannot be disconfirmed. Once the untrustworthy lens was locked in, any move on Gore's part could be interpreted as a cynical attempt to hide his true self.

As is often the case, the author of the *L.A. Times* article attributed journalists' conclusions to the voters themselves. While some political reporters spend a great deal of time talking to ordinary people, many spend most of their time among politicians, those who work for them, and—importantly—with other journalists. Ideas, interpretations, and conclusions pass among the reporters, creating a consensus on which facts are important and how stories should be reported. When asked for the source of these conclusions, many cite "the people," despite the fact that the circles in which they operate contain few ordinary citizens. For example, in a discussion after the first Bush-Gore debate on CNN's *Reliable Sources*, one of the principal forums of media self-analysis, *New Yorker* writer Joe Klein admitted that "there's a natural tendency to play toward the mistakes that reinforce our existing notions," but then went on to assert that "it was Gore's general overbearing quality in that first debate that people overreacted to." Ann McDaniel, the Washington bureau chief of *Newsweek*, added, "I don't think the media is just pushing this agenda. I think you hear voters out there raising questions about Gore's credibility and Bush's intelligence." McDaniel's perch in Washington is a vital one, but perhaps not the best place from which to judge what "voters out there" are discussing.

Early in the 2000 campaign, journalists established a frame for each candidate that found expression in reporters' stories, pundits' evaluations, and comedians' jokes. In 2000, Al Gore was a dishonest panderer and George W. Bush was a dim-witted neophyte, or as one pundit put it, this was a contest between Pinocchio and Dumbo.[3]

Of course, such uncomplimentary frames have been constructed about candidates in the past, with campaign events used as illustrations of a candidate's flaws. If a candidate does or says something that reflects his particular flaw, it is much more likely to show up in news than if his opponent did or said the same thing. This is the essence of how a press frame operates: It highlights certain features of reality and not others, determining what finds its way into news and what is omitted. If in 1996 the relatively young Bill Clinton had mistakenly referred to the Los Angeles Dodgers as the Brooklyn Dodgers, few would have taken notice. But when the seventy-three-year-old Bob Dole said, "I'm going to pitch a no-hitter from now until November 5. The Brooklyn Dodgers had a no-hitter last night and I'm going to follow what [Dodgers pitcher Hideo] Nomo did," it showed up on the national news and in dozens of newspaper articles, with reporters solemnly noting, as if correcting a beloved grandfather who was beginning to dodder, that the Dodgers left Brooklyn forty years before.

Previous research has found that the evaluations voters make of presidential candidates can be reduced to a limited set of judgments, often grouped together as "integrity," "competence," "leadership," and "empathy."[4] In order to capture the differences in the way voters evaluated the candidates, we asked respondents to the 2000 Annenberg Survey how honest, knowledgeable, and inspiring each candidate was, and how much each "cares about people like me." Our survey allowed us to track opinion change over time, as we interviewed Americans continually from the end of 1999 through Bush's inauguration in January 2001. In all, more than 100,000 interviews were conducted.

Not surprisingly, the greatest differences between Gore and Bush appeared on the first two concepts, one tapping perceptions of integrity and one assessing perceptions of competence: Gore was thought to be substantially more knowledgeable and Bush was judged significantly more honest. These evaluations, however, were not static over the course of the campaign; instead, they moved with critical campaign events and changes in the informational environment.

Gore as Lying Panderer

In their quest to identify and illuminate the candidates' characters, reporters put the candidates on the analyst's couch. After the first presidential debate of 2000, the *New York Times* published a story titled "Tendency to Embellish Facts Snares Gore." In the article, a psychology professor who teaches a class called "Detecting Imposters and Con Artists" pondered the meaning of Gore's exaggerations and concluded, "It's like the false memory syndrome when people end up believing that they were abducted by aliens."[5] Three weeks before election day, the *Times* ran a story on the first page of its Sunday Week in Review section whose headline asked about Gore, "Is What We've Got Here a Compulsion to Exaggerate?" Reporter Melinda Henneberger ruminated on various exaggerations and answered the titled question in the affirmative. Along with the many other news outlets that follow its lead, the paper of record probed the recesses of Al Gore's mind and concluded that in Gore "we see someone stretching the truth for weird, inscrutable reasons."[6]

Concerns about Gore's trustworthiness first took hold among reporters in 1988 when the Tennessean, in his first run for president, embraced New York mayor Ed Koch in what seemed like an opportunistic manner. Reporters remembered as well that Gore was the one who first raised the Massachusetts furlough program in an attack on Michael Dukakis in a primary debate. But Gore was out of the race before the perceptions could be translated into column inches. When Gore was selected as Bill Clinton's vice-presidential nominee in 1992, explorations of the "real" Gore were displaced by tactical analyses that saw advantages for Clinton in Gore's service in Vietnam and in his strong environmental record. However, the observations about Gore's integrity surfaced when, in a press conference answering questions about fund-raising calls, he uttered the phrase that would echo in attack ads of the 2000 campaign: "No controlling legal authority."

The issue of Gore's honesty brings to light the complex and often inconsistent standards applied to the statements public officials and candidates make. In her book *Lying: Moral Choice in Public and Private Life*, philosopher Sissela Bok describes the ordinary untruths politicians tell nearly every day—for instance, feigning enjoyment of a rally when one would rather be at home—as "forms of politeness that mislead few."[7] For politicians there is, however, an entire spectrum of misleading statements, each of which we judge in different ways. The veracity of the "little white lies" told in order to be polite to the listener, whether the attendants at a rally or the constituent coming to the senator's office, are not evaluated. Whether they mislead anyone or not, we do not bother to inspect them too carefully. Even when considering only what we might call self-aggrandizing lies—those told not to be polite to the listener but to enhance the image of the speaker—there are some we deem worth examining and some we do not. When a politician says, "Nothing is more important to me than the future of our children," reporters do not investigate whether she might have a more pressing priority. When candidates have declared, "I'm running because I care deeply about the future of our country," their words have not generated examination. Partly because feelings and intentions are unverifiable, we accept statements of enthusiasm and concern without investigation even when they seem faintly dubious.

Statements that have essentially the same content but different phrasing are also subject to different levels of inspection. In their campaign literature, legislators routinely claim to have "fought for" popular legislation, when in many cases the fight consisted solely of voting for the bill or agreeing to serve as a cosponsor. Does such a statement constitute a lie? Most would say no; unless the congressman actually voted *against* the bill, no one will charge him with dishonesty. What if the congressman claimed to have "led the fight"? What about saying he was "a leader in the fight," which is something less than leading the fight on one's own?

Some kinds of false statements are so accepted that few would consider them attempts to deceive. For example, it is common for officials to be asked about the political motives behind their decisions. The official will deny that political considerations entered anyone's mind; the reporter will then describe the political considerations. The original statement is discredited, but not described in terms that paint the speaker as a liar. An article from the *Washington Post*, about the Bush administration's 2002 decision to raise tariffs on imported steel (in contrast to Bush's more general free-trade philosophy), is illustrative:

> President Bush's chief economic adviser, Lawrence B. Lindsey, was asked at a recent news conference how big a role politics would play in the decision on tariffs for imported steel. "Politics will play no role," he replied.
>
> Despite his claim, several activists who met with administration officials on the matter said politics seemed important to those who calibrated the plan announced yesterday. Even a White House official, speaking on the condition of anonymity, said of the tariff decision: "Politics is part of everything any administration does."[8]

In this case, both Lindsey and reporter Mike Allen are enacting familiar roles in the political drama. Although the notion that politics had nothing to do with the tariff decision is believed by no one, Lindsey's statement is not only unsurprising but expected. Had Lindsey instead said, "Of course politics was involved. This decision will help us in 2004 in West Virginia, Pennsylvania, and Ohio," the statement would have been unusual and given greater attention. Instead he denies the political consideration, and the reporter finds other sources to contest the denial. Thus the familiar narrative is reiterated: Public officials hide their true intentions; it is those intentions which are of most consequence. Because it is so common, Lindsey's deceptive statement is not described as a lie.

In addition, in the context of a policy debate, whether an administration official is at heart a dishonest person is seldom at issue. In a campaign, on the other hand, "character" is a primary consideration for reporters. Although distinguishing the permissible exaggeration from the deceitful one can occasionally be a complex task for reporters, voters certainly have a right to expect that the same standards will apply to the statements of both candidates in a race. In 2000, the line on the spectrum of exaggeration between statements worthy of investigation and those simply ignored was in a different place for George W. Bush and Al Gore, because the frame around Gore concerned honesty and ambition, while the frame around Bush concerned experience and intelligence.

During the entire 2000 general election campaign but especially in the final six weeks, reporters judged the candidates by different standards when it came to truth-telling. Gore's claims were more closely examined to determine their accuracy, and when they were found wanting, became evidence of a fundamental character flaw. When some of Bush's claims were found untruthful they were more likely to be characterized as mistakes than as deceptions. Although the old joke says that you can tell a politician is lying when his lips are moving, not all politicians are judged according to the same criteria.

On May 5, for example, in an attempt to argue that Gore's support of gun control was hypocritical, Bush falsely asserted that Gore had been a member of the National Rifle Association. Journalists reported and corrected the false statement. What distinguishes this case, and others in which Bush made untrue statements, is not that they were ignored or excused by the press, because they were not (although they usually were given less attention than similar Gore misstatements). But nor were they used as evidence of a revealing character flaw, the way Gore's misstatements—and Bush's struggles with syntax—were.

Gore was accused of embellishing his personal and professional history, but the same charge was not made about Bush. The following example shows the kind of inaccuracy that, had the subject been Gore, would probably have been considered worthy of extended commentary by reporters. Bush's autobiography, *A Charge to Keep* (which was primarily written by aide Karen Hughes), tells the story of a night near the end of the 1988 campaign when Bush's daughter Barbara "lost her sleeping companion, Spikey, her favorite stuffed dog. She complained loudly that she could not sleep without Spikey, so 'Gampy,' better known as Vice President Bush, spent much of the night before his debate [with Michael Dukakis] searching the house and grounds of the vice presidential residence, flashlight in hand, on a mission to find Spikey. Finally, he did, and Barbara slept soundly. I don't know if my dad ever got to sleep that night." As the *New York Times* later reported, according to the senior

Barbara Bush, the toy was actually a stuffed cat, the vice president gave up the search and it wasn't found until the next day, and the incident actually took place in 1987, not 1988.[9] We were unable to find any other news outlet that repeated the *Times*'s correction of the embellished tale or questioned Bush about it.

By contrast, reporters were vigilant about pointing out occasions when Gore appeared to describe events from his personal life inaccurately. Accepting the endorsement of the Teamsters Union on September 18, Gore said, "You know, I still remember the lullabies that I heard as a child." He then cradled his arms as if holding a baby and sang the opening bars to "Look for the Union Label." The crowd laughed, perhaps understanding the idea that Gore's parents would sing him to sleep with a song from a union ad campaign to be a jest. Reporters pointed out that the song wasn't written until 1975, when Gore was twenty-seven. Gore's protestation that he was kidding was related in news stories, but given the lullaby incident's place in lists of Gore's untruths, not lent much credence.

Elsewhere in the campaign the same dynamic played out: Reporters scrutinized Gore's claims for veracity with greater vigor than they did Bush's. One of Bush's ads claimed that "while Washington deadlocked, he delivered a patient's bill of rights that's a model for America." In their final debate, when Gore said that he favored a patient's bill of rights but Bush did not, Bush replied, "Actually, Mr. Vice President, it's not true, I do support a national patients' bill of rights. As a matter of fact, I brought Republicans and Democrats together to do just that in the state of Texas to get a patient's bill of rights through." With this statement, Bush took credit for something he had actually opposed. In fact, as governor Bush vetoed one version of a patient's bill of rights, then allowed the final version to become law without his signature when it garnered a veto-proof majority. A number of newspapers pointed out Bush's distortion in post-debate analyses, but these articles were mostly simple refutations: This is what Bush said in the debate, these are the facts. How the incident might relate to Bush's fundamental honesty was not discussed.

When Gore changed his attire, journalists described it as a "reinvention" and characterized him as a "chameleon." On the other hand, when John McCain's reformist message helped him defeat Bush in the New Hampshire primary and in response Bush adopted the slogan "A Reformer With Results," it was described as a strategic move, but not one that cast any particular reflection on Bush's personality. For instance, the *St. Louis Post-Dispatch* said that with the slogan, Bush "changed both the style and substance of his campaign to counter McCain's momentum."[10] Notice, however, that it is the *campaign* that is thought to be altered, not the person. Likewise, the *Hartford Courant* referred to Bush's "new style of campaigning as a 'reformer with results' . . ."[11] Because Gore, not Bush, was cast as the dissembler, changes in his campaign were attempts to deceive; not so changes in Bush's campaign.

The consistent scrutiny of Gore's statements for inaccuracy was partly a result of successful public relations by the Bush campaign and its allies and partly a result of decisions made independently by reporters. The importance given to the allegation that Gore claimed to have "invented" the Internet is a case in point. Almost immediately after he said it, Gore's original statement was placed beyond the category of claims worthy of examination into the category of prima facie deceptions, along with "I am not a crook" and "I did not have sexual relations with that woman." Critical to this movement was the word "invented," with its implication of an engineer toiling in his basement. Gore's actual statement from an interview with Wolf Blitzer was this: "During my service in the United States Congress, I took the initiative in creating the Internet." In fact, Gore's role in securing funding for expansion of the fledgling network in the late 1980s was substantial; reporters who carefully examined his claim's veracity would have at the very least found it to be a not wholly unreasonable—if self-aggrandizing—interpretation of his role. The truth of Gore's statement rests in part on whether one concludes that the Internet was "created" by the computer scientists and engineers who designed the system, or by the politicians who provided the funding to turn a small network linking a few universities and military facilities into a global one. However, once the word "invented" became inextricably attached to the claim, it was no longer a subject of debate but an unquestioned example of Gore's dishonesty.

After the election, Gore adviser Bill Knapp explained why Gore never defended himself on the question. "We felt strongly that the more we tried to talk about it, and tried to explain what we thought in many cases were manufactured misstatements and exaggerations of human mistakes, the worse it became, and that we couldn't relitigate things from the distant past while the Republicans were stirring up new ones. We really didn't figure out a way to address it directly."[12] As Gore research director David Ginsberg argued, "Once something makes the leap from news to the late night shows, it's completely out of your hands, and no amount of argumentation, of documentation, of proof, of pleading with reporters to write the real story behind the Internet matters, because it's already in the public psyche."[13]

The misrepresentation of the Gore quote happened immediately; it was not only Republicans, but journalists as well, who took it as an opportunity for ridicule. Witness this whimsical exchange on CNN four days after the Gore statement between anchor Miles O'Brien and reporter Bob Franken:

> **O'Brien:** Senate Majority Leader Trent Lott now jokingly claims credit for taking the initiative in inventing the paperclip. And House Majority Leader Dick Armey says, if Gore invented the Internet, well then, by God, Armey created the interstate highway system. Our Bob Franken, not many people know, invented the reporter's notebook, didn't you, Bob?
>
> **Franken:** That's right. And if Dick Armey invented the interstate highway system, he should be ashamed of himself. I invented the Capitol over here, by the way.
>
> **O'Brien:** You invented the speed trap on the interstates, that's it.[14]

In this brief exchange the word "invent" is repeated six times. To say the notion that Gore claimed to have "invented" the Internet got repeated frequently would be something of an understatement. A Lexis-Nexis search seeking stories mentioning Al Gore and using the phrase "invented the Internet" captures 1,684 articles between Gore's interview with Blitzer in March 1999 and election day of 2000.

The Bush campaign deployed its indictment of Gore's credibility as an all-purpose rebuttal, including references to the Internet remark whenever possible. When in the October 3 debate Gore noted—accurately—that a couple with a $25,000 income was ineligible for Bush's proposed immediate prescription drug plan, Bush responded, "Look, this is a man, he's got great numbers. He talks about numbers. I'm beginning to think not only did he invent the Internet but he invented the calculator. It's fuzzy math . . ." When Gore charged that Bush's partial privatization plan for Social Security meant that he was promising the same money to current workers and future retirees, the Republican National Committee responded with this ad:

> **Announcer:** Why does Al Gore say one thing when the truth is another? His attacks on George Bush's Social Security plan? Exaggerations. The truth? Nonpartisan analysis confirms George Bush's plan sets aside 2.4 trillion dollars to strengthen Social Security. Newspapers say Gore has a problem telling the truth. Now Gore promises smaller government. But Gore is actually proposing three times the new spending President Clinton proposed. Why does Al Gore say one thing when the truth is another?

The Bush campaign and the RNC produced six separate ads whose primary subject was Gore's honesty. In one RNC ad, a television sitting on a kitchen counter plays clips of Gore talking, including one from his CNN interview. The female voice-over responds to Gore's claim about the Internet with a sarcastic "Yeah, and I invented the remote control." The ad thus prompts viewers to remember Gore's statement as including the word "invented" when in fact it did not. As important is the fact that this ad was used as a rebuttal to Gore's charges that Bush's proposal to permit investment of part of the payroll tax in individual stock market accounts didn't add up. A legitimate matter of contention between the candidates on a matter of concern to many was successfully recast as a question of Gore's credibility.

The announcer's sarcastic final comment ("I invented the remote control") was quoted in dozens of news stories. When it first began airing on August 31, the ad was the subject of stories on all three network evening newscasts. The ad was also played (in most cases in its entirety) on *This Week* on ABC; *Hannity and Colmes, The Beltway Boys, Fox News Sunday,* and *Special Report With Brit Hume* on Fox News; *Late Edition With Wolf Blitzer, Newsstand, CNN Today,* and *Crossfire* on CNN; NPR's *Morning Edition* and *Weekend Edition*; and NBC's *Today Show* and *Meet the Press.* Although many of the stories criticized the Republicans for attacking, they also repeated and reinforced Bush's claim about Gore's honesty.

As a cover article in the April 2000 issue of the *Washington Monthly* pointed out, the Internet remark was one of a number of Gore's exaggerations that were themselves exaggerated, often through misquotes and sloppy reporting.[15] For example, the *New York Times* and *Washington Post* misquoted a Gore comment about Love Canal, changing what Gore actually said—"that was the one that started it all" (referring to a toxic waste site in Toone, Tennessee, leading to congressional hearings about other toxic sites, including Love Canal) to "I was the one that started it all" (implying that Gore himself discovered toxic waste at Love Canal).[16] Gore's point about the positive effects of the involvement of the high school student in Toone who brought the case to his attention was changed, with one word, to another example to be used in the litany of his deceptions. The next day, the *Post's* Ceci Connelly wrote, "Add Love Canal to the list of verbal missteps by Vice President Gore. The man who mistakenly claimed to have inspired the movie *Love Story* and to have invented the Internet says he didn't quite mean to say he discovered a toxic waste site."[17] Connelly's construction of her misquote as a "verbal misstep" implied that Gore said he discovered toxic waste at Love Canal, then retracted the statement, when in fact he had claimed only to have chaired the first congressional hearings on the subject. His attempt to correct Connelly's misquote thus was framed as an admission that he had attempted to deceive with the original statement.

Another critical event in the contest over Gore's credibility occurred earlier, on March 30, 2000, when Gore stepped into the minefield of the Elian Gonzales case. The six-year-old boy, whose mother had died on their journey via raft from Cuba, had become an international cause célèbre. The Clinton administration wanted to return him to his father in Cuba, while many conservatives, particularly among the Cuban-American community in Florida, wanted him to stay with his relatives in Miami.

On March 30, Gore issued a press release supporting a bill in the Senate to grant permanent-resident status to Elian and his family. The press conclusion about this break with Clinton administration policy was that (1) Gore's statement reflected no real sentiment but was instead blatant pandering to the Cuban-American community in an attempt to increase his chances of winning Florida; and (2) as a political calculation it was extraordinarily ill-advised. A *Los Angeles Times* news story called it "a brazen move to win Cuban American votes."[18] On ABC News, reporter John Cochran sought an explanation from the author of a Gore biography. "A biographer of Gore sees a pattern in his behavior," Cochran said, introducing author Bill Turque, who then commented, "It would be completely cynical to suggest this was all politics here, but with Gore and a lot of his decisions, it is always a balance between conviction and political calculation. I think they're both in the mix here."[19] Later, on *Face the Nation*, host Bob Schieffer asked, "Is there anyone who believes that for all his pandering to Florida voters, that Al Gore improved his chances of carrying Florida? I don't."[20] Widely quoted election analyst Stuart Rothenberg declared that the Elian affair ended Gore's chances of carrying Florida. "Florida will see a lot less Democratic money and a lot less time from Al Gore," he said at the end of April.[21] After the election, Gore adviser Carter Eskew described the flap over Elian: "We managed to take a principled decision and make it look both unprincipled and stupid, which is hard to do."[22]

At times, the construction even occurred retroactively, as reporters took claims that had previously been accepted as truthful and reinterpreted them through the frame provided by the caricature of Gore. Throughout his career, Gore often related how as a boy, despite living during most of the year in Washington, he spent his summers working on the Gore family farm in Carthage, Tennessee. That he had done so had before the presidential campaign not been a matter of contention; many family members and friends had related how Al Gore, Sr., was something of a harsh taskmaster, believing that hard physical work would be good for his son. But once the Gore-as-liar motif emerged, reporters revisited this part of Gore's biography and began to treat it as if it were false. In the *Washington Post*, Michael Kelly penned a whimsical column portraying Al Gore waking up in Washington's Fairfax Hotel, then going out to farm in the District of Columbia. "It was time to herd the sheep over to Dupont Circle . . . 'Drive, James,' he said, and Carville gee-upped the mules out across the green, green grass of Massachusetts Avenue."[23] On CNN, Bruce Morton took a Gore quote—"My father taught me how to clean out hog waste with a shovel and a hoe. He taught me how to clear land with a double-blade ax; how to plow a steep hillside with a team of mules"—and implied that the fact that Gore spent most of his youth in Washington meant that a claim about specific farming details was a lie. "Summers at the family farm, yes," said Morton, "but mules and double-bladed axes? What he meant, a spokesman said, was the fact that he spent his summers working on the family farm."[24] Just as in the Love Canal case, this construction—statement, skeptical question from reporter, clarification by aide—is used to assert that the original statement was false. Why Morton believed Gore could not have used a double-blade ax or driven a mule during the summer was unclear. Three months later, Diane Sawyer interviewed Gore on *20/20*, administering a pop quiz much like the one to which Bush had been subjected on foreign policy to see if Gore knew which way the poles faced on a fence, how many tobacco plants are in an acre, what brucellosis is (a disease that affects cattle), and current cattle prices.[25] Gore performed reasonably well on the quiz, but if he had not, the conclusion would likely have been that his claim to have spent time on a farm was disingenuous.

The Democratic convention not only moved the Democratic ticket ahead in the polls, but also boosted perceptions of Gore's honesty to a level roughly equal with Bush's, with approximately 65% of those surveyed saying Gore was honest. Until that point the number of people rating Gore as honest had trailed behind the number rating Bush as honest by 15 to 20 percentage points. This movement was in all likelihood a "halo effect," in which a more positive overall impression leads to more positive evaluations on specific attributes. In addition, as a study by the Project for Excellence in Journalism showed, the theme of Gore's honesty, while briefly prominent in news at the end of his primary battle with Bill Bradley, had receded to the background leading up to the party conventions.[26]

But three weeks after the Democratic convention, four events brought Gore's honesty ratings tumbling to below 50%, where they remained until Election Day. The first was the statement about "Look for the Union Label" on September 18. That night, Gore held a fund-raiser in Hollywood with many entertainment-industry figures in attendance; the fact that he and his vice-presidential nominee and Connecticut Senator Joseph Lieberman had criticized the entertainment industry for marketing sex and violence to children not long before elicited accusations of hypocrisy from Republicans and editorial writers. "I noticed my opponent went out to Hollywood yesterday," Bush said. "He must be auditioning for a play, 'cause he keeps changing his tune."[27] In an editorial titled "Now Playing: 'Gore the Chameleon,'" the *Houston Chronicle* chided Gore for his "soft-shoe routine."[28]

On September 19, a story about a misstatement Gore made about the cost of prescription drugs broke in the *Boston Globe*. Gore had stated that his mother-in-law and his dog took the same arthritis drug but that his mother-in-law paid more for it. When the press and the Bush campaign discovered that Gore had used a congressional study and not the family bills to make his comparison, the story became the topic of stories on all three network news shows and in newspapers around the country the following day. The prescription drug story combined with the lullaby statement from Gore's Teamsters speech—which had occurred the day before—to produce numerous stories about Gore's truthfulness. "Questions about whether Al Gore exaggerates the truth have resurfaced," said *USA Today* in the ever-present passive voice. The paper provided a box with a list of Gore statements, each analyzed for its veracity.[29] *Newsweek*'s Bill Turque, the Gore biographer, wrote an article for the magazine's September 22 issue titled "Gore's Truth Troubles." The Bush campaign worked hard to describe Gore's statement as not only intentional deceptions but the latest examples in a pattern. "America better beware of a candidate who is willing to stretch reality in order to win points," said Bush. "It looks like another Al Gore invention," added Dick Cheney.[30] The Bush campaign later produced this ad:

> **Announcer:** Remember when Al Gore said his mother-in-law's prescriptions cost more than his dog's? His own aide said the story was made up. Now Al Gore is bending the truth again. The

press calls Gore's Social Security attacks "nonsense." Governor
Bush sets aside $2.4 trillion to strengthen Social Security and pay
all benefits.

Al Gore: There has never been a time in this campaign when I have
said something that I know to be untrue. There's never been a
time when I have said something untrue.

Announcer: Really?

This ad contains two misleading elements. The first is the assertion
that "the press" called Gore's criticism of Bush's Social Security plan "nonsense." This statement would imply that reporters, operating within the
standard of objectivity, had made this judgment of Gore's argument. In
fact, the "nonsense" quote appeared in an editorial by the *Wall Street
Journal*, whose editorial page is the most ideologically conservative of
any major newspaper.[31] The second misleading element is that while a
viewer might have been led to believe that the quote from Gore was offered recently, it originated in a primary debate with Bill Bradley.

A fourth event, occurring just two days after the mother-in-law story,
reinforced the press perception that Gore was untrustworthy. On September 21, in response to rising gasoline prices, Gore called for a release
of oil from the Strategic Petroleum Reserve. Like his statement on Elian
Gonzales, the SPR statement was taken by many in the press to be nothing more than cynical pandering to consumers. "How do I pander to
thee? Let me count the ways," said the editorial page of the *Atlanta Journal-Constitution*.[32] "A shameless political ploy," said the *Detroit News*.[33]
The *Providence Journal* called Gore's position "the most glaring example
yet of record presidential-candidate pandering this year."[34] The papers
described Gore's position as in conflict with his previous environmental
positions and an obvious attempt to curry favor with voters angered by
increases in the price of gasoline.

The four events occurring in rapid succession—the lullaby comment and Hollywood fund-raiser on September 18, the dog story on
September 19, and Gore's call to release oil from the strategic reserve on
September 21—locked in the press perception of Gore as a pandering,
hypocritical liar. When the candidates conducted their first debate two
weeks later, the interpretive frame for Gore's performance was in place.
During the debate, both candidates made statements that were inaccurate. The difference was in how those statements were interpreted: Bush's
were considered to be the result of a lack of information or a slip of the
tongue, while Gore's were described as deliberate fabrications.

Immediately after the first debate, Gore's advisers believed he was the clear victor. Strategist Bob Shrum said that when the debate ended "I was feeling terrific," but he quickly realized that reporters did not share his assessment. "It was clear to me right away that the Bush campaign was doing a very good job of changing the standard of judgment about the debate. The standard of judgment was suddenly: 'Did Gore make misstatements?'"[35] Coverage in the days following the debate did indeed center on a set of inaccurate statements Gore made during the debate.

The first had to do with a girl in Sarasota and a story about classroom overcrowding. Before the debate, a caterer providing food on Air Force Two gave Gore a letter and newspaper article from the *Sarasota Herald-Tribune* about his daughter having to stand in school because her classroom was so crowded that there were no more desks available. The article included a photo of the girl standing during class. In the debate, Gore related the story just as the article reported it. After the debate reporters extensively checked the story, writing articles in which the principal of the school disputed Gore's version of events. In fact, the only inaccuracy in what Gore said was a matter of verb tense: He claimed that the girl "has" to stand because of overcrowding, although by the time of the debate a chair had been obtained for her and she was no longer standing.

The other of Gore's claims to receive significant attention focused on forest fires in Texas and James Lee Witt, then Director of the Federal Emergency Management Agency. After Bush mentioned the fires, Gore said he "accompanied James Lee Witt down to Texas when those fires broke out." In fact, Gore had received a briefing in Texas about the fires not from Witt but from his deputy. However, Gore had been to a number of disaster areas with Witt during his time as vice president.

Much was also made of the fact that Gore sighed at times while Bush was speaking, as though impatient with his opponent (since the rules of the debate specified that the opposing candidate was not to be shown in reaction shots while the other was speaking, Gore had no way of knowing that his nonverbal reactions would be captured). The twin elements of Gore's demeanor and the two inaccuracies (the Witt story and the Sarasota girl) appeared in story after story about the debate. Absent in the reports was the possibility that the coverage, and not the statements themselves, might be driving changes in opinion. Instead, the fact that public perceptions of Gore's honesty declined over the course of a few days after the debate was attributed to voters simply thinking about the debate for a while, then changing their minds. This *USA Today* story was typical:

The latest USA Today/CNN/Gallup tracking poll, taken Friday-Sunday *after impressions from the last Tuesday's debate had a chance to sink in* [emphasis added], showed that likely voters rated Gore smarter, but they liked George W. Bush more . . . Catholic University of America political scientist Mark Rozell attributes the turnaround directly to Gore's "smart-alecky" performance in the debate . . . Analysts say [Gore's decline in the polls] stems from two statements in the debate by Gore that later proved inaccurate or suspect: that he accompanied James Lee Witt, director of the Federal Emergency Management Agency, on a trip to Texas to inspect fire and flood damage in 1998; and that a 15-year-old girl in Sarasota, Fla., had to stand because her science class was so crowded.

"Taken alone, they wouldn't be so bad, but Gore has a history of doing this dating back to saying he invented the Internet," Rozell says.[36]

The press coverage influenced not only voters but Gore himself. Gore responded to the negative press verdicts of his first performance by comporting himself in the second debate in a manner opposite to the way he had in the first. Where he had initially been highly critical of Bush, in the second debate he complimented him, pointing out areas of agreement between the candidates wherever he could. Where he had been aggressive in the first debate, in the second he appeared low-key. And in response to a question from moderator Jim Lehrer about his honesty, he offered an apology: "I got some of the details wrong last week in some of the examples that I used, Jim, and I'm sorry about that. And I'm going to try to do better."

When we examine one measure on our 2000 survey—Gore's honesty ratings—we see that post-debate coverage seems to have had a significant effect in altering people's judgments. While those who watched the debate had lower judgments of Gore's honesty at the outset (in part because this group includes slightly more Republicans than the sample as a whole), over the days following the debate those who didn't watch became less and less likely to describe Gore as honest. The opinions of those who saw the debate remained essentially unchanged. While the effect is limited—by the end of the period in which we asked the question approximately 5% fewer people who didn't see the debate described Gore as honest—in an election as close as 2000, such effects can play a role in determining the winner.

We see a similar delayed effect on judgments of who won the first debate. In the immediate aftermath, those not in the audience—and keep in mind this group includes fewer Republicans than the debate viewing group—were less likely to believe that Bush had won the debate. Over the following week, with each passing day more and more of this group came to believe that Bush had won. When the second debate arrived, those who did not see the first were as likely to believe that Bush won the first debate as the more heavily Republican debate watchers.

In the current media environment, no single message's effects are a result only of its original airing. Advertisements are aired to viewers, then replayed in news analyses; late-night comedians' jokes turn up on morning shows and cable news. This situation makes scholarly analysis challenging. Traditionally, scholars have relied on two methods to investigate communication effects. In experiments, they have exposed subjects to messages and measured changes in knowledge, attitudes, and opinions. In surveys, they have asked respondents to recall which media sources they use and how often, then looked for differences between people with various media diets. Each method has well-known strengths and weaknesses, but the usefulness of both is compromised by the rapid diffusion of messages across media that takes place in the real world. Some of this diffusion can be documented, but some—for instance, the cumulative effect late-night caricatures have on the perspective of reporters covering the candidates—is harder to measure. Important ideas, events, and interpretations spread rapidly through media and conversation; usually, within days those who were directly exposed to a media message are indistinguishable from those who were exposed only indirectly.

Debates offer a good case in point. As we have shown, in the few days following a debate those who saw it can differ greatly in their opinions from those who did not. As time passes, memories fade, and the debate is distilled to particular moments and interpretations that are repeated again and again, whether one saw the debate itself becomes irrelevant. In a world of multiple media outlets continually referring and reflecting one another, something akin to a single entity called political discourse does in fact exist. The primary themes and frames structuring that discourse determine the content of memory.

Obviously, citizens will not store in their memory every moment of a presidential debate; a distillation down to a few critical moments is almost inevitable. What is problematic is the basis on which those moments are chosen and the effect that choice has on the way each candidate is treated. Since the preestablished frame about Al Gore was that he was dishonest, a factual quibble over whether a young girl "had" to stand or "has" to stand was given disproportionate attention in stories that could have taken the opportunity to explicate the many consequential grounds on which the candidates differed. In typical debate coverage, the "winner" is the one who avoided the mistakes that would have high-lighted his caricature, while the "loser" made the statement proving his caricature true.

Furthermore, the fact that the Bush campaign's preferred take meshed with the journalistic interpretation heightened the likelihood that Bush's spin would be more effective than Gore's. Unlike the argument the Bush campaign made about Gore, the reasons the Gore campaign offered for voting against Bush never cohered into a single theme, particularly one that fit neatly into the reporters' frame. For example, an *NBC Nightly News* "truth squad report" by Lisa Myers detailed false statements made by each candidate in the first debate, along with quotes from experts relating the facts. But the lead of Myers's story seemed to say that Gore uttered more or worse falsehoods, something unsupported by the rest of the story: "Though both candidates took liberties with the truth, Al Gore seems most on the defensive today, accused by Republicans of embellishing." In the debate's immediate wake Bush was also accused by Democrats of embellishing, but that fact was not used to frame the story. Since the Bush message cohered with the preestablished frame, it led the story.

Appearing on *Fox News Sunday* the weekend after the debate, Bush spokesperson Karen Hughes said of Gore, "He's gaining a reputation as a serial exaggerator. The Vice President has consistently and repeatedly made up things, exaggerated, embellished facts." What had been an occasional line of attack became a central theme of the Bush campaign. As late as September 15, a Bush aide was quoted as saying, "Gore is doing better on both personality and integrity . . . We have no choice but to fight on the issues."[37] After the lullaby, the dog story, and the Strategic Petroleum Reserve, the Bush campaign focused on the issue of trust. Whenever possible, Bush sought to turn policy criticisms of Gore into attacks on his credibility. For instance, when the Gore campaign aired ads attacking Bush's environmental record, Bush responded with this ad:

> **Announcer:** While George Bush offers a positive issue agenda, more negative attacks from Al Gore. The truth? George Bush is cleaning up Texas. The Environmental Protection Agency reports that Texas leads America in reducing toxic pollution. And Al Gore? Gore has allowed mining companies to mine zinc from his property. They've been cited for polluting the source of local drinking water all while Gore has made half a million dollars in mining royalties. Even on the environment, Al Gore says one thing but does another.

Later, Bush advertising consultant Alex Castellanos explained the strategy behind the ad. "On the environmental ad, our strategy was just to deflect the attack and not really go after Gore on the environment, but to make it a hypocrisy message."[38] Attacks on Gore's credibility became the default strategy for Bush to deflect any issue attack made by Gore. For instance, in their first debate, Gore challenged Bush to join him in endorsing the McCain-Feingold campaign finance reform bill. Bush's response was this:

> You know, this man has no credibility on the issue. As a matter of fact, I read in the *New York Times* where he said he cosponsored the McCain-Feingold campaign fund-raising bill. But he wasn't in the Senate with Senator Feingold. And so look, I'm going to—what you need to know about me is I'm going to uphold the law. I'm going to have an attorney general that enforces the law. That it's the time for—the time for campaign funding reform is after the election. This man has outspent me. The special interests are outspending me. And I am not going to lay down my arms in the middle of a campaign for somebody who has got no credibility on the issue.

In making the allegation of dishonesty, Bush told a falsehood of his own: Gore did not outspend him. According to the Federal Election Commission Bush's campaign spent $185 million—more than that of any presidential candidate in history—compared to Gore's $120 million.

Our survey results indicate that the Bush strategy worked. After the debate, the number of people considering Gore honest continued the decline begun on September 19, dropping below 50% for the first time

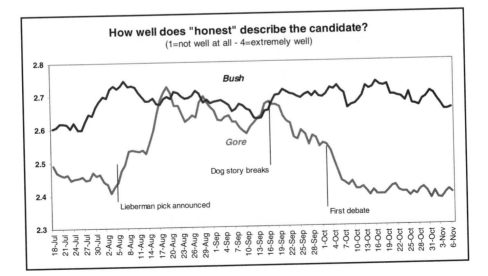

How well does "honest" describe the candidate?
(1=not well at all - 4=extremely well)

Bush

Gore

Dog story breaks

Lieberman pick announced

First debate

on October 12; it remained at or below 50% until Election Day. The few days preceding the cascade of credibility stories were the point at which Gore held his largest lead of the campaign in our tracking poll of vote intention, approximately 10 percentage points. His lead began to decline over the following two weeks, after which the candidates remained virtually even until Election Day. Although Gore did manage a slight lead in vote intentions as Election Day approached, his honesty ratings did not recover from their two-stage fall after the four stories highlighting the credibility issue and the first debate.

Bush as Inexperienced Dolt

When George W. Bush emerged as the front-runner for the 2000 Republican nomination, *New York Times* reporter Richard Berke posed the central questions that would animate coverage of the Texas governor's campaign:

> Gov. George W. Bush is appealingly self-confident. Or is he arrogant? He is engaging and fun loving. Or is he immature? He is, refreshingly, an ordinary guy who has not plotted his whole life to end up in the White House. Or is he too cavalier about the office? He is decisive and sees the big picture. Or is he shallow, impulsive, and impatient, not willing to sweat the details?[39]

"Dubya is used to being a man of whom little is expected, his name notwithstanding," wrote Howard Fineman and Martha Brant of *Newsweek*.[40] Even some who would be expected to be sympathetic trafficked in simplifications. "He's probably the least-qualified person ever to be nominated by a major party," observed talk radio host Ron Reagan, son and namesake of the former president. "What is his accomplishment? That he's no longer an obnoxious drunk?"[41] On late-night TV, Jay Leno cast the Bush-Cheney duo as the Wizard of Oz ticket with Cheney, who had suffered a major heart attack years earlier, as a person who needed a heart and Bush as the one requiring a brain.

Although reporters had entertained the idea that Bush was less than brilliant as soon as he emerged as a candidate, the press frame casting him as inexperienced and intellectually suspect can be traced most directly to an event that occurred early in the primary campaign. On November 4, 1999, Bush sat for an interview with Andy Hiller, a reporter at WHDH-TV in Boston. Hiller administered a pop quiz on foreign affairs, asking the Texas governor to name the leaders of global hot spots, including Chechnya, India, Pakistan, and Taiwan. Bush's inability to do so (he got partial credit for referring to the Taiwanese leader as "Mr. Lee") was widely reported in the national media and created a field day for the late-night shows. "Taiwan? Lee?" noted Jay Leno. "You've got a 50% chance of being right." "Bush Falters in Foreign Policy Quiz," said the *Washington Post*. "Bush Flunks World Leaders Quiz," said the *Memphis Commercial-Appeal*. A week later, the *New Yorker* published Bush's mediocre grades from Yale, prompting a second round of stories centered on his intelligence.

In November of 1999, Bush was asked in a Pizza Hut survey what his "favorite books from childhood" were. The person who filled out the survey (presumably it was a member of the staff) did not interpret the question to ask about Bush's favorite book as a child but rather his favorite children's book. The answer? *The Very Hungry Caterpillar*, which was published in 1969, while Bush was in college.[42] The week before, Bush had read the book to a class of children in a campaign appearance—as he did many other times during the campaign—so one might surmise that he thought it was a good book, a fact confirmed by his report in the *American Spectator* that he and his wife read that book to their children.[43] The critical point is that the incident was not interpreted as an accurate response to an ambiguous question; instead, the account of the survey was used as an occasion to make jokes about Bush's intelligence—the idea that as a twenty-year-old he would have been reading children's books. "When [his college roommates] pored over Kierkegaard, Schopenhauer and Kant," *San Francisco Chronicle* columnist Arthur Hoppe wrote, Bush "would defensively curl up with 'The Adventures of Peter Rabbit' or 'The Unabridged Mother Goose.'"[44] Those who assumed that he had taken the question to address his own childhood did not draw the inference that the response called into question his honesty but rather his intelligence. The parallel with Gore citing "Look for the Union Label" as a childhood lullaby is unmistakable: in Gore's case the incident was used to paint him as dishonest, while in Bush's it was used to paint him as dim.

As with Gore's dishonesty, the idea that Bush was not particularly bright gained traction in part because it meshed with certain aspects of Bush's history. An admittedly inattentive student, Bush spent the early part of his life going from one job to another. When he declared his intention to seek the presidency, he had served in public office only five years. Perhaps most important, Bush shared with his father a lack of facility with the English language that occasionaly resulted in amusing contortions. The press was particularly likely to quote what came to be known as "Bushisms" when they concerned education, as when Bush said on January 11, 2000, "Rarely is the question asked: is our children learning?" The process of tracking Bushisms was embraced by Jacob Weisberg of the online magazine *Slate*, who by the campaign's end had gathered enough to publish a book (a book of the same title and theme had been published on Bush's father). Weisberg's collection included such statements as "Will the highways on the Internet become more few?" and "We need to make the pie higher." Misstatements such as these, of course, do not necessarily indicate a lack of intelligence, but they made Bush's intellectual capacity an inviting target. His campaign's ad writers didn't help. "How come the hard things don't get done?" Bush asked in one general election ad. "Because they're hard."

Bush also seemed more disposed than most political candidates to say the opposite of what he meant to say. In his last debate with Gore on October 17, for example, he declared "I'm not sure 80% of the people get the death tax. I know this: 100% will get it if I'm the president." He also coined new forms of recognizable words and then defined them. About an impending execution in Texas, the governor noted, "This case has had full analyzation and has been looked at a lot."[45]

Mistakes that most people would probably find understandable were said to "raise questions" about Bush's intelligence, just as similar mistakes "raised questions" about Gore's integrity. When a Slovakian journalist asked Bush about his country, Bush said, "The only thing I know about Slovakia is what I learned firsthand from your foreign minister, who came to Texas. I had a great meeting with him. It's an exciting country. It's a country that's flourishing. It's a country that's doing very well."[46] Numerous stories revealed that the person Bush had met was not the foreign minister of Slovakia but the prime minister of Slovenia. The incident became shorthand for both Bush's inexperience and his intelligence. One *Washington Post* article was subheaded, "The Question Dogs George Bush: Is He Smart Enough?"[47] Other interpretations were certainly available: had it been Al Gore, reporters might have described the remark as a deceptive attempt to ingratiate himself with the Slovakian journalist. Reporters might also have described it as an honest mistake that even an intelligent person might have made; after all, neither Slovakia nor Slovenia had been an independent nation ten years before, and during his tenure as governor Bush met with many dignitaries. The frame around Bush's character determined the interpretation given to the facts.

Just as reporters interviewed psychologists to plumb Gore's "compulsion" to exaggerate, speech therapists were quoted on Bush's struggles with the language. Even his own aides acknowledged that "his brain works faster than his mouth does."[48] One magazine article speculated that Bush was dyslexic, a diagnosis Bush either underscored or cleverly parodied when he said, "The woman who knew that I had dyslexia—I never interviewed her."[49]

When Bush was ahead in the polls, as he was for most of the 2000 season, the resilience of his campaign muted the doubts of press and pundits about his intelligence and competence; when he fell behind, as he did after the Democratic convention and through much of September, the doubts bubbled to the surface of stories. For example, on August 24 Frank Bruni of the *New York Times* wrote a piece that commented on Bush's naps, early bedtime, and days off. When he departs from his script, noted Bruni, "and sometimes when he mangles the words within it, he can seem fuzzy on specifics, less than forceful in his thinking, tired."[50]

Apart from Gore's claim about the Internet, no single remark drew more attention during the 2000 campaign than Bush's response to questions about a Republican Party television ad on September 12, a time when his campaign had been trailing Gore's in the polls for more than two weeks. In the ad criticizing Gore's Medicare prescription drug plan, phrases, including "bureaucrats decide," dance frenetically around the screen. In one of the ad's final frames, the screen is momentarily filled with the word "rats." Faced with the accusation that the Bush campaign was attempting to implant subliminal messages in viewers' minds, Bush dismissed the idea. But in doing so he pronounced "subliminal" as "subliminable," not once but three times. The clip was played on two of the three network news broadcasts, then repeatedly on cable news shows, talk shows, and comedy shows. Such instances primed—and faltering polling numbers licensed discussion of—questions about Bush's intelligence that had been temporarily set aside when he led in the polls.

By choosing a running mate with far greater experience than he, Bush simultaneously assuaged doubts about his lack of experience and reinforced them. As a former member of Congress, White House chief of staff, and secretary of defense, Cheney provided the ticket with "gravitas," but also gave the inexperience caricature new life. Cheney's deft answers to foreign policy questions in the vice-presidential debate prompted speculation that the parties would have been better served had the vice-presidential nominees headed the tickets. Republican consultants report that after the debate, Cheney's appearances drew large crowds and had a discernible impact in the polls. But the notion that Cheney was more qualified than Bush to head the ticket and lead the country opened a narrative captured initially in cartoons that featured Bush as a child and Cheney as the adult, Bush as the puppet, Cheney as the puppeteer. Bush attempted to combat the caricature by raising his right hand during campaign appearances and reciting parts of the oath of office, just as another candidate criticized for his lack of experience—John F. Kennedy—did forty years before.

There was a critical contrast in the media environment between the twin questions of Gore's honesty and Bush's intelligence. While in both cases the press was vigilant about finding statements that would highlight the perceived character flaw, the question of Gore's honesty was central to the Bush message, particularly after the third week in September. In contrast, the Gore campaign was reluctant to attack Bush's intelligence, perhaps for fear of being charged with deploying elitist, personal attacks. In the second debate, Jim Lehrer invited Gore to criticize Bush on the question, but Gore demurred. In a fascinating exchange, Lehrer invited the candidates to address both issues, first by pointing out that Bush's campaign had referred to Gore as a "serial exaggerator."

> **Bush:** I don't believe I've used those words.
> **Lehrer:** No, but your campaign has.
> **Bush:** Maybe they have.
> **Lehrer:** Your campaign officials have. And your campaign officials, Vice President Gore, are now calling—now calling the governor a "bumbler."
> **Bush:** Wait a minute!
> **Lehrer:** I mean, is—my point it, should this—is this—
> **Gore:** I don't use language like that, and I don't think that we should.
> **Lehrer:** It's in your—it's in your commercials.
> **Gore:** I understand.
> **Bush:** (Laughs.) Yeah.
> **Gore:** I haven't seen that. In my commercial?
> **Lehrer:** Yes. Yes.
> **Gore:** Well, the—
> **Bush:** You haven't seen the commercial?
> **Lehrer:** And your—
> **Gore:** I think that what—I think the point of that is that anybody would have a hard time trying to make a tax cut plan that's so large, that would put us into such big deficits, that gives almost half the benefits to the wealthiest of the wealthy, I think anybody would have a hard time explaining that clearly in a way that makes sense to the average person.

While pointing out that he had not personally used the phrase "serial exaggerator," Bush displayed no displeasure at its use by his staff. When Lehrer said that Gore's commercials had called Bush a "bumbler"—which in fact was untrue, a mistake for which Lehrer publicly apologized at the opening of the third debate—Gore seemed momentarily ready to deny the accusation. When he realized this, Bush nearly leaped out of his chair, thinking he might have caught Gore in a lie, and asked incredulously, "You haven't seen the commercial?" The implication of Bush's question was that the Texas governor had seen a nonexistent ad. Perhaps unsure of whether the word did appear in one of his commercials, Gore didn't deny it, but gave a somewhat tortured explanation of his staff's criticism of Bush.

In the exchange, Bush eschewed a particular phrasing of the attack on Gore's honesty but maintained the substance of it. Gore, on the other hand, denied that he and his campaign were making an attack on Bush's intelligence and attempted to shift the focus to a policy disagreement. At various points over the course of the campaign Gore attempted to raise doubts about Bush's qualifications, but mindful of the pitfalls of engaging in a personal attack, seemed unable to bring himself to make the critique explicit. In an April interview with the *Los Angeles Times*, Gore said of his opponent, "I think a lot of people are asking that question: Does he have the experience to be president?" But he quickly added, "It's not for me to answer that question."[51] Gore's attempt to question Bush's experience without actually questioning his experience was a modified form of a rhetorical technique known as *paraleipsis*, in which a speaker draws attention to something with the act of pretending to avoid it—for example, "I won't bring up my opponent's recent troubles with the law . . ."

But reporters, prodded by the Bush campaign, would not allow Gore to claim that he had not in fact raised the question. The first question moderator Jim Lehrer asked Gore in the first candidate debate was this: "Vice President Gore, you have questioned whether Governor Bush has the experience to be president of the United States. What exactly do you mean?" Gore responded with a denial: "I have actually not questioned Governor Bush's experience, I have questioned his proposals . . ." Reporters fact-checked Gore's claim and referred back to a pair of interviews in the *New York Times* in which Gore said Bush's tax-cut proposal raised the question of whether he had the experience to be president.[52]

The Gore campaign finally found the vehicle to mock Bush's intelligence five days before the election, when Bush said on the stump, "They want the federal government controlling the Social Security, like it's some kind of federal program." Until that point, the Gore campaign had not identified an attack on Bush's intelligence that tested well enough to air. "Trust me," said Gore advertising consultant Bill Knapp after the campaign had ended. "We tested ad hominem attacks against him. They were not effective . . . We tested spot after spot where we showed his screwups and his inability to communicate smoothly and effectively. We used that technique in '96 against Dole very effectively, but we could not get ads that worked well in 2000 against Bush for that."[53] When Bush made the remark about Social Security, the Gore campaign quickly produced the following ad:

> Announcer: Is Social Security a federal program? Of course it is. But it seems George Bush doesn't understand that. Here he is talking about the Gore/Lieberman plan.
> George W. Bush: They want the federal government controlling the Social Security, like it's some kind of federal program.
> Announcer: But the bigger mistake is what Bush wants to do to Social Security. Take a trillion dollars out. Promising it to young workers and seniors at the same time.
> George W. Bush: They want the federal government controlling the Social Security, like it's some kind of federal program.

In contrast to the multiple ads the Bush campaign aired attacking Gore's credibility, this was the only Gore ad that questioned Bush's intellectual capacity. Gore himself cited the Bush quote in speeches during the campaign's final week. A *New York Times* reporter covering Gore finally granted Bush the benefit of the doubt reporters had seldom bestowed on Gore, when she wrote, "The Vice President never allowed that Mr. Bush's comment might have been a slip of the tongue or a poorly worded thought, instead milking the idea that it was just plain dumb— and that it was further evidence that Mr. Bush is blank on the basics and not equipped to be president."[54]

When we examine people's judgments of Bush's level of knowledge in our survey, we see only two significant turning points. At the point of the announcement of Joe Lieberman as Gore's running mate evaluations of how knowledgable *both* candidates are begin to move: Gore's knowledge ratings grow and then flatten after the convention ends, while Bush's steadily decline all the way to Election Day. In the short term, the shift in vote intention toward Gore is manifest in changing evaluations of how knowledgable candidates are. However, among Democrats and those exposed to high levels of news media, there is a significant drop in evaluations of Bush's intelligence after the third debate.

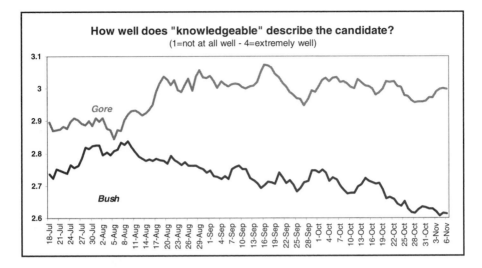

Before the Lieberman announcement Gore was approximately thirteen points behind Bush; by the end of the convention he had pulled even. For most of the campaign, most people nonetheless found Gore reasonably honest and Bush reasonably knowledgeable. Voters tend to be fairly generous in their evaluations; although they may like one candidate more than another, they are usually willing to give both the benefit of the doubt until persuaded otherwise.[55] Apart from honesty and knowledge there was relatively little movement over the course of the campaign in the trait evaluations.

A Pox on Both Your Houses:
Comedy and the Candidates

After a Pew Research Center poll found in February 2000 that 47% of eighteen- to twenty-nine-year-olds reported gaining political information about the presidential campaign from late-night talk shows,[56] speculation increased that this was a form of communication that might draw its persuasive power in part from the fact that we so persistently question that any such power exists. The same survey reported that 28% of young people were getting some political news from late-night comedy shows such as *Saturday Night Live*.

Other evidence of the effects of late-night comedy followed as the campaign progressed. After the first general election debate of 2000, Gore's advisers sat their candidate down to watch the *Saturday Night*

Live parody as a way of convincing him that he had been too aggressive. Late-night comedy thus matters in part because the campaigns take it seriously. " 'We read the transcripts of those shows and watch them,' said Chris Lehane, the Gore campaign's press secretary. 'The monologues are evidence of when a story really breaks through. If it makes it into Leno or Letterman, it means something.'"[57] So we see that the comedy shows may affect not only the opinions of citizens and reporters, but the behavior of candidates as well.

In 2000, late-night comedy telegraphed substantive information as it reinforced a limited range of candidate traits, introduced into public discussion some assumptions unwarranted by existing evidence, and invited cynicism about the quality of those who seek public office. In the process the late-night comics cast Bush as a death-penalty-supporting, not-too-bright reformed drinker and possible cocaine user, and Gore first as robotic and then as a self-aggrandizing panderer. Both directly and through replay in news, these portrayals reinforced a press frame that was more readily surmounted in the debates by Bush than Gore.

We conducted a content analysis of jokes on *Late Night With David Letterman* and the *Tonight Show* during the campaign. Overall, Bush was the target of more jokes than Gore; while 49% of the jokes about the presidential campaign on the two shows mentioned Gore, 62% mentioned Bush.[58] By far the dominant theme of humor about Bush was that he was stupid, unqualified, or inexperienced. In fact, these jokes made up 40% of all those in which Bush was mentioned. Twenty-nine percent of jokes about Gore played on his caricature as a stiff policy wonk, while 15% mocked his exaggerations. However, from the week of September 19 on, the dominant theme of jokes about Gore was his perceived tendency to lie. Similarly, over half of the jokes about Bush from the beginning of September to Election Day portrayed him as stupid.

The stance of late-night humor is fundamentally cynical; each politician is defined only by his or her most glaring weaknesses, and the system produces only venal, corrupt candidates unfit for the office. The implication? Neither candidate is actually worthy of high public office. "You have a clear-cut choice," said Letterman. "You have the choice of one candidate who babbles incoherently, and then a second candidate who babbles incoherently." Leno was even more cynical, both toward the candidates themselves and, by implication, toward politicians in general. Before the first debate, he said, "I guess the local NBC station had the option of either carrying the debates or the playoff baseball game. So you want to watch guys lying, or guys stealing? Pretty much that's what it is." After the final

debate, Leno seemed positively angry: "And in last night's debate, they spent the entire ninety minutes lying . . . They called it the 'presidential town hall debate.' Shut up! It didn't take place in a town hall, it wasn't really a debate, and neither of those guys is presidential."

The context of humor allowed Leno, Letterman, and other comedians to raise questions and insinuate claims about the candidates that would be roundly criticized if uttered by reporters. The question of Bush's youthful drug use provides a clear example. Rumors that the Texas governor had done cocaine in his earlier days were gingerly explored during the primary campaign, but when reporters were unable to substantiate the rumors the subject disappeared from news reports. Jay Leno, on the other hand, continued to find fruit in the subject of cocaine up until Election Day. The revelation a few days before the election of Bush's drunk-driving arrest brought a golden opportunity to bring the candidate's alleged drug use and his problems with alcohol together. "They had the police officer on the news today who arrested him," said Leno. "He said Bush was conservative, very polite, gave no resistance. Well, sure—Bush was just happy the guy didn't find the cocaine under the seat." While reporters were more likely to describe Bush's flaw as inexperience than lack of intelligence, the comedians pushed the caricatures to their logical extremes.

In 1992, candidates began to look beyond the traditional news media for places they could appear that would allow them relatively unfiltered access to voters. These included not only news interview shows such as *Larry King Live* (on which Ross Perot announced his candidacy), but entertainment shows as well. Bill Clinton played the saxophone on *Arsenio* and answered questions from teenagers on MTV; Al Gore would do the latter eight years later.

The candidates also appeared on numerous other non-news programs. Bush went on *Live With Regis*, both candidates sat with Oprah Winfrey, Jay Leno, and David Letterman, and together they taped a skit for *Saturday Night Live*. While the appearances were intended in part to counteract the caricatures that had developed, they attempted to do so in part by reiterating them. To show what good sports they were, Bush and Gore poked fun at themselves on the same bases that the comedians had been mocking them. In his appearance on *Late Night With David Letterman* on September 14, for example, Gore included in his "Top Ten" reasons to vote for him, "I gave you the Internet and I can take it away." Gore's decision not simply to appear on the show but to make the same jokes about himself that the comedians had been making was no doubt a strategic move intended to diffuse the caricature's power. The belief that this strategy can be successful is long-lived. Richard Nixon appeared on *Laugh-In* in 1968 to say, "Sock it to me!" Nancy Reagan appeared at the White House correspondents' dinner early in the Reagan administration and sang a self-mocking song. After being heavily criticized in the press for spending money on renovations and new china for the White House and accepting expensive gowns as gifts from designers, Reagan sang a tune parodying her preference for haute couture (titled "Second-Hand Clothes," to the tune of "Second-Hand Rose"). As Hedrick Smith reported in *The Power Game*,[59] everyone had a good laugh and reporters softened their criticism of the First Lady considerably.

While the late-night caricatures typically reflect the criticisms being made elsewhere in the media, in 2000 late-night humor was brought to a wider audience as excerpts from the monologues were played and re-played on the cable news networks. MSNBC, for example, repeatedly played segments from NBC's *Saturday Night Live*. The *New York Times* and the AP recapped recent late-night jokes. Beginning during the Republican convention, *CBS Evening News* aired weekly roundups of the "telling campaign comedy" of the late-night comedians who, said anchor Dan Rather, "this year, more than ever, [are] helping shape public perceptions of the presidential candidates, for better or worse." Jon Stewart, the host of *The Daily Show* on Comedy Central, was interviewed by the likes of Wolf Blitzer, Larry King, and Katie Couric. When asked in an April 22, 2001, *60 Minutes* interview why so much late-night humor was added to news in 2000, Stewart answered, "Because there are five twenty-four-hour news channels. At some point, they have got to turn and go, 'Does anybody have a joke about this?'"

The seriousness with which news reporters took late-night comedy is evident in a comment by ABC's Cokie Roberts immediately following the last debate. "I think," she said, "we have to wait and see what the next couple of days bring and how people are reacting, and I have to say we have to see what the late-night comedians are saying, as well, because sometimes they have a lot more effect than any of us political analysts." In a similar vein, Matt Lauer introduced a *Today* story on October 6 about the effect of comedy on the campaign by saying, "We've heard this morning and all week, for that matter, from the political analysts about the two debates. But what did the men who really matter think? You know, the men who influence public opinion through late-night television?"

Candidates' Ability to Determine Press Frames

Political scientist John Zaller argues that "the harder presidential campaigns try to control what journalists report about their candidate, the harder journalists try to report something else instead."[60] It may also be true, however, that campaigns are more successful at dictating what journalists will report about the *other* candidate than about themselves. Given the press's addiction to conflict, attacks—both the legitimate and the illegitimate—inevitably elicit focus in the press. Spin becomes conventional wisdom when reporters begin to couch one side's arguments in the passive voice ("Questions are being raised . . .").

When one campaign attacks another, the coverage follows a predictable pattern. Journalists report the attack, then ask a series of questions: Why has the campaign chosen this line of attack? Is the attack working? How will the other candidate respond? The result is a series of stories centered on the subject of the attack—for example, Gore's credibility or Bush's experience. Since reporters spend a great deal of time analyzing candidates' strategies—particularly with regard to the attacks they launch—campaigns that have a consistent message about their opponents will see that message highlighted in news. This was particularly true in 2000, when strategy coverage may have been at an all-time high.

We see this pattern in action when Katie Couric of NBC's *Today* show asks reporter David Gregory on November 1, "What is [Bush's] main message going to be in the next couple of days?" Gregory responds, "Keep up the attacks on Al Gore. He's got a new ad up in the battleground states that challenges Gore's credibility. Suggests really that he's been lying for political gain, specifically on Social Security, which is a message they hope resonates in Florida. They want to do this. They want to remind voters on the stump that Al Gore will say anything to scare them to get them into the voting booth." Gregory's ostensible goal is to explain to viewers what the Bush campaign's strategy is, but in doing so he repeats the campaign's message virtually word for word.

Implicit in many analyses of public opinion in presidential campaigns is the notion that when voters make their decisions primarily on issues, they are deciding reasonably and responsibly; when they decide based on personal characteristics, they are allowing irrational whims and potentially inaccurate impressions to move their votes. In fact, some research has found that highly educated voters, despite knowing more about the issues, are more likely than those with less education to cite personal characteristics as reasons for voting for a particular candidate.[61]

Among television's many effects on presidential politics has been the personalization of candidates and thus an increased disposition among voters to judge them based on personality and character.[62]

A great deal of time and attention is spent in any presidential campaign in the attempt to understand who the candidates really are at heart. This emphasis on character is not problematic per se. It is the simplification involved in the way character is explored that raises questions. The search for the candidates' "true" selves leads journalists to home in on one or two personal characteristics that come to define each candidate, then explore them, and ultimately frame coverage through their assumptions.

When Jack Ford asked Al Gore on *Good Morning America*, "As the vice president of the United States, you've had a distinguished career in the House and in the Senate, and yet you find yourself on stage in front of family members and tens of millions of people with a moderator asking questions about your integrity and your credibility. Does that hurt?" we should not be surprised if the answer was as unenlightening as Bush's response to Ford's question for him: "You've heard questions throughout this campaign raised by the Gore campaign about your intelligence, your ability to grasp presidential issues. With twenty-seven days or so left till the election, how do you assure the American people that you have that presidential grasp of issues?"

The simplifications and caricatures infuse interpretation of statements and events in a variety of ways. Witness this discussion of the latest poll results from reporter Gary Langer on ABC's *World News This Morning* on October 17: "Amid some criticism of his debate performance, the number of registered voters who think of Gore as honest and trustworthy is down from 63% to 49%. The more surprising result is that Bush's credibility rating is down as well, down 9 points to 53%." The fact that Gore's credibility ratings have declined is expected and understandable. The fact that Bush's have declined, on the other hand, is "surprising." It is in word choices and interpretations such as this one that press frames operate.

At some point in every presidential campaign, the images of the candidates take shape in the news. Using a combination of hard evidence and gut feeling, reporters arrive at a consensus on the features of each candidate's personality that are the most important. Subsequent information that fits each candidate's stereotype then becomes far more likely to pass through the news filter to reach readers and viewers. The larger narrative determines decisions about not only how to deal with claims, but about how to interpret the conclusions at which reporters have arrived. Once a factual determination had been made—for instance, "Al Gore's mother-in-law pays more for her drugs than the Gore family pays for the dog's," the question is what to do with the conclusion. By pairing the conclusion with a comment from a Bush campaign representative about "another Al Gore invention," the narrative, which can be reduced to "Al Gore is untrustworthy," proceeds. When Gore stumbled in a speech late in the campaign trying to recall the word "mammogram," reporters—if they noted it at all—did not say that the incident "raises questions" or pair the quote with one from someone alleging that Gore was insufficiently knowledgeable. Reporters might argue that the Bush campaign alleged Gore was a liar but did not allege that he was stupid, but even if true this does not mean that the reporters are not the ones constructing the narrative. It is they who describe events, select and assemble quotes, and arrive at conclusions. The journalistic project—particularly in the context of a campaign, which has a beginning, middle, and end—is ultimately a literary one.

Like all caricatures, those constructed to describe presidential candidates reduce a complex individual into one plausible facet of his personality, then exaggerate it for effect. The question is not whether Al Gore never exaggerated or George W. Bush was a figure of towering intellect, but first, what important facts are left out by the portraits, and second, whether the portraits so distort their subjects that voters are left with a misleading picture of those vying for the country's highest office.

CHAPTER 4

The Press as Soothsayer

O n the evening of November 7, 2000, the television networks presented their viewers with an evolving story built on a series of assumptions about events taking place in real time. Just as they had in elections past, they presented descriptions of these events as facts. Just as it had in years past, the viewing public accepted these descriptions as facts. But as we soon learned, these descriptions were actually guesses about what had occurred—careful, educated guesses, but guesses nonetheless.

The role of soothsayer is one that reporters have inhabited with increasing frequency in recent years. As cable news shows have proliferated, reporters have been called upon to predict political events in the near and distant future. Citizens have become used to seeing journalists tell them not only what has happened or is happening, but what will happen. The word *soothsayer*—one who predicts the future—is derived from the Old English word *sooth*, meaning truth. So perhaps journalists could be forgiven for forgetting that when they describe what has yet to occur they set aside the custodianship of fact and move into a less certain domain.

If news is a rough draft of history, the draft written on the night of November 7, 2000, was rougher than most. "Bush Wins" declared the *Boston Herald* and the *New York Post*. "Bush!" said the *Austin American Statesman*. The printed *New York Times* was among those adding a qualification: "Bush Appears to Defeat Gore."

Journalism's reputation for getting it right was preserved by the oldest of the national news outlets, the Associated Press. Although it followed the networks in the first mistaken call of Florida for Gore, the 152-year-old news organization that has been reporting on elections since Zachary Taylor's in 1848 did not call Florida or the election for Bush. Instead, at 2:37 A.M. the AP reported in an urgent update that "the race was still up for grabs" and at 3:11 A.M. dispatched a cautionary advisory to its subscribers warning that the outcome was still in doubt:

> The lead in Florida for George W. Bush has dwindled to about 6,000 in the vote count. A small percentage of the vote has yet to be reported in several counties, including two predominantly Democratic counties.
>
> AP believes the uncounted votes in Broward and Palm Beach counties could allow a change of the lead in the Florida vote. We are watching the resolution of the actual vote count to assure if there is a change in the Florida results, which could yet have an impact on the outcome of the presidential election.

The AP advisory served as a warning to the networks that the call for Bush was questionable. In an unusual recognition of the value of another news source, both CBS's and NBC's post-election reviews of Election Night coverage suggested that in the future each would pay more attention to independent sources such as the AP.

Does the coverage of Election Night and the morning after matter? The experience of 2000 shows that the simple answer is yes. It mattered first as an indicator of the extent to which we assume the accuracy of news reports, even in an age in which many say they distrust the media and a smaller subset persist in holding that the media are biased. When the networks called Florida for Gore, the first response of viewers was not a "we'll see" attitude. Instead the call was taken at face value. So, for example, Supreme Court Justice Sandra Day O'Connor "visibly started when CBS anchor Dan Rather called Florida for Al Gore," reported Evan Thomas and Michael Isikoff of *Newsweek*. "'This is terrible,' she exclaimed. She explained to another partygoer that Gore's reported victory in Florida meant that the election was 'over,' since Gore had already carried two other swing states, Michigan and Illinois."[1] Gore's election would have thwarted O'Connor's plans to leave the Court with the assurance that a Republican president would appoint her replacement.

So pervasive is our confidence in the mediation of the networks in matters electoral that Vice President Gore not only took the second mistaken call—this time of the election for Governor Bush—at face value, but called the Governor to concede, entered a limo to drive to the location at which he planned to make a concession speech to his assembled

followers, and aborted that mission and retracted the concession only
when an aide watching the actual vote tabulations realized that there
remained a possibility Gore would pull ahead.

The mistaken calls may also have had an effect on the outcome of the
post-election battle. Gore supporters believe that the call of Florida and
the election for Bush, in *Newsweek*'s words, "gave Bush a key psychological
advantage going into the post-election."[2] Alternatively, Bush supporters
believe that the first call of Florida for Gore drove down the Bush vote in
the West. What the numerous books written about the Florida debacle
and the various recounts of the ballots confirmed was that the election's
outcome was by no means the foregone conclusion that some in the press
would have had us believe. Had they happened differently, any number of
events and decisions could have resulted in a Gore victory. The performance of the press was therefore of some consequence.

The press's expectations and behavior were influenced both by polls
and by the behavior of the campaigns. For much of the 2000 election
year, Bush led Gore in the head-to-head polls. In the final week, even as
the difference between the two remained within the margin of error, the
fact that Bush was ahead of Gore within the margin was interpreted by
many in the news media as a Bush lead. For instance, in a typical story
the day before Election Day *USA Today* described a two-point lead—
half the poll's margin of error—as a "Bush Holds Slight Lead."[3]

Although the "lead" that Bush held was usually characterized as small,
particularly in the final week, it was described as a lead nonetheless. In
fact, in a poll with a margin of error of plus/minus 3%, any lead smaller
than 6% is not a lead at all but a statistical tie. Plus/minus 3% is the
figure for *each* candidate's position. This means that the poll had insuf-
ficient power to determine who is in fact ahead; if Bush is shown with a
one-point advantage, the poll tells with 95% certainty that the true margin is somewhere between a 7-point Bush lead and a 5-point Gore lead.
For example, if Bush is at 47% and Gore is at 46%, we know only that
the true Bush position is somewhere between 44% and 50%, while the
true Gore position is somewhere between 43% and 49%.

The attempts to explain this inherent feature of survey sampling
were confusing at best. For example, the night before Election Day Tom
Brokaw said, "Over the weekend the NBC News-*Wall Street Journal* poll
had Governor Bush leading the Vice President by three points. But today's
MSNBC-Reuters overnight tracking poll shows a slight lead for the Vice
President [3 points]. Both polls have a built-in margin of error. That
means those results could flip." It would be difficult for most viewers to

understand what Brokaw meant when he said that the results "could flip." Many probably assumed they could flip not if one conducted another survey of an identically sized sample (which is in fact the case), but that they could flip if some last-minute event occurred in the campaign. In 2000, journalists were no less likely than they had been in the past to explain the meaning and operation of the margin of error, but their failure to do so was of greater import in the closest election in decades, particularly given the lead changes the polls identified.

A second factor circumscribed reporters' expectations. The Bush campaign, whether through calculation, hubris, or poor polling of its own, led reporters to expect that Bush anticipated winning as many as 320 electoral votes. This perspective was reinforced in the final week by Bush's visits to states that the Democrats and the press believed they had secured, including New Jersey and California. On ABC and NBC the expectation that Bush would win led to a contrast effect and an overreaction when it seemed that Gore had taken Florida, Michigan, and Pennsylvania. On CBS the presumption that Bush would win led to the assumption even as Gore was within striking distance that the presidency was Bush's to lose and a longer shot for Gore. The reactions to the evening's calls would show that reporters' expectations—based on what they thought the polls had told them—colored their interpretation of Election Night.

Weaknesses in Network Coverage

In addition to their mistaken calls, five factors undermined the credibility of the networks' election coverage in 2000: the pseudocertainty the anchors ascribed to their predictive methods, the illusion created by each of the networks that it had its own unique source of data, taking credit for success but attributing failure to outside forces, the anchors' astonishment at pro-Republican states placed in the "too close to call" category, and in the case of NBC, ABC, CNN, and Fox, metaphors that equated victory with taking Florida, Michigan, and Pennsylvania.

Certainty About the Accuracy of Projections

The network news operations' overconfidence in the accuracy of their projections left them unable to protect viewers from misinformation. Early on Election Night the anchors spoke a language of absolute confidence.

Tom Brokaw said, "We make these decisions based on interviews that we conduct with the voters as they leave the polls. But we have to be *absolutely certain* [emphasis added] that they match up with the actual returns, as well, that they fit the models that have worked so well for us over the years." Similarly, in the first hour of Election Night coverage, Dan Rather said, "Let's get one thing straight right from the get-go. We would rather be late in reporting returns than to be wrong. And again our record demonstrated that [to be] true. If you hear someplace else that somebody's carried a state and you're off, as you shouldn't be, watching them, then come back here, because if we say somebody's carried a state, you can pretty much take it to the bank, book it, that that's true."

The networks also tended throughout Election Night to treat projections as actual results. Since no one has actually won a state until all votes are counted and certified, the calls by the networks in most states are projections or estimates based on a reading of exit polls in sample precincts adjusted for assumptions about absentee ballots and in close states confirmed by checking the exit polls against actual precinct-level vote counts. Reporting that winners *are projected* is not only accurate but increases the likelihood that voters will not feel misled when a call is withdrawn or reversed.

Where the networks initially "projected" Florida first for Gore and then for Bush, the reporters and anchors quickly shifted to language that assumed that the projected winner was the actual victor. In the initial call CBS treated Florida as an estimate. Rather said, "Florida goes for Al Gore. Now, folks, the equation changes. CBS News estimates when all the votes are in and counted, the Sunshine State will have plenty of sunshine for Al Gore." Shortly after the call, Rather again qualified it, saying, "Now having won Florida, by the CBS News estimate." However, the Florida call was quickly translated into a given, not an estimate or projection. Between the first call and the retraction, Rather and others on air at CBS referred to their projection as an actual event: "Gore has won Florida . . . Florida went for Gore . . . Gore—blue—has captured Florida . . . Florida dropped for Gore . . . Al Gore's victory in Florida interrupted us . . . Gore got Florida."

CBS's second call in Florida was also phrased as an estimate. Rather said, "Bush wins. Florida goes Bush. The presidency is Bush. That's it. CBS News estimates when all the votes are in and counted that George Bush will have won the presidency of the United States . . . If our CBS News estimates are correct up and down the line tonight, and we believe they are, George Bush—George W. Bush, son of President George Bush

. . . One of the closest elections in American history, Bush has won it."
On ABC, Peter Jennings's announcement was similarly qualified: "Unless there is a terrible calamity, George W. Bush, by our projections, is
going to be the next president of the United States." Tom Brokaw was
only slightly more emphatic: "George Bush is the president-elect of the
United States. He has won the state of Florida, according to our projections." Brokaw then raised the issue of Florida's mandatory recount pro-
vision, but dismissed it. "In Florida, if there's a difference of less than
half of one percent, there is an automatic recount of the vote. But given
the way that it was moving for Governor Bush at the end, that probably
won't be necessary."

The subsequent talk also included qualifiers. Referring to Bush, Ed
Bradley said, "If, indeed, he has won . . ." Bob Schieffer said, "If we don't
have to take back this call, as we had to take back Florida earlier in the
evening . . ." However, the fact of a win was soon expressed as a given and
CBS's reputation pegged on it in categorical and certain language. In the
most emphatic declaration of the evening, Rather proclaimed, "Sip it,
savor it, cup it, photostat it, underline it in red, press it in a book, put it
in an album, hang it on the wall, George Bush is the next president of the
United States."

Rather then stood behind the call even as the numbers in the Florida
vote closed. "Now, Florida, with 99% of the precincts in—and I want to
repeat this what Bob Schieffer said a moment ago—Bush leads by 11,000
votes out of 6 million votes cast in Florida—smelling salts for all Democrats, please. One-fiftieth of 1 percent made the difference in Florida,
which in turn made the difference in the whole presidential race." Since
this margin triggered an automatic recount in Florida, one-fiftieth of
one percent had not made a difference—at least not yet. Seeing the same
information, Tom Brokaw was plainly worried: "Look at this in Florida,
here we are, 99 percent of the vote in. We have projected it, obviously, for
George W. Bush. Good grief. Look at that."

CBS was not alone in treating outcomes that were projected as if all of
the votes were in and the outcome certain. Peter Jennings, for example,
noted, "You've heard us talk endlessly throughout the campaign about the
big three, of Florida and Michigan and Pennsylvania. Florida goes to Mr.
Gore, Michigan goes to Mr. Gore. And Pennsylvania is too close to call."

Until they were reversed, the networks continued to treat their projections as facts not only with the force of reality, but occasionally with
legal standing. Fighting this impulse was ABC's Mark Halperin, who said
while waiting for the Gore concession speech, "I feel like I'm the sole

person here standing in the way of the Bush transition, but, you know, we see here, the Florida State Department Division of Elections Web site shows a very small margin." While reporting the fact that Gore had called Bush back to retract his concession, NBC's David Gregory referred to Bush as "at this point still the president-elect," implying that that status is a function not of votes but of the networks saying that it is so—until they decide that he is not the president-elect, he still is. Even as the network projections were being revealed as faulty, the press continued to discuss them as though they were descriptions of reality.

Between sundown and sunrise, anchor confidence in the process was shattered. Dan Rather crafted a memorable statement of regret: "We've lived by the crystal ball and learned to eat so much broken glass tonight that we're in critical condition." "It was acutely embarrassing," noted NBC's Brokaw in late December, "and we're still sorting out exactly what happened and why. I take some small comfort in the public reaction, which seems to be more disappointed than angry."[4] In the early hours of the morning after retracting the call of the election for Governor George W. Bush, Brokaw said: "We just don't have egg on our face. We have an omelet all over our suits." Where eggs were the entrée of preference on NBC, on CNN tastes were avian. Judy Woodruff asked her coanchors: "Could you pass the crow?" Jeff Greenfield proclaimed: "Oh, waiter, one order of crow."

Two on-air moments suggest the transformation in the persona of the anchor between Florida I and the end of Florida II. When Florida was called for Bush, Rather said, "Sip it, savor it . . . George Bush is the next president of the United States." After reporting that Gore had contacted Bush to take back his earlier phoned concession, Rather noted: "Now the situation at the moment is nobody knows for a fact who has won Florida. Far be it from me to question one of our esteemed leaders, but somebody needs to begin explaining why Florida has not now been pulled back to the undecided category. When you get to these computer models, you may as well be speaking Swahili or High Norse to me, and there must be some reason why we stick in with Florida for Bush, but somebody in due time will, no doubt, confirm that . . . at last report, fewer than 300 votes separated the two in votes actually counted down there."

Comparable moments occurred on NBC, ABC, and CNN. On NBC Tom Brokaw observed that "the votes have been counted, and it's not up to the networks to get them there; the networks tonight, I think that it's fair to say, I think I indicated earlier we don't just have egg on our face, we've got omelet all over our suits at this point, and on our face, and everywhere else. We awarded Florida erroneously at one point, and came back, and managed to make everything equal by awarding it erroneously a second time." At 4 A.M. ABC's Peter Jennings admitted, "We're not absolutely sure quite what to do next."

In the aftermath of what some characterized as the Election Night network debacle, CBS News president Andrew Heyward promised, "We'll trade some of this air of omniscience for greater credibility . . . I think we just got slightly overconfident in the infallibility of the system." But his other statements suggested that the confidence in the perfectibility of human systems remained. "This election was unique in so many ways and it exposed flaws in a system that had been very accurate up to now. The Swiss watch didn't work on Mars, so we're going to build one that does." Heyward seemed to argue that the problem was only with the system of projections, and not with the way those projections were interpreted and presented to viewers.

Implying a Competitive Advantage Where None Existed

The networks also created the illusion that each had its own polling operation when instead most of what they were getting was pooled Voter News Service data with some special questions added for each network. This put the individual network's credibility on the line more so than VNS's when a call was incorrect. So, for example, Rather said, "As you and your neighbors have gone to the polls, we've been conducting our own national poll, part of our exit poll operation throughout the day." Anthony Mason then reported on the responses to some of the CBS questions on the VNS exit poll. But a viewer could be forgiven for concluding that the calls being made in the individual states were also from this CBS exit poll and not information received at the same time by ABC, NBC, CNN, and Fox. After Florida had been called incorrectly twice, but before it had been withdrawn from the Bush column, Rather continued to amalgamate VNS and CBS. "We put this data, this information precincts into computers and then we—we make judgments on whether a race is over or not. No doubt, after this is over, there's going to be a lot of rethinking about how these races are called . . ."

The Voter News Service was created after the 1988 election, when the three broadcast networks and CNN, in a cost-cutting move, decided to consolidate their exit poll operations (the organization was originally called Voter Research and Surveys). After the 1994 election, all the networks formed their own "decision desks" to assess the data and recommendations arriving from VNS and make an independent judgment on when to call each state. Each projection is therefore based on data gathered by VNS, evaluated by VNS, then evaluated again by the network's own staff of analysts.

Until the predictions proved incorrect there was no allusion to VNS at all on any of the networks. Indeed, when Rather said, "Whether we'll have announcement of decisions or not, we just don't know whether they have enough information," it was unclear who "they" were. When Rather said of Florida "no indication we'll have the decision anytime soon," it was unclear who was to make the decision he was awaiting. On CNN, moments after the call of Florida for Gore was retracted, Judy Woodruff asked analyst Bill Schneider to explain VNS to viewers. Only Fox News mentioned VNS before the Gore call was retracted.

There was also no adequate explanation of how the exit polling process works. In the absence of such an explanation, when all of the networks made the same call, a viewer might well have assumed that five separate exit polls had drawn the same conclusion from independently gathered evidence. This was yet another way in which voters could have been fooled into thinking that what the networks told them were not predictions and projections, but statements of fact.

Data, Not People

"But Florida has been pulled back into the undecided column because of bad data, let me say suspect data, from the precincts in Florida," said Rather. The wording became more telegraphic on CBS as the evening progressed: "Because of bad data, suspect data out of some precincts in Florida, we pulled Florida back . . ." "Florida up in the air, some bad data from some precincts suspected. That's the reason it goes in the undecided column." "Suspect data went into the computers." On NBC Tim Russert joked about the dry-erase board on which he scribbled electoral calculations: "If you just stayed with these simple boards, you wouldn't have those problems. It's those highfalutin computers, Tom. This is the answer."

When in his resignation speech President Richard Nixon noted that "mistakes were made," the network anchors were quick to indict that deflection of responsibility. On November 7 and 8, as the errors in Florida were compounded, each network did as Nixon had done and shifted responsibility to unnamed outside forces, the equivalent of saying "mistakes were made." But, Rather said, we will fix it: "We're going to redo all mathematics, all the computer business, all the data business and see how it comes out." This suggested that the problem was with VNS, not with the precinct report of the vote count.

Too Close To Call

The scene was a committee chamber in the House of Representatives. As part of its review of Election Night coverage, the staff of the House Committee on Energy and Commerce played a video digest of the networks' battle with their own best and worst instincts on Election Night and the morning after 2000. There is, of course, a delicious irony in watching network anchors reduced to the sound bites that are their stock-in-trade but here fashioned into a whole by someone who is selecting instances to build an indictment. Because the tape was edited by the staff of the Republican majority, its focus was not on the implications of the call of the election for Bush but of the initial call of Florida for Gore. Hence most of the sound bites in it focus on that earlier process. Included, however, are segments that are particularly damning.

> **Bernard Shaw:** Look at this. Look at the war in Georgia. Vice President Gore, Governor Bush, this race for CNN at this hour, too close to call.
> **Jeff Greenfield:** And this has got to be a shocker in Austin. They've had this race put away in their pocket for weeks, if not months. We'll see.
> **Bernard Shaw:** Let's go to Thomas Jefferson's state. What's happening in Virginia? Again, the race. Too close to call.
> **Jeff Greenfield:** Bernie, Virginia has not voted for a Democrat for president since Lyndon Johnson in 1964. It is the heart of the Republican base of the South. They should have won this one going away.
> **Tom Brokaw:** The idea that North Carolina is too close to call does come as a surprise this evening.
> **Tim Russert:** The fact we projected Florida and Michigan before we projected Ohio for Bush is very telling.
> **Tom Brokaw:** Surprising.

Each of these states—Virginia, North Carolina, and Ohio—was won by Bush by a comfortable margin. So why did the network anchors get it wrong? The problem may have lay in a misunderstanding on the part of those speaking on air, or a lack of communication between them and the decision teams. For instance, when the decision teams saw an exit poll showing a Gore lead in North Carolina, they quite reasonably waited to make a call until actual vote counts arrived. Bush would win North

Carolina easily, and the decision teams correctly identified the prelimi-
nary exit poll results as anomalous. The delay was not a result of the North
Carolina result being "too close to call," as the anchors described it; instead, the decision teams were simply not *ready* to make a call based on
the data available at that moment. "Too close to call" is a statement not
about the networks' exit polls or computer models, but about an objective
reality. "Not ready to call"—or however the networks might consider referring to this status in the future—is more properly a statement about
their analysis, not about the votes themselves. The anchors went on to
interpret the fact that these states were "too close to call" as though Bush
had performed worse than expected, which was not in fact the case.

Metaphors Driving Interpretations: The Trifecta

Continuing the "horse race" metaphor that drives much campaign coverage, the organizing metaphor used by some in the networks to describe three decisive states that would supposedly decide the election
was the "trifecta." A trifecta pays when the horses that win, place, and
show are selected in the correct order. Picking a trifecta at the track is a
highly unusual stroke of luck that generates huge winnings. Within the
frame of this metaphor, the election was effectively over with a victory
for Gore in Florida, Michigan, and Pennsylvania. By focusing on the
indispensability of Florida, Michigan, and Pennsylvania, Election Night
analysts followed the pattern set by nightly news in the weeks leading up
to the election. On ABC, for example, George Stephanopoulos reported,
"Three big states we've talked about all year: Pennsylvania, Michigan,
and Florida. This is where the candidates spent the most money and the
most time. Bush went there fifty-three times. Gore went there sixty-six
times. Whoever wins two out of three of these states should be in the
driver's seat tonight, especially if he wins Florida." The same assumptions were in play at the other networks. On NBC Tim Russert noted
that "if, for some reason we knew that George Bush won Florida, won
Pennsylvania, won Michigan, it'd be very difficult for Al Gore. But if Al
Gore wins Florida, then Bush must win Pennsylvania or Michigan." Although he would give Tennessee an importance missed by his competi-
tors, on CBS Dan Rather also focused on the big three, with his early
observation that "if you want three to watch, those are the three: Florida,
Pennsylvania, and Michigan."

The metaphor of "the big three" became a way of seeing the election
for ABC. Its power was evident in an exchange between Mark Halperin

and Peter Jennings. Jennings said, "Al Gore has now Florida and Michigan, Pennsylvania to come of the big three. If he wins the big three of these battleground states, does that put him up to 270?" Halperin responded, "It gets him really close. It gets him really close."

The controversy surrounding the early-night call of Florida for Gore rested on the assumption that the call elicited network coverage suggesting that the election was effectively over. If that were the case, reasoned the Republicans, their supporters would stay home. Why Democrats would not stay home as well is of course a reasonable question.

This question was raised after the 1980 election, when NBC called the presidency for Ronald Reagan shortly after 8 P.M. eastern time. While the polls remained open on the West Coast, Jimmy Carter went before the cameras and conceded the election. Researchers attempting to investigate the consequences of the Carter concession found very small if any effect on turnout. It should be noted how different the cases of 1980 and 2000 are—while many had yet to go to the polls, Carter conceded; no one declared the election over while polls remained open in 2000.

Speculation on either side hinges on the assumption that a person paying attention to network news would believe the election was over after the Florida call. A close reading of the transcripts does not support that conclusion. Instead, since the reporters were focused on Florida, Michigan, and Pennsylvania with the assumption that the person who took all three would be all but unbeatable, it is not the call of Florida, which came at 7:50 P.M., that created a sense of inevitability for Gore but rather the call of Michigan at 8:00 and Pennsylvania at 9:00 that invited that conclusion. In other words, between 9:00, when Pennsylvania was called, and 10:15, when Florida was put back in the undecided category, the rhetoric of the reporters strongly implied a likely but not inevitable Gore victory. The exception to this was CBS, with Dan Rather and Ed Bradley believing, correctly, that if Gore lost Tennessee he would not win even with two of the big three in his column.

The Frame Adopted by CBS
Differed From That of the Others

So similar were the Election Night perspectives of the networks that a number used identical metaphors to forecast the same probable results. Nonetheless, the differences were as noteworthy as the similarities. While their assumptions and metaphors biased ABC's and NBC's coverage against Bush after the mistaken call of Florida for Gore, CBS's perspective produced the opposite effect—the assumption, even after the first mistaken Florida call, that Gore was a long shot and the election was Bush's to lose. This difference is particularly interesting in light of the fact that CBS was relying on the same source of data—the Voter News Service—as the others, and shared key members of their decision team with CNN. In this instance of live television, then, there was a high level of consistency in framing by CNN, NBC, ABC, and Fox, with Rather on CBS an interesting outlier.

One of the reasons that CBS did not adopt the frame that Gore would probably win after the first mistaken call of Florida is that Rather had defined winning or losing Tennessee as central to Gore's prospects. Where the other networks cast Florida, Pennsylvania, and Michigan as the "iron triangle" or the "trifecta," Rather did not.

During the same period, CBS was less likely to interpret Florida, Michigan, and Pennsylvania as a sign that Bush was in trouble and more likely to take projected wins for Gore there as a sign that he was viable but had a long way to go in a close race. When asked by Rather to give him three to watch, Ed Bradley said, "Pennsylvania, Michigan, and Tennessee." Rather said, "Mark well Tennessee. Al Gore's in the fight of his political life in Tennessee. It could be—nobody's predicting it—that if Tennessee . . . if Tennessee should go to Bush, it could wind up denying Al Gore the presidency." However, if the call of Florida for Gore had held, Gore would have been president without Tennessee.

The notion that Gore might lose the presidency by losing his home state of Tennessee created an ongoing narrative theme for Rather. In retrospect, Rather was right. "It would be Shakespearean if Al Gore were to lose the presidency because he lost his home state. But it's too early to say whether he's even going to lose it, much less whether it's a decisive state."

When Gore was projected as the winner of Florida, Rather said, "There are many people who believe and would tell you that Al Gore, in order to be viable in this presidential race, needed to win Florida, Pennsylvania, and Michigan. Florida has gone for Gore." Moments later, Rather called Illinois and Michigan for Gore. Did he now have an advantage? No. "A big win for Gore [in Illinois] helps keep his hopes of the presidency alive." Winning Illinois and Michigan was described as "the heart of the Gore comeback."

Of the calls in Florida and Michigan, CBS's Bob Schieffer said they kept "Al Gore in the game." John Roberts, who was in Nashville with the Gore campaign, said, "So if they [the Gore campaign] get Pennsylvania and if they get Minnesota, then all bets are off, and I—they—they really believe that with the remaining battleground states, they can pull out a win." Rather responded, "Well, hope springs eternal, and we shall see." With Gore at 119 projected electoral votes and Bush at 121, Gore was described by Rather as "surging back."

Before Pennsylvania was projected, Rather said, "Still hard to see, maybe impossible for Al Gore to win the presidency without carrying California. He's got to have California. Things have not—not yet reached the stage where George Bush can't win it without carrying Pennsylvania." After Florida, Michigan, and Illinois were called for Gore, with the electoral vote projected at 130 Bush to 119 Gore, Rather said, "There's still plenty of room on the board for George Bush not only to win the presidency but to win it comparatively early."

Because Rather believed that the presumed Florida win made Gore viable but did not guarantee him the presidency, he refused to buy in to the metaphors of "big three," "iron triangle," or "trifecta" to describe Florida, Michigan, and Pennsylvania. He also placed symbolic weight on Gore's prospective loss in his home state. As a result, CBS's coverage between the call of Florida for Gore and the retraction of that call was not biased against the possibility of a Bush win but biased against the possibility of a Gore win.

Rather's unique take on election night and the morning after may have been partly the result of effective Republican spin. With the electoral count projected at 192 for Gore to Bush's projected 185, Rather noted, "But the states still out there, where the polls have closed and decisions are not yet in, include a number of states that Bush feels confident he's going to take. He thinks he'll get five in West Virginia, thinks he'll get five in New Mexico. Also thinks he'll get eight in Arizona and another eight in Colorado. Those—those are his hopes. He's also hoping to get the eleven in Wisconsin. Bush seems almost certain in his own mind—the polls are still open out there—he's, in his own mind, fairly certain he's going to get Montana, Idaho, and Utah. And Oregon—the Bush people seem very confident before the polling actually started that they'd get Oregon. This is a reason we can say at this hour while Gore leads with 192 and Bush has 185, this is still anybody's race. It's cardiac arrest time in this presidential campaign." Where Rather saw Bush as confident, he saw the Gore campaign as more tentative in its projections. "The Gore people thought they might have some shot at getting New Mexico." By contrast, "the Bush people are very confident they can carry Arkansas."

This raises the question, Why did the confidence of the Bush campaign frame Rather's forecasts and the confidence of the Gore campaign—for example, that it would carry California—did not? The example we have cited is representative. With the projected count at 192 for Gore and 185 for Bush, Rather said, "Keep in mind that the Bush people are fairly confident—or at least they were before people actually started voting—that partly because of Nader's strength in Oregon, that they might be able to carry Oregon. We'll see about that." After Florida was pulled back into the undecided column, Rather said that "the Bush people are still confident that they're going to win it." "The Bush people were fairly confident they have Arizona, but the polls have closed, we haven't called it yet . . . The Bush people are feeling, once again, very confident that they've got Florida, but if the Gore—if—if Gore actually winds up carrying Florida, which is now in some doubt, we can't say . . ."

The exceptions to reports of Bush confidence typically include statements about both campaigns and occur after the West Coast polls had closed. For example, about Florida, Rather noted, "The Bush people think they'll win it on the strength of majority and absentee ballots. The Gore people think they'll win it because they ran so strong in southeast Florida."

Late in the evening the Gore campaign either began to communicate with CBS or began to be heard. Rather noted that "the Gore people insist that most of the votes not actually counted so far in Florida are from the so-called Gold Coast in southeast Florida, where the Gore people think they'll do very well."

Not all of the Bush information was reliable. Before CBS pulled back Florida for the second time, Rather reported that "Jeb Bush is on the phone with operatives in Florida and they say that their numbers show that Bush has won the state by more than 2,000." This raises the question: Would CBS have pulled Florida back from the Bush column sooner had it not received misinformation from the Bush campaign?

The First Florida Call

The least conclusive statement made by a network anchor when Florida was called for Gore was uttered by Dan Rather, who interrupted a guest to report, "I'm so sorry to interrupt you, Mike, you know I wouldn't do it if it weren't big. Florida goes for Al Gore." He then added, "Now, folks, the equation changes."

By contrast, CNN's Jeff Greenfield defined the Florida win for Gore as a large barrier to a win by Bush, and the other networks suggested that winning Florida was necessary for the Texas governor. When CNN called Florida for Gore, Greenfield said, "This is a roadblock in the size of a boulder to George W. Bush's path to the White House. They had counted these twenty-five electoral votes from the moment George Bush entered the campaign before he was even nominated." On Fox Scott Rasmussen observed, "Well, that's one of the two states that George Bush needed if he wants to become president, so there's one more, and that means Pennsylvania becomes very, very important." ABC's Dean Reynolds noted, "Well, all along, Florida was one of the key pieces to their electoral puzzle. I mean, this is a shocking defeat for them in Florida tonight. There's no question about it." On NBC Tim Russert set up a predicate to explain why Al Gore was still campaigning in Florida at 4 A.M. of Election Day. "Because George W. Bush knew," said Russert, "that he had to win Texas and Florida, his linchpins . . ."

Those who criticize the rhetoric surrounding the call do not dispute the fact that winning Florida turned out to be decisive for George W. Bush. Instead, they claim that calling Florida for Gore may have affected enough votes in other states to create a self-fulfilling prophecy—making it necessary for Bush to win Florida to become president.

Michigan for Gore

On CNN Judy Woodruff noted at 8 P.M. that "the stunner at this hour is that we can call Al Gore the winner in the Wolverine State." The sense of surprise was palpable on the other networks as well. On CBS reporters noted, "And in Michigan, again, John Engler was supposed to erect another firewall, and as happened in the Michigan primary Governor Bush ran right into the firewall." That left Pennsylvania. "Still watch Pennsylvania," noted Halperin, "in the East it's really, at this point, it's almost the whole election. If Al Gore can win Pennsylvania, [he] probably only needs to find one more state out there on that map to win this. If he loses Pennsylvania he can't win."

Pennsylvania for Gore

On CBS Bill Whittaker called Pennsylvania "the linchpin for the Bush strategy." "All eyes on Pennsylvania," said Russert, "and the question the

Republicans are asking across the country is, if George W. Bush lost Pennsylvania, too, and Gore won the trifecta—Florida, Pennsylvania, Michigan—could he still win the election? The answer is yes, but barely."

When Peter Jennings projected Pennsylvania for Gore, he added, "So that gives him the big three. That gives him Florida, and Michigan, and Pennsylvania. Those are the toughest battleground states of the year, and ABC News projects that Mr. Gore has won in Pennsylvania." A few moments later Jennings refreshed the metaphor. "As you know, just a few minutes ago we projected that Pennsylvania would go for Mr. Gore, giving him the trio of the big battleground states."

If Gore had won the trifecta, what were the chances that Bush could win the presidency? Three metaphors used to express Gore's presumed victory in Florida, Michigan, and Pennsylvania conveyed the notion that it was extremely unlikely that Bush could now win the presidency. Doing so was described as the equivalent of shooting down enemy warheads, hitting a bull's-eye, and running the table. On NBC Brokaw noted, "Big call, Tim. Pennsylvania goes to Vice President Al Gore. NBC News is projecting that Al Gore is the winner in Pennsylvania . . . It's still not over by any means, but with Florida, Pennsylvania, and Michigan in his column, Vice President Gore begins to build a foundation that could get him to 270 electoral votes, and it begins to look like, well, the missile defense shield, that in fact the governor has to hit every state with a laser beam and not miss any of them." On NBC Tim Russert mixed a metaphor from horse racing with one from archery to suggest the difficulty Bush would have in winning: "Well, the bull's-eye is needed, Tom, with Gore winning the trifecta . . ." The notion that Bush was a long shot was expressed as well by those on air at CNN, where Judy Woodruff's metaphor of combination became Jeff Greenfield's notion that Bush would have to run the table.

> **Judy Woodruff:** And we are able to call Pennsylvania for Vice President Al Gore. Twenty-three electoral votes go to the Vice President. Jeff Greenfield, Bernie Shaw, this is a major disappointment for George W. Bush, and Jeff, it makes it all the harder for him to put together a winning combination.
> **Jeff Greenfield:** It absolutely does. It means that the states that are now undecided, we can begin to say that George Bush has to more or less run the table on them.

On Fox William Kristol said, "If Gore wins Pennsylvania and gets the trifecta, Bush could still win, but he'd have to win an awful good—

you know, he'd have to run the table with a lot of these medium-sized states."

Trifecta? Bull's-eye? Run the table? All highly unlikely. As interesting is the possibility that two of the three metaphors made more sense to those speaking them than to some listening. While it is reasonable to think that most know what a bull's-eye is, "trifecta" and "run the table" are tied to forms of gaming with less than universal appeal. Perhaps the full extent of Bush's posited difficulty was lost on viewers less familiar with racetracks and pool halls than the males on air appear to be. That Bush was in trouble would, however, have been clear from the context in which the metaphors were used. When asked, both Russert and Greenfield indicated surprise at the assumption that some might have found the metaphors confusing.

Florida Back to Undecided

At 10:15 the networks began pulling Florida back into the undecided category. On NBC Tom Brokaw observed, "What the networks giveth, the networks taketh away." Note the plural. Throughout Election Night and the morning after the networks adopted a posture that assumed that *when we're right we're right; when we're wrong, everybody is wrong.* On CBS reporters noted, "Everybody that we know of had put Florida into the Gore column some time ago." "But everybody in the business virtually had called Florida for Gore based on data that turns out to be suspect." "Florida's twenty-five electoral votes were put in Gore's column, based on what we believed and most other people believed at the time—I know of nobody who didn't believe it—data from various precincts in Florida. It turns out that some of that data is suspect, and so to be as cautious as we can, and to level as straight as we can with you in the audience, we pulled Florida back its twenty-five electoral votes, put in the undecided column." "Everybody we can think of, everybody in the business had moved Florida into—everybody we know of had moved Florida into the Gore camp." "Everybody we know of said some time ago, okay, Florida's going for Gore . . ."

Like CBS, ABC noted that most other news services called Florida for Gore: "We and most other news services had called it for Mr. Gore." After Karl Rove came on air at NBC to suggest that Florida had been called for Gore prematurely, Tim Russert made the same move, saying, "But every network looked at this based on the samplings we're getting and awarded it to Vice President Gore . . ." On Fox Brit Hume noted, "We, and other networks, are now saying that Florida, which we and others had called for Vice President Gore, is now too close to call. Florida, the state of Florida, is back in play. So the world is a changed place . . ."

The networks took credit for their track record of accurate calls and made calls throughout the evening as if they were responsible, but shifted responsibility to bad data and computers when the Florida call for Gore was pulled back. Early in the morning ABC finally put on Carolyn Smith, who led the ABC team interpreting the VNS data, to explain that "we thought—we—we—we thought we had it a little bit before eight. And it is one of those things that we don't like to see happen. Everything began to fall—began to fall apart." Peter Jennings prodded her to absolve ABC of sole responsibility: "I don't mean to get us off the hook here for a second—but so many news agencies made the same projection."

In our day-to-day lives most of us live with a simple accounting system: If you take credit for what goes right, you should take responsibility for what goes wrong. On Election Night and the morning after the networks took credit for being right but deflected responsibility for what went wrong. Dan Rather said, "Florida pulled back into the undecided column. Computer and data problem. One of the CBS News headlines of the hour . . . Big trouble down there with data and computers in Florida. To err is human—is human, to really foul up requires a computer. And that's what's happening in Florida . . . bad data came from certain precincts in Florida . . . that's what was spitted out of the computers with the data, but data from some precincts turns out to be suspect, we pulled it back."

Public Perception

The coverage affected viewers' perspective on the news media themselves. In a Pew Research Center poll taken during the primaries, 63% rated the news media's coverage of the campaign as good or excellent. In the week after the election, Pew asked people to grade the news media again. This time 69% gave them a grade of C, D, or F. After the election, we asked our survey respondents the following question: "As you may know, early in the evening on Election Day, the media declared Al Gore the winner in Florida. Later in the night the media reported that George W. Bush won Florida. Finally, the media said the race was too close to call. In your opinion, what best explains why the news media made mistakes in reporting the Florida election results?" Just over one in five (21.4%) replied that it was an honest mistake because the race was very close. A majority (56.1%) attributed the mistakes to carelessness or reporting results before knowing for sure who won, an assessment that while not the most generous avoids an imputation of bias. Just over one in ten (12.4%, mostly Republicans) said it was because reporters personally wanted Al Gore to win.

Unsurprisingly, people's own political predispositions affected whether they found the media suspect. When we asked if they found the coverage of the uncertainty over the election outcome biased, Republicans were evenly split between those who said there was a bias for Gore (46.2%) and those who found no bias (45.7%), with almost none seeing bias in favor of Bush. Most Democrats, on the other hand (65%), found no bias in coverage of the election results, but those who did find bias were, like their Republican counterparts, disposed to see it favoring the other party's candidate. A similar number of independents (61%) saw no bias, while those who did were evenly split on whether it favored Gore or Bush.

The claims and counterclaims of the Democrats and Republicans about the influence of the coverage on the outcome of the election also seem to contain at least the possibility of truth. Consistent with the Democrats' view, our poll shows that as the recount was beginning and even as Bush's presumed lead narrowed, a majority of the public—including over half of all independents and nearly one in five Democrats, combined with nearly all Republicans—believed that Bush should have been declared the winner. Consistent with the Republicans' view, our poll shows that 8% of those who voted had been following election returns before going to the polls. At one point on Election Night, CNN anchor Judy Woodruff asked reporter John King, standing with Bush supporters in Austin, "What's that noise in the background?" King answered, "Um, that's me. They've got CNN broadcasting on the big screen, so there's an echo."[5]

Scholars have noted that the amount of analysis in news has increased over the past half-century.[6] Journalists spend an increasing amount of time explaining the why of politics, as opposed to the who, what, where, and when. In and of itself, this evolution is not necessarily harmful to their fundamental mission of describing the world to the public. At times, however, the assumptions and perspectives carried by those explanations can suppress the factual information citizens need to make sense of the political world.

Although reporters pride themselves on being recounters of important fact, they increasingly take on the role of pundits, forecasting the future. Even some who have not become part of the talking-head culture of television commentary have shifted reporting toward speculation about future consequences. This future-oriented approach, however, does not include a strong commitment to forecast the likely consequences of campaign promises to governance. Instead, it focuses on political consequences—the outcome of elections and congressional votes, the movement of public opinion, and the rising and falling fortunes of political figures. The debacle of Election Night 2000 illustrates how comfortable major news organizations have become with generalizing from inexact data to certain statements about the future. On-air reporters did not say at 2 A.M. on November 8, 2000, that George W. Bush *would be* the president *if* their predictions turned out to be correct; instead, they said, in the words of Dan Rather, "Sip it, savor it, cup it, photostat it, underline it in red, press it in a book, put it in an album, hang it on the wall. George Bush is the next president of the United States."

As Tim Russert said to Tom Brokaw the night before the election, "The exit polls, if they show a dead-even race or a candidate up a point or two, throw them out. We won't know anything." Had the networks followed Russert's pre-election advice, they would have sacrificed a small measure of certainty but been able to better serve their viewers. If the networks would be willing to delay their statements about who won which state until any risk of a mistake could be eliminated—even if it might mean not calling the election until the next day—they could separate preconception and prediction from fact and better preserve the public's trust.

5

The Press as Shaper of Events

The press both covers events and, in choosing what to report and how to report it, shapes their outcome. In 1959, Douglas Cater dubbed the press the "fourth branch of government," arguing that reporters were not merely observers but also were participants with a substantial degree of independent political power.[1] The reporter, Cater wrote, "can choose from among the myriad events that seethe beneath the surface of government which to describe, which to ignore. He can illuminate policy . . . he can prematurely expose policy and, as with an undeveloped film, cause its destruction. At his worst, operating with arbitrary and faulty standards, he can be an agent of disorder and confusion. At his best, he can exert a creative influence on Washington politics."

Forty years later, Timothy Cook expanded on Cater's notion, arguing that "the American news media today are not merely part of politics; they are part of government."[2] Cater, Cook, and scores of other scholars assert what some in journalism prefer to downplay or deny: that with the choices they make in carrying out the enormously difficult task to which they have been assigned, journalists help determine the course of events.

The more important the role public opinion plays in the progression of a political conflict, the greater the potential of journalists' choices to move events. As Walter Lippman famously described it, press attention is "like the beam of a searchlight that moves restlessly about, bringing one episode and then another out of darkness into vision."[3] Through what they illuminated, the press helped determine the outcome of the 2000 post-election battle in Florida. In leaving some critical pieces of information in darkness, the press also failed in carrying out its investigative role.

By the early hours of Wednesday, November 8, the country knew that the 2000 election had produced 267 probable electoral college votes for Al Gore and 246 for George W. Bush, with Florida's 25 electoral votes undetermined (Oregon and New Mexico were not yet final but leaning to Gore). On December 18, in each state capitol, the 538 electors would cast their votes. The votes would be read and accepted in a joint session of Congress January 6.

We will argue that in the thirty-six days following the election the Republicans exercised sufficient control over politics and the press to license five conservative justices of the Supreme Court to end the election without fear that their decision would undercut the credibility of the Court in public opinion. Among the forces acting on public and elite opinion were the networks' November 8 early-morning call of the election for Bush, Republican control of the positions of governor and secretary of state in Florida, and the fact that throughout the post-election counting process, the tallies consistently favored Bush, however narrowly. While recognizing the importance of these factors, our focus here will be on the role played by partisan rhetoric in shaping the perspective of journalism's elites. We will argue that the strategic dexterity of the Bush forces produced a pro-Bush perspective among key elites, in turn producing polls whose biased questions reinforced a perception in the public and press that since Bush had won it was time to end the process. Trusting that the public would accept Supreme Court action, five justices took the case of *Bush v. Gore* and, consistent with these elite cues, decided it for Bush. The success that the Republicans had in casting overseas absentee ballots as "military ballots"—and the arguments and presumptions that framing carried, including the idea that Gore was unpatriotic for wanting to disenfranchise the votes of those in uniform—proved to be decisive in the election. Reporting on the so-called military ballots also represented a failure on the part of the press: a failure first to ascertain the facts and then to contextualize them.

Because they feature those speaking for each side, include extended discussions, are watched faithfully by other reporters and opinion leaders, and are widely quoted in day-after news stories, the three major Sunday-morning interview shows offer a synopsis of the rhetorical field on which political actors compete. Rivaled only by the nationally distributed *New York Times* and the hometown paper of Washington elites, the *Washington Post,* the three Sunday network shows—*This Week* on ABC, *Face the Nation* on CBS, and *Meet the Press* on NBC—influence the discourse in other media by featuring those at the center of the national debate engaging the issue of the moment and the positions of the other side. Each Sunday, congressional leaders, White House staffers, and other key political actors make their pilgrimage to the network studios to offer what amounts to the official line of the various factions of American politics.

The national audience for the Sunday shows is relatively small; they are viewed on average in around 8.5 million homes combined, or 8% of U.S. households. But those in the circles of power—White House and congressional staff, interest group members, lobbyists, reporters, and scholars of politics—watch the Sunday shows religiously. By doing so they learn both the arguments being marshaled to defend the issues on the national agenda and the parameters of debate. Digests of this discourse then spread to other media outlets in the form of Sunday-evening news segments and Monday-morning newspaper reports. In short, the Sunday shows reflected the evolving rhetoric and the press perspectives on it in the thirty-six post-election days in a forum that has the added advantage of not being characterized by edited sound bites.

The Impact of the Networks' Declaration
That Bush Had Won

When the networks called the election for Bush at 2:20 A.M., televisions were on in fifteen million American homes. Those who were still awake heard the individuals they trust for their news—Peter, Tom, Dan, Brit, Brian, and Bernard—solemnly intone that George W. Bush was the next president. Graphics with Bush's picture and the words "George W. Bush—43rd President of the United States" flashed on the screen. This image was then replayed in stories recapping the events of election night. When this call was retracted at 3:50 A.M., 8.5 million homes still had their televisions on.[4] In 6.5 million homes, viewers went to bed thinking Bush had won but awoke to find instead an unsettled election.

Gore partisans believe that the network call of the election for Bush created a presumption that the Texan had in fact won, a perception that haunted Gore in the post-election period. Gore adviser Bob Shrum argued that "it made a big difference that Dan Rather said, 'Let's give a big

hearty Texas welcome to the new president of the United States, George
W. Bush,' and all these explosions went off." Gore pollster Stan Greenberg
agreed that the "media perception . . . made it very difficult for the Gore
campaign in those thirty days, because they were now fighting against a
presumption that already was stated."[5] While, as Gore representatives
believe, elite opinion may ultimately have been affected by the early-
morning call for Bush, evidence to that effect is difficult to marshal. There
was no identifiable anti-Gore or pro-Bush bias immediately evident in
the discourse of the Sunday shows.

Who Is the Presumed Winner?

The press had a number of possible frames available to it to discuss the
outcome of the vote the weekend after the election. In the first, Gore had
won the popular vote, was ahead in the electoral college, and the outcome in the electoral college was uncertain. That position was expressed
by Senate Minority Leader Thomas Daschle, who noted, "I'm also worried about the prospect of inaugurating a president who's won neither
the popular vote or a rightful claim to the electoral vote."[6] The alternative perspective held that Bush was ahead in the state that would cinch
the electoral college and as such was the presumed victor until Gore
proved otherwise. In the streets of Florida, Bush supporters expressed a
stronger view with signs and T-shirts that proclaimed "Sore Loserman"
in type identical to the Democrats' Gore-Lieberman signs. A final possible frame would have telegraphed that neither candidate was ahead.

   Our first reason for doubting that the call for Bush had an immediate
effect on the public is that the Gore frame was as prominent as the Bush
one on the Sunday-morning talk shows on the first Sunday after election
day. In fact, a pro-Bush tilt did not take hold until the controversy over
overseas absentee ballots was cast to favor Bush and Katherine Harris certified the Florida vote for the Texas governor on November 26.

   In the background of the debate over popular versus electoral vote
was the posturing of the two campaigns in the days before the election.
In the weeks leading up to Election Day, journalists posited a scenario in
which, buoyed by a large turnout in Texas, Bush might win the popular
vote but lose the electoral college. On the day before Election Day, the
Boston Globe said, "The race remains neck and neck with the growing
possibility that George W. Bush could win the popular vote but lose the
electoral vote to Al Gore."[7] The *Christian Science Monitor*'s analysis was

the same: "This year, the presidential race is so quirkily close that it's possible one candidate, George W. Bush (R), could win the popular vote, and another, Al Gore (D), could win in the Electoral College."[8] "The scenario runs something like this," wrote the *Atlanta-Journal-Constitution*. "Gore scores an electoral victory based on wins in a handful of states . . . Bush loses out in the Electoral College, but actually gets more votes nationally . . ." "I think there would be an outrage," commented Republican congressman Ray LaHood of Illinois.[9] In the course of speculation about that possibility, Democrats went on record reiterating that, under those circumstances, the victor in the electoral college would be the president. Had Gore repudiated that position in the post-election period, he would have been branded both a hypocrite and the opportunist Republican campaign rhetoric had made him out to be.

Because an electoral vote victory but popular vote defeat had not been projected as a possibility for Bush, the Republicans were not constrained by pre-election position-taking. The opposite scenario may have been a possibility contemplated within the campaign, however. In the closing weeks of the campaign, word leaked to a reporter for the *New York Daily News* that the Republicans had planned for the possibility that Bush would win the popular vote but lose the electoral college. According to the report, under that circumstance the Republicans would air ads arguing for the legitimacy of the popular vote. "A massive talk radio operation would be encouraged," reported the article. "'We'd have ads, too,' says an anonymous Bush aide."[10] When asked about the article at the Annenberg School election debriefing on February 11, 2001, senior Bush adviser Karl Rove said the possibility of a campaign to persuade Gore electors to vote for Bush "was never discussed. It may have been discussed at a higher level of the campaign, like the interns and the mail room clerks, but I never heard it discussed until I read it in the newspaper."[11] Rove's denials notwithstanding, others report that Republicans were gearing up for the possibility. CNN analyst Jeff Greenfield indicates that "at least two conservative commentators were specifically briefed by the Bush campaign shortly before taking to the airwaves about the line of attack to be taken in the event that Bush wound up losing the Electoral count despite a popular vote lead." Kenneth Duberstein, who served as the elder George Bush's White House chief of staff, said, "It was part of the talking points."[12]

Perhaps constrained by his campaign's pre-election arguments, Gore foreclosed the popular vote claim to legitimacy in a press conference the day after the election. "Despite the fact that Joe Lieberman and I won the popular vote," he said, "under our Constitution it is the winner of the Electoral College who will be the next president. Our Constitution is the whole foundation of our freedom and it must be followed faithfully, toward the true result ordained by the American people with their votes in our respective states."[13] Perhaps following Gore's signal, on the Sunday-morning shows the Democrats noted but did not argue aggressively that because Gore had won the popular vote, Bush was not entitled to the presumption that a continuing lead in the vote-counting process in Florida gave him a privileged position. Even though the fact of the Democrat's popular-vote victory was noted fourteen times by those on the Sunday shows, it did not persist as a dominant theme and was used primarily to justify a continued count, not the presumption that Gore had a more legitimate claim to the presidency than Bush.

By contrast, the notion that Bush had won not once but multiple times was a central part of his supporters' argument. On twelve occasions on the weekend after the election, Bush supporters on the Sunday shows reiterated the fact that he had been declared the winner on election morning—a first indication that the call would provide a rhetorical footing for the case that Bush had in fact already been elected.

The Late-Night Call Did Not Frame the Discussion on November 12 or November 19

The assumption that Bush had won Florida eventually did take hold on the Sunday shows, but not on the first two weekends after the election and not as a by-product of the early-morning call. Had the early-morning call had a decisive and immediate influence, the anti-Gore, pro-Bush assumptions would have been apparent on the first Sunday after Election Day. Instead, as Cokie Roberts said, "So, we're really talking about a tied election." "George Bush leads by 279 votes. That's unofficial, but it's very close . . . [there are] more than 400,000 votes [uncounted in Palm Beach County]." On *Meet the Press*: "Gore gained thirty-six votes, Bush lost three . . . in the hand recount, it appears that Gore is gaining more disproportionately than Bush."

In this initial period, both campaigns were asked about the possibility of concession. On *This Week*, for example, Sam Donaldson asked, "Do you—do you believe that Governor Bush will concede if he's behind? And if he does not, if he wants to contest in the other states that Cokie mentioned, what's your strategy?" The possibility that Bush would fall behind led to the question "If Governor Bush finds himself behind after these hand counts are counted, should he back off, throw it in, show himself a good loser?"[14] The same Sunday, Tim Russert asked James Baker, "Why does Governor Bush fear a hand recount?" Baker was also asked, "Isn't there somewhere along the line here when you're going to have to step back and say 'This is the way it is and you can't tie this up in the courts for a matter of months'"? On November 12 on *Face the Nation* John McCain was even asked whether if Al Gore were to win he would consider being his secretary of defense. On *Face the Nation* a week later, both sides were questioned about whether the other was trying to steal the election.

Indeed, during the first two post-election Sundays, hosts' questions more often associated "president" and "presidency" with Gore than Bush. Following the adversarial form characteristic of Sunday-morning questions, the hosts presented proponents of a position a difficulty they or their candidate would face under various scenarios. For example, Tim Russert asked Mary Matalin on November 12 whether "if in the end" Gore was declared the victor and "he wins the presidency, could you and your fellow Republicans ever truly accept him as a legitimate president?" The assumptions shifted after November 26. In the last three weeks of the post-election contest, those associations were more likely to tie Bush to the presidency. For example, on *Face the Nation* on December 12 Bob Schieffer asked James Baker whether if Bush is "declared the president, isn't it going to be awfully hard for him to govern?"

However, in the early weeks, three notions that weakened the Democratic position began to take hold. They included the assumption that the process in Florida was chaotic and unfair, the presumption that the process was a recount not a count, and the supposition that Bush not Gore might consider challenging the outcome in other states.

The Chaos Frame

The Republicans cast the post-election count as unreliable and chaotic. "Those were not thirty-four days of reflection," noted a reporter for the *New York Times* who was in Florida for the recount. "It was part of the Bush campaign strategy to create a sense of chaos . . . You heard from Bush campaign spokespersons almost every day a quote that involved the word 'chaos' or something similar."[15]

By and large, the Sunday hosts accepted the Bush assumption that the hand count was fundamentally flawed and unfair. Where forty-four of the moderators' questions implied that the counting process was being handled in a unfair way, only sixteen assumed that the process was a necessary means of determining the will of the voters of Florida.

The unfair/chaos frame was captured by the Republicans' 1996 standard-bearer Bob Dole, who on November 12 analogized the Gore strategy to a carnival game. The Democrats were "going to keep—they control the machinery in these counties and they count to—to—want to keep counting until they get enough to win and they say, 'Well, it's over. We won.'" New York governor George Pataki noted on *Face the Nation* on November 26 that "all these efforts to count and recount and change the standards are simply an effort not to try to have a fair and accurate recount, but to try to find votes for Gore." The same point was made by Montana governor Marc Racicot (*Meet the Press*, November 19), who asserted that "ballots have been used as fans" and "have Post-it notes stuck on them." Baker said, "You're divining the intent of the voter with respect to whether it has two chads hanging down or whether it's punched or whether it has indentations. I mean, it's crazy" (*Meet the Press*, November 12).

Hosts reiterated the dramatic, concrete, visual Republican charges. "Ballots were used as fans," said Sam Donaldson, recapping the Republican position on November 19. "Post-it notes stuck over presidential spots. Bush ballots have been found in Gore piles." The Republican frame was effectively advanced by conservative regulars on the shows as well. On November 12 on *This Week*, George Will forecast that "if this highly sophisticated vote-manufacturing procedure goes ahead, Gore will win." On the twenty-sixth, the process in Florida was described by Will as a "circus-like fiasco."

Host disapproval of the process was sometimes plain. On November 12, Tim Russert showed a clip of election officials holding a ballot to the light to examine voter intent. "These are the counters holding up ballots," he said. "Looking at them, turning them around, looking at them through the light . . . If the chad, the piece of paper that was poked, was hanging, swinging or a tri-chad, pushed three-fourths of the way through, it would be counted. If it, in fact, was bulging, pregnant, or dimpled, not counted. Is this any way to elect a president?" Gore adviser Warren Christopher, to whom the comment was addressed, responded that "it is not very useful to parody what they're trying to do there." The difference in assumptions about the two campaigns was evident when earlier in the show Russert gave the same description to James Baker, then asked him a question that invited criticism of the process: "What does that say to you? What does that say to you?"

On ABC on the same day, Cokie Roberts noted, "It is so much going on with the chads and the holding them up to the light and all that stuff that it's becoming a laughingstock. And this is the American presidential election." Donaldson said, "Ask not what your chad can do for you, ask what your chad can do for your country." The comments of the hosts, in other words, were consistent with the frame of such Bush partisans as Mary Matalin (who later joined the Bush White House), who decried the "human manipulation" of the recount. James Baker made the same point when he stated that there were "no uniform, objective standards . . . and it's all subjective . . . presents terrible problems of human error and potential for mischief" (*Meet the Press*, November 12).

When asked to explain the vote-counting process in Florida on November 12, ABC reporter Jackie Judd responded with the question "Do you have an hour?" and added, "It was pretty complicated." Bush representative James Baker translated "complicated" as "flawed." Referring to Judd's report, he noted that the "lead-in made the case very effectively I think [that the recount process] is deeply flawed." On November 29, Russert asked a Gore representative, "When you see a voting inspector with a magnifying glass looking at a ballot, holding it up to the light, does it trouble you?"

The process in Florida was characterized as "turmoil" (*This Week*, November 12) and as "spinning out of control"(*Face the Nation*, November 19). The chaos frame was tied to the notion that Gore championed procedures that were producing disorder. Once in the words of a host (*Meet the Press*, November 19) and once in a quote on the screen (*This Week*, November 19), the proposition that Gore would do anything to win was offered.

Whatever they might have felt about the relative merits of human judgment and the accuracy of machines prior to 2000, voters sided with the campaign they favored. Although election laws around the country assume that hand counts are more accurate than machine counts (many states mandate hand counts when machine counts show a small margin between candidates), those who voted for Bush adopted the Bush campaign's position that machines are more accurate. We asked our survey respondents this question: "As you may know, ballots are being counted by machine and by hand in Florida. Which method do you think is more accurate? To count ballots by machine, by hand, or do you think both methods are equally accurate?" Those who voted for Bush swore to the accuracy of machines, while those who voted for Gore placed their faith in human tabulation or said the two methods were equally accurate. (See details on next page.)

	Machine count more accurate	Hand count more accurate	Both equally accurate
Voted for Bush	75.2%	5.7%	16.8%
Voted for Gore	21.5%	44.3%	28.7%

The Recount Frame

There were hints of a problem for Gore in the November 12 transcripts when on ABC, reporter Dean Reynolds described Gore as attempting to "overturn the results of an election." Used four times more often in the Sunday shows than the words "hand count," "manual count," "complete count," "total count," "full count," or even "hand recount," the word "recount" reinforced a central assumption of the Bush forces: that the ballots had been counted and were being tallied again.

By contrast, Gore's case pivoted on the assumption that this was a count, not a recount. In this perspective, some of his votes, such as those on the butterfly ballot, had been miscounted; in the case of the so-called under or over votes, others had not been counted at all. As Gore's running mate saw it, they were seeking a "full, accurate, honest count" (*Face the Nation*, November 19) or alternatively simply wanted "every vote to be counted" (*This Week*, November 19). Occasionally hosts adopted the pro-Gore language of hand recount, as Tim Russert did on November 19: "But if you want to eliminate any cloud of illegitimacy over a potential president, why wouldn't a statewide hand recount settle the issue once and for all for the American people?" But that comment was the exception.

In press conferences and interviews the Bush campaign advanced the Bush-winner, Gore-sore-loser frame. Bush had won every count, said his representatives. Why was there a need for further proof that he was the president-elect? Although the Bush campaign persisted in saying that the ballots in Florida had been counted not once (on election eve) but twice (in the mandated statewide recount), instead as the *Los Angeles Times* revealed on November 21, sixteen of the sixty-seven Florida counties did not conduct a recount but instead simply reviewed their original tallies. Of these sixteen counties, eleven were won by Bush and five by Gore. Nonetheless, the Bush rather than the Gore language predominated on the Sunday shows.

In all, in the fifty-four times during the five post-election weeks that the show hosts questioned the positions of the two camps, a Gore spokesperson was almost twice as likely to be challenged as was a person defending the Bush position.

Why an Additional Bush Challenge
but Not a Gore Challenge?

Gore could have lost Florida and still won the electoral college had he taken New Hampshire's four electoral votes, which Bush won by 7,211 votes. However, on the Sunday shows the hosts instead focused on the possibility that Bush would contest Gore's close wins in New Mexico (366 votes), Oregon (6,765 votes), Wisconsin (5,708 votes), and Iowa (4,144 votes). For example, on November 12 Tim Russert asked James Baker if a Bush request for an injunction to stop the count was denied with Gore ahead, whether the Bush campaign would ask for a recount in other states. He asked Warren Christopher whether he thought the Bush campaign "has every right to seek recounts in New Mexico and Oregon and Wisconsin and Iowa?" On the same day, Sam Donaldson asked whether Bush (but not Gore) should consider contesting other states if he lost Florida, a prospect that Cokie Roberts saw as a "temptation" for Bush. And on CBS John McCain was reminded by Gloria Borger that "there are lots of other states, as you well know, that are very, very close, in which the Bush campaign might well demand a recount."

The Turning Point for Bush:
"Overseas Absentee Ballots" Become "Military Ballots"

Between the nineteenth and twenty-sixth the sentiment of the hosts on the Sunday shows turned against Gore. A debate over the counting of overseas absentee ballots, many of which came from members of the military, changed what had been to that point relatively evenhanded presentations to forums in which the Gore campaign was assumed to be acting beyond the pale, while the Bush campaign was assumed to be defending the honor of America's servicemen and -women. The Republicans effectively framed "overseas absentee ballots" as "military ballots" not subject to the literal provisions of Florida law, and further, unbeknownst to the Sunday hosts, applied that standard only when it advantaged Bush. At the same time, the Bush forces successfully cast Gore's attempts to enforce the law as an unpatriotic assault on those who were risking their lives in defense of their country. Missing half the story, elite journalists sided emphatically with the Bush campaign.

Early in the post-election process, some in the press recognized that the overseas absentee ballots might prove decisive. On the *Today Show* on November 8, for example, Tom Fiedler of the *Miami Herald* noted that "the outstanding issue is going to be those absentee ballots that are going to be coming in from overseas or out of state." Fiedler would turn out to be prescient; whatever its effect on the outcome of the Florida count, the issue of overseas absentee ballots dealt a severe blow to Al Gore's ability to maintain legitimacy in the press for his effort to prevail in the Sunshine State.

Two types of ballots could be sent back from overseas: county ballots and federal ballots. Provided for in the Uniform and Overseas Citizen Voting Act, Federal Write-In Absentee Ballots had a space to indicate the date; county ballots did not. On the twenty-first of November the *Orlando Sentinel* reported that "most" of the military ballots were "standard county-issued ballots." The *New York Times* reported on the same day that having no postmark was the "most common reason for rejecting overseas ballots" but added that "very few military ballots were thrown out purely for that reason."

The overseas absentee ballots were not necessarily from the military. Section 101.62 of the Florida Statutes specifies that an "absent qualified elector overseas" means a person registered and qualified by law who is a member of the armed forces in active service, a member of the merchant marine or "other citizens of the United States, who are permanent residents of the state and are temporarily residing outside of the territories of the U.S. and District of Columbia." In the immediate wake of the election it was not clear whether there would be a large number of such ballots from U.S. citizens in Israel—ballots presumed to be Democratic votes—or whether the overseas absentees would be overwhelmingly military ballots—presumed to favor Republicans.

According to Florida law, overseas absentee ballots had to be received by ten days after the election. On November 17, canvassing boards began counting those ballots. Media reports indicated that Gore representatives were attempting to exclude as many ballots as possible. Since absentee voters have to follow a detailed set of instructions, there are many grounds on which a ballot can be excluded. According to an analysis by the Associated Press, when canvassing boards in Florida's sixty-seven counties counted overseas ballots on November 17 and 18, they excluded 39% of the overseas absentee ballots (1,420 out of 3,626).

Nonetheless, practices varied from county to county; counties carried by Bush excluded 29% of the overseas ballots, while counties carried by Gore excluded 60%.[16] Even as it reported the different rates of exclusion, the press failed to draw the inference that the Republican claim that there should be a uniform counting standard was being selectively applied. Instead, the *New York Times* on November 18 suggested that each party was unevenly applying standards. Heavily Republican counties tended to include military ballots without postmarks, said the article, where heavily Democratic counties tended to exclude them. Meanwhile the *Times* editorialized in favor of a liberal standard in counting the overseas absentee ballots.

Part of the confusion was caused by a memo Katherine Harris sent to the canvassing boards before the count on the seventeenth stating that overseas ballots did *not* have to be postmarked prior to Election Day. Canvassing boards in some Republican counties followed her instructions, while boards in some Democratic counties ignored them, judging that the edict contradicted first the rules counties had used in previous elections in Florida, and second Florida law, because Harris seemed to be declaring it legal to vote after Election Day.[17]

On November 22, the Bush campaign filed suit in Tallahassee, asking the state of Florida to force counties to accept absentee ballots submitted by members of the military, regardless of whether they were postmarked or had postmarks after Election Day. The suit "asked for the overseas military ballots to be ruled valid even if they have illegible, late or domestic postmarks, lack a handwritten date, have 'minor differences' in signatures compared with the ballot requests, and whether or not the counties concerned know whether the voters requested absentee ballots in time."[18]

The reason for the postmark is clear. What otherwise prevented a person from voting after the results of the November 7 election were in and the "virtual tie" a reality? Indeed, long after the election was resolved the *Washington Post* located a sailor who admitted to casting a late (and hence illegal) ballot and found as well a number of ballots postmarked after the legal deadline. Some military personnel sent their ballots in—after Election Day had passed—by express mail services such as UPS and DHL.

Unexplained by the press at the time was a difference in the practices of the two campaigns. Where the Democrats tried to convince the canvassing boards to strictly follow the letter of the law on the overseas ballots, the Bush campaign made the case for ignoring the law when it advantaged Bush, even to the point of including ballots cast after Election Day. At the same time, the Republicans argued that the law should be followed to the letter when doing so helped Bush.

Representatives of the Bush and Gore campaigns had little difficulty telling which of the overseas absentee ballots came from military personnel. First, each ballot envelope[19] indicated the address to which it had been originally mailed; many indicated a military base. Second, those that had valid postmarks showed either an APO (Army Post Office) or FPO (Fleet Post Office). Finally, Federal Write-In Ballots sent to the members of the military were printed in red ink, while those mailed to members of the foreign service or other nonmilitary personnel were printed in black ink. Consequently, in most cases it was possible to tell whether a ballot came from someone in the military.

When the first count of late-arriving ballots took place on the seventeenth, Republicans and the press realized that the Gore campaign was demanding that the canvassing boards adhere strictly to the law on overseas ballots. On *Meet the Press* that Sunday (November 19), Tim Russert quoted from a Democratic memo on, as he put it, "how you knock out ballots from military people overseas." "How can a campaign who insists on the intent of the voter, the will of the people, not disenfranchising anybody, accept knocking out the votes of the people of the armed services?" he asked Gore's running mate. Why had the Democrats made this move? The Republicans had an explanation consistent with their original frame, paraphrased by Gloria Borger on CBS: The Gore campaign attempted to have those ballots disqualified "because they expected not to get those votes." The Sunday hosts clearly disapproved of the Democratic tactic. And on November 19, Gore's running mate appeared to agree with them. Overall the Sunday hosts raised twenty-three questions about the challenge of absentee ballots. Overall, the Sunday shows assumed the illegitimacy of the Democrat's challenge of the absentee ballots—which were presumed to be military ballots. Thirteen disapproving comments were lodged against Gore. Bush's interpretation of Florida law was questioned eighteen times, Gore's twenty-six.

The memo in question, written by Democratic lawyer Mark Herron, outlined the rules of Florida law covering overseas ballots, including the various grounds on which a ballot could be challenged. Days before, in a press conference arranged by the Republican National Committee, Jim Smith, who had served as both secretary of state and attorney general for the state of Florida, gave reporters essentially the same information, detailing the rules of Florida election law. While the content of the Herron memo and the Smith press conference were virtually the same, the Smith press conference was little noted and not taken as evidence of an intent on the Republicans' part to disqualify legitimate votes. The Herron memo, on the other hand, was used by Bush representatives as proof that Gore sought to disenfranchise military personnel. Members of the press then accepted and amplified this interpretation, further placing the focus on those absentee ballots cast by members of the military. Montana governor Marc Racicot said, "I am very sorry to say, but the Vice President's lawyers have gone to war, in my judgment, against the men and women who serve in our armed forces." A *Washington Post* news story described the memo as "coaching Democrats on how to disqualify votes from overseas military personnel."[20]

A post-election investigation by the *New York Times* discovered that Bush campaign lawyers had produced their own memo instructing their representatives on the vagaries of Florida law regarding absentee ballots. Unlike the Gore campaign's memo, which listed only the grounds on which ballots could be excluded, the Republican memo gave instructions both for excluding civilian overseas ballots and defending identically questionable military ballots. The Democratic memo included a sample form representatives could use to challenge a ballot; the Republican memo included two forms, one for challenging civilian ballots and one to demand the inclusion of military ballots.[21] Had reporters uncovered the Republican memo, they would have had to report that both campaigns were seeking to knock out votes unlikely to favor their side. An observation of the two campaigns' representatives participating in the vote counting would have produced the same conclusion.

Conflicting Frames: Disenfranchise Military Voters or Follow the Law

The Republicans succeeded in casting the Gore campaign memo insisting that canvassing boards strictly follow the law as an attempt to disenfranchise members of the armed forces. The Gore campaign argued instead that, in the words of Rhode Island Senator Jack Reed, "you have to follow the rules to cast a valid vote . . . It's not aimed at military or overseas civilians. It's aimed at valid voting."[22] As evidence of the Democratic intent to discount military ballots, the Republicans argued that these ballots had been rejected at a higher rate in 2000 than in earlier years. In actuality, the rate of rejection of overseas ballots was the same in 2000 as it had been in previous years.[23]

On November 19, Joe Lieberman appeared on *Meet the Press*, where he was met with the following question from Tim Russert: "Will you today, as a representative of the Gore campaign, ask every county to relook at those ballots that came from armed services people and waive any so-called irregularities or technicalities which would disqualify them?"

The presumption behind Russert's reference to "so-called irregularities or technicalities"—and the arguments the Bush campaign was making—was that any ballot coming from a member of the military should be included, regardless of whether it was legally cast. The regulations on absentee ballots are meant to ensure that the ballot is cast by the person in question, and cast before election day. Although all the requirements have a legitimate purpose, some are more critical than others to ensuring the integrity of a ballot. For example, absentee voters are instructed to sign across the flap of the envelope; if such a signature is not present, election officials can still ascertain with relative certainty whether the ballot is legitimate. On the other hand, if the ballot has no postmark and arrives two weeks after Election Day, there is no way to determine whether it was mailed before the election deadline. According to the *Times*'s post-election investigation, among the ballots arriving from members of the military that were accepted and counted were some mailed after Election Day and even a few sent by individuals who had already voted.

Had Russert posed a question about overseas absentee ballots from the Gore perspective to a Republican on the same show, we would be hard-pressed to argue that he had embraced the Bush frame. A question of that sort might have asked, "Will you insist that all ballots be assessed using the standards set by Florida law and as a result insist that those sent from within the United States or postmarked after Election Day be excluded? Consistent with your arguments about the recount, will you insist that the same standards be applied to overseas ballots in counties carried by Gore and by your campaign? And do you believe that serving in the armed forces entitles a person to have a ballot counted this year when by the standards applied in past elections it would have been thrown out?" But Russert asked no such question.

Lieberman's reply to Russert undercut the efforts of his campaign's representatives in Florida. While Gore staffers were challenging overseas ballots that did not conform to the requirements of Florida law, Lieberman told election officials to include as many ballots as possible:

> I would give the benefit of the doubt to ballots coming in from military personnel . . . [M]y guess is that every one of those election officials in each of those sixty-seven counties in Florida wanted to really do this, count the absentee ballots by the letter of the law so they wouldn't be subject to question. And if they have the capacity, I'd urge them to go back and take another look.

The Bush frame captured elite opinion. On the same show, Russert asked Lieberman, "How can a campaign who insists on the intent of the voter, the will of the people, not disenfranchising anybody, accept knocking out the votes of people of armed services?" When Lieberman appeared on *This Week* the same day, Sam Donaldson said to Lieberman, "Now it is correct, your officials did tell county officials what to do to disqualify ballots." On *Face the Nation*, Bob Schieffer asked him, "But shouldn't you and the Vice President put out some statement or something to the effect—some guidance, even to—to—to Democrats who think they're doing—following the letter of the law that says, 'Look, we need to give our military people the benefit of the doubt'"?

The Democratic insistence that the law be followed was successfully recast by the Republicans as an unpatriotic attempt to discriminate against those risking their lives to defend the nation. In a statement released by the Bush campaign, Racicot and Gulf War general Norman Schwarzkopf said, "It is a very sad day in our country when the men and women of the armed forces are serving abroad and facing danger on a daily basis . . . yet because of some technicality out of their control, they are denied the right to vote for the president of the United States who will be their commander in chief."[24] Republican congresswoman Tillie Fowler of Florida stood before the memorial to Duval County's war dead and charged that "there was an organized Democratic effort throughout this state in every single county to get military ballots thrown out."[25] The irony of these statements is that they contradict those of Jim Smith, who in the press conference arranged by the Bush campaign on November 12 said, "The privilege to vote abroad comes with the corresponding duty to follow practices adopted by the state of Florida to assure timely and fair elections."[26] Bush allies also attempted to portray military personnel overseas as hurriedly filling out their ballots while dodging bullets and torpedoes,[27] though the United States military was not involved in any hostile action at the time and each unit in all of the armed services has a voting-assistance officer assigned to help personnel satisfy all regulations when voting.[28]

While the Republicans were applying different standards in different counties, they were tagging the Gore campaign with hypocrisy. So, for example, retired General and prospective Bush Secretary of State Colin Powell found the exclusion of military ballots troubling. "All those GIs in Broward County, Florida, are going to learn that 75 percent of their absentee ballots were thrown aside. At the same time, we're trying to divine the intent of dimples on the other ballots." On *NBC Nightly*

News on November 26, Medal of Honor recipient Bob Ingram made the same argument: "If you're going to count a dimple, then they need to count a vet's vote."

The press accepted this logic, despite the fact that the Bush campaign was pointedly arguing that dimples made by civilians should not be counted. About Florida Attorney General Bob Butterworth's opinion that ballots should be counted if they were dated but had no postmark,[29] Howard Fineman of *Newsweek*, appearing on MSNBC's *Hardball* on November 20, said, "Legally they had to do it because logically their argument is, the intent of the voters is what matters here . . . You can't argue for dimpled chads on the one hand and be rigorous about postmarks on the other." The logic that would follow would say, use the liberal standard in both cases, so give Bush the military ballots that didn't pass legal muster and give Bush or Gore the hanging and dimpled chads, depending on which seemed to express voter intent as reviewed ballot by ballot. Although each was seeking to impose the standard most favorable to it in one case but not in the other, the hypocrisy charge was leveled only at the Gore campaign.

In fact, both campaigns made strikingly hypocritical arguments when it came to which ballots could be counted. On the question of those cast at polling places, the Gore campaign argued that maximum leeway should be granted to the voter, and that ballots should be scrutinized to determine each voter's intent. The Bush campaign argued that any irregularity in a ballot—even if, for instance, the voter had properly punched the hole next to a candidate's name and also written the same candidate in—was the voter's own fault and justified excluding the ballot. When it came to the overseas ballots, on the other hand, the Gore campaign attempted to have any ballot that did not precisely conform to every last regulation excluded, while the Bush campaign argued that what mattered was the intent of the voter regardless of whether the rules had been followed.

The Republicans Succeeded in Determining the Frame

What was the effect of the Republican assault on Gore's effort to ensure that those casting overseas ballots followed the letter of the law? Almost immediately, journalists both adopted the Republican frame—that overseas ballots equaled military ballots, and that Gore was attempting to disenfranchise servicemen and -women—and declared the Gore effort a "public relations disaster," a phrase used again and again in print, on radio, and on television. On NBC Tom Brokaw asked, "What about those disqualified absentee ballots? They may be counted after all, after a weekend of public relations disasters for the Gore campaign" (*NBC Nightly News*, November 20). The notion that what the Democrats were doing was illegitimate was clear in a statement on ABC's *World News Tonight* on November 20 by Peter Jennings, who noted that "the Democrats are getting banged around on the ground, at least anecdotally, for interfering as best they can with the absentee ballots from the military and trying to knock them out." Cokie Roberts responded, "The public relations effect of seeming to be trying to take votes away from our men and women in uniform, who are serving the country in danger's way overseas, could not be worse for Democrats." Did the Democrats recognize that the Republicans had won public opinion on the issue of overseas absentee ballots? On CNN John King reported that on Capitol Hill "many Democrats raised alarm there because Republicans have been making the case that the Democrats are anti-military . . . Democrats in Washington urged the Gore campaign to take care of this because of the perception the party would be viewed as anti-military no matter how this turns out."[30] Georgia Democratic senator Zell Miller said that he didn't "care when it's dated, whether it's witnessed or anything else. If it is from someone serving this country and they made the effort to vote, count it and salute them when you do."[31]

Such statements by a few Democrats led Republican attorneys to characterize the calls for reconsideration as bipartisan. On *NBC Nightly News* November 25, Bush attorney Ben Ginsburg observed that "some county boards have sought to evade bipartisan calls to count overseas military ballots by raising procedural issues concerning venue, challenging the court's jurisdiction and posing other obstacles."

In short, using public opinion which their comments had helped create as pressure, media elites pressed such visible Democrats as Lieberman to capitulate. At the same time, the Republicans got canvassing boards to reconsider and count previously disqualified ballots even though, had the court cases gone to a ruling, these ballots would probably not have been counted. The dominant frame assumed inaccurately that there had been a higher level of rejection of military ballots in 2000 than in previous elections. In fact, the exclusion of many overseas absentee ballots for failure to comply with regulations was a regular feature of vote counting in Florida, as it is in many states.

The military ballot controversy had a direct effect on the counting of ballots. In twelve counties, canvassing boards went back to review the ballots they had rejected for not meeting the requirements of law. Public opinion coupled with the capitulation of the Gore representatives had their effect. As a result of that second look, Bush netted an additional 109 votes. The reexamination of absentee ballots to include more, which occurred over the Thanksgiving holiday, came to be known as "Thanksgiving stuffing."

We interviewed the Gore campaign staffer covering heavily Republican Escambia County, who kept careful records of the results of the various counts. When the initial count of late-arriving overseas ballots took place on November 17, the Gore campaign challenged the validity of many ballots on the basis of improper signatures and postmarks; the Escambia canvassing board agreed with 58% of those challenges. In most of the challenges that the board rejected, there was no postmark or the ballot had been mailed from within the United States. When the board revisited the ballots a second time, the Gore campaign renewed its challenges to the same ballots, but this time the board agreed with only 32%. Included in the ballots that the canvassing board accepted and counted were ballots with no postmark, ballots on which witnesses had failed to give their address, and seven ballots that had postmarks after election day.

By focusing so much attention on the strategic implications of the conflict over overseas ballots, journalists failed to fulfill their investigative role. This excerpt from a cover article from the November 27 issue of *Newsweek* illustrates the focus: "The blow was hard—and, some would say, low . . . the Bushies accused the Democrats of running a dirty campaign to disallow the absentee ballots of soldiers and sailors stationed abroad . . . Was the latest offensive clever—or desperate?"[32]

An alternative explanation accounts for the belief that military personnel should have their ballots counted even if they failed to comply with voting regulations, while the same was not true of ordinary citizens, by attributing these press sentiments to the complicated feelings many journalists have about the military. In recent years, respect for the military among citizens has increased dramatically. Military successes in Kuwait and Kosovo have enhanced the image of the armed services. Reporters—many of whom are not veterans—may have been, consciously or unconsciously, deferential to servicemen and -women, and thus receptive to a story line that extended extra-legal privileges to them.

Bush won in public and press opinion what he probably would not have won in court, because the law was not on his side. On November

25, the Bush campaign withdrew the suit it had filed days before, which asked the state to force canvassing boards in fourteen counties (ones with the largest numbers of overseas military voters) to reexamine the overseas ballots. Bush lawyers said they dropped the suit because it had had its intended effect: canvassing boards were reconsidering and including previously excluded military ballots. Others believed the suit was withdrawn because it was likely to lose. According to the *New York Times*, "In a hearing on [November 24], Judge L. Ralph Smith of the Leon County Circuit Court said Bush's lawyers had failed to present any evidence that the local elections officials were violating the law when they rejected ballots for such reasons as lack of proper postmarks, dates and signatures."[33] Instead of interpreting the dropped suit as evidence that the Bush case was legally suspect, the networks gave that action little play. For example, on *NBC Nightly News* on November 25 Kelly O'Donnell notes that "Republicans dropped one suit against fourteen county canvassing boards, less than two hours before an expected ruling this afternoon, and now favor fighting it out county by county, hoping to force local officials in each county to reexamine disqualified military ballots."

Nearly eight months after the deadline for receipt of overseas absentee ballots, David Barstow and Don Van Natta, Jr., of the *New York Times* reported the results of their extensive investigation of the tabulation of the overseas absentee ballots. "A six-month investigation by the *New York Times* of this chapter in the closest presidential election in American history," they concluded, "shows that the Republican effort had a decided impact. Under intense pressure from the Republicans, Florida officials accepted hundreds of overseas absentee ballots that failed to comply with state election laws."[34] Among the 680 questionable ballots were "ballots without postmarks, ballots postmarked after the election, ballots without witness signatures, ballots mailed from towns and cities within the United States and even ballots from voters who voted twice." The *Times* also located two ballots that were counted despite the fact that they arrived at the canvassing board by fax. Since Bush's certified margin of victory was 537 votes, the overseas absentee ballots may have made the difference.

The turning point in the battle to shape public opinion was the November 19 Lieberman interview with Russert on *Meet the Press*. "Lieberman Put Democrats in Retreat on Military Vote," read the headline in an explanatory article by the *Times*'s Rick Berke.[35] Curiously missing from the *Times*'s explanation was the role of the media in framing the dispute over the overseas absentee ballots on Bush's terms. In an editorial eight months after the election, the *Times* noted, "This page argued for allowing as many votes to be counted as possible under the imperfect circumstances prevailing at Florida polling places, and we also called for a liberal standard in counting overseas absentee ballots from members of the armed forces. But the study found that Republican counties were far more likely to count the flawed overseas ballots than were the Democratic counties—a difference attributable in part to the relentless, aggressive efforts of Mr. Bush's Florida advisers . . . [T]he same standards should have been applied to all absentee ballots from abroad, not just those in Republican dominated counties."[36] The *Times* should have told us that that was what was happening while it was happening. As admirable as is the *Times*'s post-election investigation of the overseas ballots, it shows journalists acting as historians rather than watchdogs. Had reporters more aggressively investigated the military ballot story at the time, readers and viewers would have been better served.

November 26:
The Prospective Florida Certification

The last week in November began with the idea that the candidates each could legitimately claim to be the victor still prevailing. The November 20 issue of *Newsweek* offered a clear illustration of the neutral frame: Under the title "The Winner Is . . ." the cover combined photos of Bush and Gore to create a single figure, half each candidate, standing before the White House. But the prevailing frame would soon shift in Bush's favor.

Sunday November 26 ended with Katherine Harris, the Florida secretary of state, certifying Bush as the winner in Florida by 537 of the almost 6 million votes cast. On that Sunday morning Tim Russert reminded Democratic senator Tom Daschle, "But the Vice President argued against allowing this case to go before the Supreme Court." He then asked, "How can he now use that as an excuse or reason not to concede?" On ABC the same week, Sam Donaldson referred to the Democrats' attempts to "dig up enough votes for Al Gore."

On November 26, broadcast news began reinforcing the notion that Bush was the presumptive president and Gore the loser. Illustrative is the difference between the questions asked of Bush and Gore representatives by Bob Schieffer on *Face the Nation*. To the Bush spokesperson: "If the count shows that George Bush is ahead in Florida tonight, will he declare himself the president?" Gore's prospects are bleaker: "If Al Gore *somehow* comes out ahead at the end of the day today, will he declare himself president?" (emphasis added)

A survey of *Roll Call*, one of the two newspapers covering Capitol Hill, confirms that elite opinion shifted between November 17 and 26. On Thursday, November 9, editor Morton Kondracke wrote that "the presidency is still up for grabs in the Florida recount."[37] Stuart Rothenberg said that "uncertainty" is "clouding the outcome of the presidential contest." The following Monday, Kondracke called the election a "virtual tie," condemned the rhetoric, which he saw as being ratcheted up, and noted that "the consequences will likely be that the next president, whether it's Vice President Al Gore or Texas Gov. George W. Bush, will have his legitimacy constantly and bitterly questioned by the opposition."[38] On Thursday, November 16, Kondracke noted that "whoever ends up being president, it behooves both him and the barely ruling Republican Congress to end the toxic partisanship that's dominated Washington for the past 15 years and collaborate on a moderate policy agenda."[39]

But after the disputed certification, the assumptions changed. On Monday, November 30, the front page of *Roll Call* carried the headline "Bush Looks to Democrats." "Confident that he will be the next president," said the story, "Gov. George W. Bush is targeting 'four to five' House Democrats for top posts in his administration, according to GOP sources."[40] Below the fold, a second headline read, "Impatience with Gore Growing." "While Hill Republicans this week expressed confidence that the tide of public opinion had turned against Vice President Al Gore and his crusade for the presidency, Democratic leaders scrambled to staunch a wave of defections and allow him one last chance to gain the legal upper hand."[41] The wave of defectors? According to the article, "Rep. Julia Carson (D-Ind.), Sen Russ Feingold (D-Wis.) and former Clinton administration Labor Secretary Robert Reich have called on Gore to surrender." Of the 211 Democrats in the House, one; of the 45 Democrats in the Senate, one; and of dozens of current and former Clinton cabinet members, one.

In the same issue Kondracke wrote that "Republicans should quit trying to hustle Vice President Al Gore into conceding the election. He's not likely to win his vote contest in Florida, but he might."[42] Rothenberg noted that "if he is sworn in as president, Bush may find in the nation's GOP governors a reservoir of political talent and experience that he can use to get his administration off on the right foot."[43] By December 7, a Bush victory was seen as inevitable. Kondracke wrote that "if Bush ends up president, as now seems likely, all hopes for policy achievement and reduced rancor in sharply divided Washington will depend upon the Bush-Daschle relationship."[44] A headline in the paper read "Bush May Face Census Battle."

December 3:
The Prospective Bush Cabinet,
Transition, and Administration

By December 3, nine days before the Supreme Court decision ended the process, the Sunday shows were beginning to talk about a Bush but not a Gore cabinet and a Bush but not a Gore presidency. On December 3 and 10, Tim Russert asked nineteen questions that posited a Bush presidency, and none that made the same assumption about Gore; the journalists on ABC did the same twenty-seven times. On *This Week,* reporter Aaron Brown stated incorrectly that "the Gore side has to convince this judge to overturn a certified presidential election." What had been certified, of course, was not the presidential election but the Florida count. On *Meet the Press* on December 3, Russert asked Cheney, "Should you be here today as vice president, based on your health?" Russert also presumed that Colin Powell is "going to be secretary of state."

On December 3, the notion that Bush was the victor in everything but name was in place. "Oh, there's no Democrat who thinks Gore is going to win . . . I mean, that they are clear on that. Not—not any that I've talked to, anyway," said Cokie Roberts on ABC. Driving the assumption were the certification of November 26 and the fact that Bush had begun to act the part. On the shows that weekend his chief of staff designate, Andrew Card, was interviewed. Gore had not designated a chief of staff. On ABC Roberts asked Card whether there might be a Democrat named as secretary of treasury. On *Meet the Press,* Russert asked Dick Cheney, "Won't you have to scale down your tax cut to pass it?" and "When will you make appointments to the cabinet?" On the same show House Minority Leader Dick Gephardt was asked, "If Al Gore loses this election, is he the Democratic front-runner in 2004?" No comparable question was asked about Bush's prospects if he lost.

The December 3 Sunday shows were filled with speculation about a prospective Bush cabinet. On *This Week,* Cokie Roberts asked Card, "There are those who say that the best way to put together a team under these circumstances is essentially a coalition government, to put a lot of

Democrats in his cabinet. Is that going to happen?" Roberts noted as well that "since the election, there seems to be some doubt on the part of Americans about whether Governor Bush is, in fact, calling the shots for his own administration." Russert also asked, "When will you make appointments to the cabinet . . . ?" and responded to Cheney's answer by saying, "You'll have some well-known Democrats in the cabinet?" Of Richard Gephardt, the *Meet the Press* host asked in the same program, "[W]ill a 1.3-trillion-dollar Bush tax cut pass the Congress if Bush is the president?" On the same Sunday, Bob Schieffer asked Senator John Breaux, "Well, do you think there's any chance that the Senate or the House would pass the kind of tax cut that George Bush talked about in the campaign?" Recognizing the presupposition in the question, Breaux responded. "Probably not the tax cut that either George Bush or Al Gore talked about."

The assumption that Bush would prevail was also evident in the way the Sunday hosts discussed the next Congress. The hosts came to assume a 50/50 split in the Senate, an outcome that would have resulted only if Bush was the winner. If Gore were to win, his running mate, Connecticut's Joseph Lieberman, would give up his seat to become vice president, the Republican governor of Connecticut would appoint a Republican to fill his seat, and the Senate would be split 51/49 in favor of the Republicans. On November 26, Russert said, "It appears that the U.S. Senate will have fifty Republicans and fifty Democrats." He inquired of Republican vice-presidential nominee Dick Cheney, "Now that the Senate is 50/50 Democrats/Republicans and the Republicans control the House by eight or nine votes, won't you have to scale down your tax cut in order to pass it?" The next week he said, "Now that the Senate is 50/50 . . ." Bob Schieffer predicted on *Face the Nation* on November 26 that "in the Senate, split 50/50 among Republicans and Democrats . . . McCain will be the swing vote." The host who eventually caught the assumption was Schieffer, who on December 10 posited "a Senate split evenly—50/50, that is—if George Bush does become president." With the media elite of the Sunday shows presuming that Bush was all but president-elect, the five decisive justices in the *Bush v. Gore* decision were in respectable company when they stopped the count and took the case on the assumption that Bush would be disadvantaged if the count were to proceed.

The selection of sound bites followed the shows' slant. On two of the three December 3 shows, the quote of Gore's that was featured is not the strongest one that he had made in the previous week. The exception was *Meet the Press*, which showed Bush saying, "I'm soon to be the president" and Gore reporting, "I believe we're going to win this election." *This*

Week carried the same statement by Bush but a less positive one by Gore: "We're making quiet progress." In each case, the statement by Bush was the more confident, but where Bush and Gore were cast as prospective winners by NBC, ABC featured a Gore statement that mentioned neither election nor the presidency.

Who Is Stealing the Election?

Across the five weeks of Sunday shows, the programs implied that Bush might be "stealing" the election three times while making that assumption about Gore on twelve occasions. Some form of the word "steal" was used to refer to Gore's effort six times and Bush's twice. The extent to which the Republican rhetoric of theft had put that charge into play was evident when Sam Donaldson noted on November 26, "People saying this election's being stolen by the Democrats—isn't that inflamed rhetoric? Does that help the process?"

In our post-election survey, we asked Americans whether they thought each candidate was trying to steal the election. The results show how people embrace the positions of the partisans with whom they agree. Consistent with the Bush take, 75% of those who had voted for the Texas governor agreed that Gore was trying to steal the election. Only 9% of Democrats concurred. On the other hand, with Gore representatives not making a similar charge against Bush, only 43% of those who voted for Gore responded that Bush was trying to steal the election.

Here, too, the Sunday shows tipped toward the Bush spin with the hypotheticals to the Gore campaign, phrased as "If Bush is successful, will you concede?" By contrast, the Bush stand-ins were asked, in effect, "If Gore is successful, would it be a crime?" So, for example, on *Meet the Press* on November 12, Tim Russert asked Bush spokesperson Jim Baker, "If, in fact, Florida is eventually awarded to Vice President Gore, will there be a sense in the Bush campaign and throughout the country the election was stolen?" On December 3, he asked Cheney, "Do you think Al Gore's a sore loser?" That same week Donaldson on ABC closed an interview with Lieberman by saying, "Excuse me, we've got to go and yet you've made it clear that you're not prepared to say that you'll accept the result." A Bush victory was assumed to be legitimate, while a Gore victory was assumed to be questionable.

Meanwhile, on the Sunday before the Florida Supreme Court ruled that the manual count of votes should proceed, Russert asked Democratic vice-presidential nominee Joseph Lieberman whether, if the Court ruled against Gore, the Democrats would concede that Bush had won. "It ends there. The Supreme Court has spoken. Why not accept that decision?" asked Russert. "Why keep dangling out there future litigation?"

Who Should Concede?

In the five Sunday shows aired by the three networks, the word "concede" appeared in twenty-three questions. In twenty of them, concession was tied to Gore. The others were nondenominational. In this category, on the first Sunday after the election Sam Donaldson asked Dick Gephardt, "[W]hen we find out who actually won Florida as certified by the secretary of state, should the other guy concede?" Twenty-one of the twenty-three questions about concession were posed to Gore's representatives.

On the issue of concession, the rhetoric of his supporters undercut Gore. By implicitly accepting the assumption that Gore would eventually concede, some Gore representatives reinforced the concession frame. So, for example, when Bob Schieffer asked Warren Christopher on December 3 if Gore would concede if he lost a pending court decision, Christopher did not challenge the premise in the question but instead replied, "I can assure you that the vice president, when the time comes, will concede in a very gracious way." On six occasions someone on a Sunday show quoted someone else calling for a Gore concession. So, for example, former senator Dale Bumpers was quoted as saying "There might come a time when the vice president would be well served to say the country's interest is more important than the interest of one person or political party and go ahead and concede."

The Differing Rhetoric of the Two Campaigns

The structure of the Sunday shows is adversarial. In this format, the host poses questions from the perspective of the opposing side. Since both sides are represented, the show is balanced, with the host maintaining a consistent posture. In practice, since the host often confronts a guest with quotes from the other side, if one side engages in stronger rhetoric than the other, the tone of the show shifts to favor that side. Even in a forum in which an ostensibly neutral arbitrator controls the discussion, partisans can seize an advantage with their rhetorical choices.

In the thirty-six days following the election, Bush gained a tactical advantage from Republican rhetoric that was more categorical, more strongly worded, and more consistent than that of the Democrats. For example, speaking for the Republicans on *This Week* on November 12, 1996 Republican nominee Bob Dole defined the Gore strategy as "count till you win." On *Meet the Press* James Baker sounds the same theme: "We will, therefore, vigorously oppose the Gore campaign efforts to keep recounting over and over until it happens to like the result."

The notion that the election was being stolen was dramatically stated by House Minority Whip Tom DeLay of Texas, who said, "The Democratic Party is prosecuting a war to reverse the results of a fair, free election . . . Make no mistake, we are witnessing nothing less than a theft in progress." The quote was replayed on the Sunday shows November 19. The same day, Sam Donaldson said to Joe Lieberman, "The Republicans say that you and Vice President Gore are trying to steal this election in Florida." He then repeated the charge in an exchange with George Will. By refusing to repeat the words, some Republicans on air appeared moderate while the idea itself lingered. So, for example, when Cokie Roberts asked Republican House Majority Leader Dick Armey on November 26 whether he thought the election was being stolen, he responded, "I'm saying that I'm a Republican. I couldn't use a word like that. You'd never tolerate it. But you used the word, Cokie, and I don't disagree with you." Where on November 19 Donaldson premised questions on the fact that Republicans were saying Gore was stealing the election, by the twenty-sixth the subject had broadened. "People [are] saying this election's being stolen by the Democrats," noted Donaldson to Bob Dole.

Since frames are the product of a give-and-take between political actors and reporters, those actors have the ability to shape the frame through their rhetorical choices. This is particularly true in a presidential campaign, where the foci of the candidates are by definition newsworthy. Just as during the campaign Bush ensured that questions about Gore's integrity would be given prominent play by discussing it himself—while Gore left criticisms of Bush's experience largely to others—in the thirty-six days, the Bush campaign made Al Gore the issue by tagging his acts as products of Gore's personal cynicism and ambition.

Notice that the Gore campaign never charged that the Bush campaign was "waging war" on African-Americans, or on the poor, or on Holocaust survivors in Palm Beach County, all of whom seemed to be having their votes excluded at higher-than-expected rates. Instead, their arguments were abstract ("Count every vote") and not directed at Bush or his representatives. It was the Bush campaign that charged that votes were being manipulated, implied that Al Gore was unpatriotic, and said that the election was being stolen. Simply by accurately reporting the rhetoric of the two campaigns, reporters constructed an unequal playing field, one in which Gore's good faith and character were in question but Bush's were not. As a *New York Times* reporter later said, "Those 'Sore Loserman' signs were ubiquitous. They were on TV all the time . . . We wanted to tell our readers what the campaigns' respective strategies were so it was plain."[45] We cannot divine the impulses behind Gore's rhetorical strategy; one interpretation that has been offered is that Gore was more concerned with his standing among Washington elites than with the war on the ground, and thus took the high road.[46] Whatever the decisions behind the rhetoric, the Bush campaign's personal attacks on Gore made his intentions and behavior the topic of discussion, while the same was not true of Bush. Democrats raised similar questions about Bush allies—Katherine Harris, Jeb Bush, the Republican majority in the Florida legislature—but chose not to do the same about the Texas governor himself.

The presumed partisans on *This Week*, George Will for the Republicans and George Stephanopoulos for the Democrats, also differed in the harshness of their claims about the other side. On November 12, for example, Stephanopoulos said that if the election "is counted fairly, Al Gore won more votes in Florida." Will said that the Gore campaign has "put in place a mechanism [that won't] . . . fail to deliver the requisite number of votes once they invent what the meaning of a vote is down there . . . It is a selective, third recount . . . presided over by partisan Democrats, who just yesterday, changed the rules on—on how the chads would be counted." The comparative tentativeness of Gore's defenders, coupled with the categorical and strongly worded rhetoric of the Republicans, worked to Bush's advantage.

Reading and Misreading the Polls

As interpreted on the Sunday shows, the polls were a death knell for Gore. On December 10, Russert stated, "By 51 to 40, people think that George Bush ought to be president . . . 63% think he won legitimately. Only 48% think Gore won legitimately." He then asked, "Has the country coalesced around the idea of Bush as president?" If 63% thought

Bush won legitimately and 48% thought Gore did so, then either 111% of the public was being represented by the poll or some must have thought that both of them legitimately won. In an election decided by a handful of votes, why did Russert preface the 48% for Gore with "only"? If half the public thought Gore won, "the country" could hardly be said to have "coalesced around the idea of Bush as president."

An alternative poll question focused on whether Gore should concede. On December 3, Cokie Roberts translated responses to this question into a series of challenges to Gore representative and former senator George Mitchell. "You've seen polls saying—huge majority say the vice president should concede . . . Well, then how do you account for the large majority saying that the vice president should concede? . . . 60 some percent say he should concede and the ABC poll shows that, the Gallup poll shows 57% . . ." She then asked Mitchell, "Let me just ask you a question as somebody who has dealt with Northern Ireland and the difficulties there. You know that people there hold on to their—their rights and the injustices that have been committed against them and sometimes that's not wise. Is it wise—obviously Al Gore has the right to do what he's doing—is it wise for the country for him to be doing what he's doing?"

Roberts's conclusion that 57% constituted a "huge majority" was repeated elsewhere; in print and on television, commentators assumed that a slight majority in favor of a Gore concession—made up of virtually all those who voted for Bush and a handful of those who voted for Gore—constituted a sentiment on the part of "the American people."

National news organizations sponsored a number of polls asking about the possibility of a candidate's concession. The majority fell into one of two categories. The first asked whether, at the moment the poll was being taken, Gore should concede. This question was asked by polls conducted for CNN, ABC News, NBC News, CBS News, Fox News, the *New York Times*, the *Washington Post*, the *Wall Street Journal*, *USA Today*, Reuters, and *Newsweek* magazine.

The second type asked whether, given a hypothetical set of circumstances, Gore should concede. So, for example, polls assessed whether Gore should end his challenge if he fell short in hand counts or if court decisions went against him. Questions of this type were asked in surveys for CNN, ABC News, *USA Today*, the *Washington Post*, and *Time* and *Newsweek* magazines. News organizations began polling on these questions a few days after the election and continued until the Supreme Court decision on December 12 ending the counting.

The first of these survey questions was asked on November 10, just three days after the election. Once Katherine Harris certified the Florida count for Bush on November 26, multiple organizations asked the question every night. Whether and when Bush should concede, on the other hand, attracted little interest from news and polling organizations. Where court decisions and counts disadvantageous to Gore were posed to poll respondents as possibilities, Bush did not receive the same treatment. The key question in the polls was not "Who will win this count/decision/etc.?" but "Will this be it for Gore?" On November 30, a Fox News poll asked people, "If Gore concedes, do you think he will do it like a statesman or a sore loser?" Only two organizations—the Pew Research Center and the CBS News/*New York Times* poll—repeatedly entertained the possibility of a Bush concession.

The neutral question by the *New York Times* found that the country did not share the presumption that Gore should give up. Instead, whether or not Gore should concede was a function of partisan disposition and not a matter of national consensus. The CBS News/*New York Times* poll taken three weeks after the election asked, "Based on what you know so far, do you think one of the candidates should concede now or is it too soon for that?" Those who said one should concede were then asked which one. Eighty-three percent of those who had voted for Bush answered that Gore should concede, while 12% said it was too soon for a concession. In contrast, 77% of those who had voted for Gore said it was too soon for a concession, with an additional 13% saying Bush should concede. Only 5% of Gore voters thought the vice president should concede.

Our survey asked two relevant questions from November 28 to December 12: "In your opinion, should George W. Bush/Al Gore concede the election and let Al Gore/George W. Bush become president or not?" Our results were similar, with 92% of those who had voted for Bush saying Gore should concede, and 75% of those who had voted for Gore saying he should not. Twenty percent of Gore voters thought Bush should concede, while virtually no Bush voters (3%) agreed.

In addition to Pew and CBS News/*New York Times*, Gallup released a poll December 4 that asked separately, "As of today, do you think Al Gore/George Bush should concede?" Eighty-four percent of Bush supporters and 27% of Gore supporters said Gore should concede; 10% of Bush supporters and 16% of Gore supporters said Bush should concede. Gallup asked about Gore conceding repeatedly, but this was the only time that organization reported asking the same question about Bush.

The outlook in news was similar, typified by a piece in the *New York Times* on the first Sunday after election day, titled "The Limits of Patience." It would be in the nation's best interest, suggested the scholars and politicians interviewed for the article, if the outcome of the election were determined within the following week. "We have been through this kind of thing before," said historian David McCulloch, "and thank God we had people then who put the country first."[47] On ABC, Cokie Roberts interpreted the polls to say the same thing, telling Tom Daschle on November 19 that "our polls are showing that the longer it goes on, the less confidence people have in the confidence of the count." On December 3, she reiterated the polled perception: "The public does seem to be losing patience with this." Once again, the sentiments of a bare majority made up of virtually all those who voted for Bush and a sliver of those who voted for Gore was taken to constitute the will of "the public."

A central question about the polls was posed by Roberts: "Well, then, how do you account for the large majority saying that the vice president should concede?" The answer: Biased polling questions and strong cues from elite media probably played at least some role in eliciting those polled responses, whose meaning was then exaggerated by journalists.

The Supreme Court and Public Opinion

Much attention has focused on the fact that the Supreme Court's decision to take the case of *Bush v. Gore* as well as its ruling placed the five conservatives in the majority in the odd position of arguing for federal authority in a case in which the Constitution gives the states primary responsibility. Because of those justices' decisions articulating a federalist philosophy in which state power is preferred to federal, their position struck some as inconsistent. We believe that the consensus that had emerged in the media and the responses elicited by biased polls eased the decision to take the case and to rule to end the election contest. Despite their lifetime appointments, members of the Court are sensitive to public opinion, as evidenced by the majority's decision in *Planned Parenthood v. Casey* (1992), in which it said, "The Court's legitimacy depends on making legally principled decisions under circumstances in which their principled character is sufficiently plausible to be accepted by the nation."[48]

If not through a reading of public opinion, how did the court come to its presumption in accepting the case that Bush, not Gore, would be "irreparably harmed" were the counting not halted? Justice Scalia stated in the 5–4 ruling on the application for the stay that "the counting of votes that are of questionable legality does in my view threaten irreparable harm to petitioner [Bush], and to the country, by casting a cloud upon what he claims to be the legitimacy of his election." But it is Justice Scalia's next sentence that interests us more. "Count first, and rule upon legality afterwards, is not a recipe for producing election results that have the *public acceptance* democratic stability requires" (emphasis added).

Some have observed that the majority's reasoning in issuing a stay halting the recount on December 9—that it was Bush and not Gore who would suffer the greater harm, and therefore the count should not be allowed to go forward (questionable legitimacy versus losing a rightfully won election)—presupposed that Bush would assume the presidency regardless of what a count might reveal. As David Strauss wrote,

> The premise of the argument is that there is a legitimate interest in suppressing truthful information—information about what the recount ordered by the Florida Supreme Court would have disclosed—in order to protect the President of the United States from political harm . . . There is only one circumstance in which the balance of equities might have favored Governor Bush: if a majority of the Supreme Court had already decided how it was going to rule. If there had been any chance that the Vice President would win in the Supreme Court, the stay was indefensible.[49]

A "cloud" that might be cast on Bush's legitimacy is not a question of law but one of public opinion. If public acceptance was on the mind of the justices who accepted the *Bush v. Gore* case, then we think it plausible that the consensus of the elite media and the presumed sentiment reflected in the polls contributed to a climate in which five conservatives would intervene in what their previous decisions indicate would ordinarily have been cast as a matter for state or congressional resolution. If the Rhenquist court has been marked by any single feature, it is a devotion to federalism, the philosophy that wherever possible power should be shifted from the federal government to the states. The first question, then, is why the Supreme Court found the case of the Florida election within its purview.

The anxiety of the conservative majority was evident when Justices Rehnquist, Scalia, and Thomas noted that "in most cases comity and respect for federalism compel us to defer to the decisions of state courts on issues of state law." In *Bush v. Gore*, however, they carved out an exception. Their discomfort with applying the Fourteenth Amendment's equal-protection clause to the means by which votes are tabulated is apparent in this now famous statement from the majority's ruling: "Our consideration is limited to the present circumstances, for the problem of equal protection in election processes generally presents many complexities." Many, if not most, legal problems present complexities, but the Court does not ordinarily assert that its own decision and logic may not be used as precedent. This can be seen as a message to those who might attempt to cite *Bush v. Gore* as a precedent in future suits asserting that different voting methods constitute a violation of equal protection: This is the reasoning we are using here, but don't ask us again. One assumes the majority was aware that an application of that logic to future voting rights cases would demand that all the citizens of a given state vote by means of identical technology, with their votes counted by a single standard, a situation that many states moved to implement after the election, but one that existed in only nine states in 2000.

Even some conservatives were troubled by the majority's ruling, if not by the result. Writing in the *Weekly Standard*, John DiIulio, Jr., whom Bush later tapped to head his Office of Faith-Based Initiatives, noted that "the arguments that ended the battle and 'gave' Bush the presidency are constitutionally disingenuous at best. They will come back to haunt conservatives and confuse, if they do not cripple, the principled conservative case for limited government, legislative supremacy, and universal civic deference to legitimate, duly constituted state and local public authority."[50]

If the majority in *Bush v. Gore* was wavering in its impulse to take the case, the polls conveniently provided reassurance. A late-November poll suggested that even Gore supporters would favor Supreme Court intervention; the CBS poll found 54% saying it was a good idea for the Supreme Court to get involved in the presidential election. Sixty-one percent of Gore voters and 48% of Bush voters supported the idea.[51]

Before they knew how the Supreme Court would rule, Gore voters were more likely than Bush's to favor the Court's intervention, as one might expect if one were applying the generalized liberal and conservative views on the role of the federal judiciary. Once the decision was handed down, opinions shifted dramatically. The day after the December 12 ruling, 54% of Gore voters in a Gallup poll said the decision made them lose confidence in the Supreme Court (only 5% of Bush voters agreed).

If the majority of the Supreme Court believed that public and elite opinion considered Bush the legitimate victor, it was only half right. Just as the election was a dead heat, Americans on both sides believed their candidate had won. When we asked our respondents if there could be a perfect recount, who would be shown to be the winner in Florida, the answer was simple: those who had voted for Gore said Gore, and those who had voted for Bush said Bush.

In sum, whether Bush should in fact have been declared the winner in the electoral college, his supporters were more rhetorically dexterous than Gore's in the thirty-six post-election days. This dexterity created a climate on the Sunday-morning shows more hospitable to the Republican case than the Democratic one, elicited polling questions biased to the assumption of a Bush win, and may have helped overcome the ideological reservations of the five conservatives on the Supreme Court who ended the count and with it the dispute over the outcome of the 2000 presidential election.

In the five weeks following Election Day 2000, the Bush and Gore campaigns fought to determine which frames would structure news coverage and debate about the election. The results of that battle determined which information was deemed relevant, which actions were considered acceptable and which beyond the bounds of propriety, and how events would be interpreted. The Bush campaign's ultimate victory was due in no small part to its success in getting its preferred frames adopted by the news media. That success can also be attributed in part to the press's failure to fulfill its investigative role on the topic of overseas absentee ballots. The post-election events suggest that the frames guiding news coverage can shape the outcome of events. The side more successful at convincing the press to adopt its preferred frame is the one more likely to prevail.

The Press as Patriot

W hen President George W. Bush threw out the first
ball at the third game of the World Series in New
York City in October 2001, reporters could have
written that Bush's well-placed throw reflected his
love of the sport. After all, he was the owner of the Texas Rangers and as
a child reportedly aspired to play professional ball. The reports could
have suggested that presidents, including Bush, use appearances at sporting events to establish their identification with ordinary Americans and
in particular to appeal to blue-collar men. Alternatively, the story could
have averred that the time the President took in the days before the game
to practice the pitch was evidence of a person whose priorities were mis-
placed and who was insufficiently focused on dealing with the post–
September 11 threat. Or the stories could have concentrated on the signal
the playing of the Series sent the world about American determination
and resilience. In this frame what was important was the President's intent to send the message that neither he nor the country was cowering in
fear of possible terrorist attacks.

With the patriotic lens created by September 11 still in place, reporters chose the latter focus. "Amid Tight Security," said the headline in the
Houston Chronicle, "Bush Pitch Is Perfect for Start of Game 3." On *Good
Morning America*, Charles Gibson reported that Bush "certainly signaled
a sense of normalcy, I think, to the nation by going to the game last night
with that patriotic pitch." In ordinary times, the press adopts a distanced
stance to those it covers. However, in times of crisis reporters abandon

irony, cynicism, and occasionally even skepticism to see the world through a nationalistic and patriotic lens. The lens focuses on some stories and frames that are substantially different from press practice as usual.

We believe that most journalists, whether consciously or not, report from a sense, perhaps visceral, perhaps cerebral, that their reporting should instill public faith in the proposition that, despite its flaws, the democratic system does work. Investigative journalism is premised on the notion that corruption revealed is corruption constrained. The press's institution-sustaining role, which is our subject here, is evident both in the accounts of the media recount and in coverage of the leadership of President George W. Bush on and after September 11.

Once the Supreme Court ruled in *Bush v. Gore* and the time clock ran out on any possible recount of Florida's votes, George W. Bush was, under U.S. law, the president-elect. This was true whether he had in fact been the choice of the majority of those who cast a legal vote in Florida or not. Were the various reexaminations of the ballots by press organizations to show that in fact the majority of Florida's votes went to Gore, that finding would not dislodge Bush from the Oval Office. It would, however, cast a shadow on his presidency, running the risk that he, like Rutherford B. Hayes, would be known as His Fraudulency. Such a scenario would make it more difficult for him to lead and raise troubling questions about a democratic system that had given the White House to the wrong person. Despite the fact that major news organizations undertook extensive reviews of the surviving ballots, their editors and headline writers were disposed to set aside the ambiguous outcome produced by their analysis and find that the person in the Oval Office was the one who belonged there.

The press's conclusion that Bush was the legitimate victor in Florida in the face of ambiguous evidence illustrated a shift in perspective. Once Bush became the president, he was no longer simply an individual, but also in some ways the embodiment of democracy itself. At issue in his fate were the institution of the presidency and the electoral system. Against the backdrop of these implications, the press reframed the question over the Florida contest from who won to whether the system worked. Discussion of the results of the media recounts affirmed democracy's success in navigating what could have been a constitutional crisis. We got it right after all, the stories said; the Supreme Court did not select the president. This was true both of the *Miami Herald* "recount" reported before September 11 and the consortium "recount" whose release was delayed by the aftermath of the terrorist attacks.

Editors and headline writers cast the findings of these review processes as confirmation that Bush had indeed won, despite the fact that the evidence before them argued as plausibly that Gore could have been the president. Had the evidence overwhelmingly favored Gore, these reports probably would have made that point. But faced with data suggesting that the question of who "really" won Florida did not have a single answer, but rather depended on which ballots were counted and how, news outlets wrote the "democracy works" story.

The issue of the Florida vote and the attendant questions about George W. Bush's legitimacy offer a case study in how the press deals with ambiguity and contested interpretations of history. When the results of both media recounts were released, reporters sought a firm conclusion, even one that was not fully supported by the facts. It was no accident that the conclusion was one that vindicated the system in which they play such a critical part.

As the thirty-six post-election days progressed, commentators noted that whatever the standards canvassing boards employed, and whatever the decisions of the courts in Florida and Washington, eventually the truth of who really won Florida would be known. Because Florida has one of the more comprehensive "sunshine" laws of any state, making state meetings and documents available to the public, it was assumed that some group would count all the Florida ballots to produce an historical record. After the election concluded, two media consortiums took on the task and eventually produced comprehensive sets of results. The data demonstrated that what constitutes a "vote" is a matter of some interpretation. The way in which the results were reported demonstrated that ambiguous and contradictory information is occasionally molded by the press into a clear and coherent narrative in which ambiguity is downplayed.

The first media recount to be completed was conducted by the *Miami Herald*, *USA Today*, and Knight-Ridder, who contracted with an accounting firm to count more than 60,000 undervotes from Florida. This count did not include ballots that had been read by counting machines, or those on which more than one vote for president was read by the machine. Using various standards for judging ballots, the study produced eight sets of results, five of which showed Bush ahead and three of which showed Gore ahead.

Despite the ambiguities in their own data, the *Herald* aggressively pushed the interpretation that Bush was the clear winner. *Herald* executive editor Martin Baron made the rounds of news shows, telling them, as he did Fox News on April 4, "The almost certain result is that George Bush would have still emerged the winner in a manual recount throughout the state of Florida." Although they had all the data available, other news organizations followed the lead of the *Herald* and *USA Today* to focus only on the set of results that showed Bush ahead. Peter Jennings said, "The first major independent review of the Florida vote has found that President Bush would have won by an even greater margin if the Supreme Court had not stopped the recount." NBC reporter Kerry Sanders said, "The conclusion: ballots say Bush."

Newspaper stories were no less emphatic. "Bush Prevails in Ballot Check," said the *Arizona Republic*. "Papers' Recount Says Bush Still Is Winner," said the *Boston Globe*. The headline in the *Los Angles Times* read, "Recount Would Have Increased Bush Win, Papers Say." From *Newsday*: "Review: Bush Really Won." The *Washington Post*, which had titled its first story about the *Herald* recount "In Ballot Audit, Bush Prevails," was one of the few papers that ran a follow-up story examining the data more closely. The next day, it looked at all eight scenarios and published an article titled "From Election Audit, Mostly Uncertainty" that amended its piece of the day before to discuss in more detail the scenarios under which Gore would have won.

When reporters discussed the *Herald* recount, however, the consensus frame was a statement of fact leading to a subjective conclusion. The statement of fact—"Bush would have won Florida anyway"—was not borne out by the *Herald* data with anything approaching the clarity with which reporters described it. The conclusion that followed, although debatable—while the post-election events may have been messy, democracy worked in the end—became the elite consensus. Indeed, on April 4 *USA Today's* Web site titled one of its articles "Review Shows Right Man in White House." The short time frame—the data were released on the evening of April 3 and rushed into the next day's papers—may have led reporters and editors to accept the *Herald's* interpretation instead of making an independent judgment of the data.

A more comprehensive media count, including not only the undervotes tallied by the *Herald* but the overvotes as well, was conducted by a consortium of news organizations that included the Associated Press, the *New York Times*, the *Washington Post*, and the *Wall Street Journal*. After many delays, the counting, which was conducted by the University of Chicago's respected National Opinion Research Center, was completed just after the World Trade Center attacks in early September 2001. In the wake of the attacks and the ensuing spirit of national unity, the release of the results was "put on hold indefinitely."[1] However, on November 12, 2001, the results were finally released.

This study produced an even more ambiguous set of results. The consortium released data showing eleven different scenarios, including some that incorporated the methods each Florida county used to count ballots. Within each, results for four standards of agreement between the coders who examined the ballots were also reported. Therefore, there were a total of forty-four separate results. As befitted the election of 2000, Bush was ahead under twenty-two of those scenarios, and Gore was ahead under twenty-two. In general, however, Bush was ahead in scenarios in which only the undervotes were counted, while Gore was ahead when all the ballots, both overvotes and undervotes, were counted.

So who *really* won Florida? The question has no single answer. Rather, the response depends on the more specific question one asks. Who would have won if the Supreme Court had allowed the recount ordered by the Florida Supreme Court to go forward? Who would have won if all the ballots were counted using a strict standard, or a lenient standard, or the standards each county actually used? For whom did more Floridians attempt to vote? Each of these questions should have been of interest to reporters discussing the results. One could make a reasonable argument in favor of each being the most important question. The consortium recount was undertaken with the goal of counting all the votes in Florida to provide a historical record; its goal was not to come to a single conclusion. When the results were announced, however, the overwhelming majority of news outlets focused on the scenario—a statewide recount of undervotes but not overvotes—that produced a Bush victory.

The frame was clearly in place in the newspaper headlines announcing the result. "Bush Still Had Votes to Win in a Recount, Study Finds," said the *Los Angeles Times*. "A Review of Controversial Election Shows Bush Winning a Recount of Florida Ballots," said the *Wall Street Journal*. From the *Washington Post*: "Florida Recounts Would Have Favored Bush." The *New York Times* said, "Study of Disputed Florida Ballots Finds Justices Did Not Cast the Deciding Vote." The *St. Petersburg Times* headline said simply, "Recount: Bush." While a few papers went with headlines emphasizing the ambiguity of the results (the *Chicago Tribune's* story was headlined "Still Too Close to Call"), the vast majority proclaimed a vindication of the Bush win.

On television, the frame was equally clear. On the *Today* show, Matt Lauer said, "A yearlong study by a consortium of news organizations has concluded that the Supreme Court did not cast the deciding vote in the presidential election. The winner is, and was, George W. Bush." On *Good Morning America*, Antonio Mora managed to make it seem as though the consortium had produced many scenarios resulting in a Bush win but only one with a Gore win, as opposed to the actual twenty-two: "Finally, a comprehensive media review of last year's presidential election in Florida indicates that under all recount scenarios but one, the results probably would not have changed. The review shows that Al Gore might have won only if he had asked for a statewide recount, a request he did not make." Like Mora and many others, Brit Hume of Fox News used the term "*would* have won" to describe the scenarios favoring Bush, but the term "*might* have won" to describe those favoring Gore, despite the fact that both occurrences were hypothetical. He also noted that Gore did not request a count of the overvotes: "A ten-month study into the uncounted Florida ballots in last year's election shows that George W. Bush would have won, even if the U.S. Supreme Court had allowed a hand count of all so-called undervotes statewide, as requested by the Florida Supreme Court, or ballots in four counties, as requested by Al Gore . . . the study . . . showed Gore—quote—'might have won,' if there had been a hand count of all mismarked ballots, something neither Gore nor the Florida high court ever requested."

There was one problem in the contention that the overvotes would not have been counted had the Supreme Court allowed the recount to go forward: it may not have been true. Judge Terry Lewis, who would have overseen the Florida recounts, later disclosed in interviews that he was inclined toward ordering the canvassing boards to review overvotes as well as undervotes in order to comply with the Florida Supreme Court's order to determine the "intent of the voter." Communications between Lewis and the canvassing boards before the U.S. Supreme Court halted the recounts confirm his account. "I would have addressed that issue," Lewis said later. "Logically, if you can look at a ballot and see, this is a vote for Bush or this is a vote for Gore, then you would have to count it."[2]

But when the consortium results were released, the overvotes favoring Gore were dismissed. On CNN, Paula Zahn said, "Well, now a comprehensive review of the Florida outcome shows that if the U.S. Supreme Court had allowed a hand recount, a statewide recount, George W. Bush would still have won the presidency." She then interviewed Jeffrey Toobin, author of a book about the events in Florida, and asked him whether he held to his book's contention that the wrong man was elected. When Toobin responded in the affirmative, asserting that the most important question was whom more Floridians intended to vote for, Zahn asked him incredulously, "Jeffrey, how can you say that? How can you say that given the conclusion of this analysis . . . ?" In a matter of moments, the complexity of the consortium study was stripped away, leaving only the conclusion that Bush had won.

In a story such as this, where different sets of facts compete for primacy and interpretations could vary, the initial consensual frame is critical because it is what persists in memory. When recalling the 2000 election, reporters and commentators repeat the claim that "Bush would have won Florida anyway," as ambiguity and contradictory information dissolve over time. The assertion "Bush would have won Florida" is not false, but nor does it represent the complete truth. The parallel assertion "Gore would have won Florida" is no less true, and no less worthy of becoming the dominant frame around the issue.

Why was the "Bush won" frame chosen? Part of the answer lies in the fact that reporters are for all their cynicism members of the establishment who have an investment in the legitimacy of the system, more so during a crisis. The notion that the presidency could have been granted to the wrong person is a serious threat to that legitimacy. Witness the way CNN political correspondent Candy Crowley closed her story on the consortium results. "Maybe the best thing of all," she said, "is that the messy feelings at the Florida ballot box have really only proven the strength of democracy." We then see the sergeant-at-arms, on the floor of the House of Representatives, announcing in a booming voice, "Mr. Speaker, the President of the United States!" as Bush enters to applause. He is president and democracy is strong, as indicated by his role in the ceremonial rituals of power. This interpretation of recent history vindicates the electoral system.

Journalists may express cynicism toward the *individuals* who seek and hold power, but they are reverent toward the *institutions* of power.[3] Thus, when the results of the two media studies were announced, the competing potential frames pitted not so much Al Gore against George Bush as systemic failure against systemic success. In this way, the press implicitly moved from "is"—the realm of fact—to "ought"—the realm of value. It made a statement about both the past and the present, that Bush "really" won Florida, and therefore he should be the president.

Would the interpretation of the consortium recount have been different were it not for the terrorist attacks on the World Trade Center and the Pentagon? While the take on the *Herald* recount—coming as it did in April 2001—suggests not, the desire on the part of reporters to renew and uphold popular faith in the system became particularly strong after

September 11. Journalists emphasized that the legitimacy of Bush's election was no longer up for discussion. "Clearly, if the issue of legitimacy wasn't resolved the day the president was sworn in, it was certainly resolved September 11," said the Washington bureau chief of the *Wall Street Journal*. "It doesn't exist anymore."[4] Tim Russert agreed: "You know, I thought Al Gore two weeks ago in Iowa stood up and said, 'George W. Bush is my commander in chief,' pretty much put to rest any questions about the legitimacy of George W. Bush. People of this country know that they have one president, one commander in chief. The country's united behind his leadership."[5] After September 11, the consensus became all the more categorical, to the point where raising the question was defined as out of bounds. The conclusion that remained was not false, but represented only one version of the truth.

September 11: The Transformation of the Press

Why was the photo of firefighters raising the American flag, Iwo Jima–like, and not that of the burning towers chosen as the image that would represent September 11? Why no indictment of Bush's faltering performance of September 11 and no extended exploration of the president-like functions performed by the vice president? Why an acceptance of the language of war even before a congressional resolution had been passed? And how did discourse that in the campaign was problematic become instead emblematic of leadership? By examining coverage of the government and the president in the hours, days, and weeks following the terrorist attacks, we hope to answer these questions. Our answer will argue that September 11 propelled the press into the role of patriot.

September 11 produced extended commentary about the presumed "death of irony." Like everyone in the United States, journalists were affected by the changed climate. Where the press ordinarily casts a wary eye on those it covers, for a brief time on and after September 11, the press showcased a less familiar role: that of champion of the nation, its leaders, and its institutions. This change was reflected in the pictures chosen to encapsulate events, the stories that were not written, the extent to which the frames offered by the president were embraced by journalists, and the critiques that were suppressed.

Scholars have observed in the past that during times of national crisis, press coverage becomes more favorable to the president, as a "rally round the flag" effect occurs not only in public opinion but in news pages as well.[6] When the president comes to embody the country—as he does when traveling abroad, for instance—public approval increases and news coverage sounds approving notes.[7] We seek to explore the possibility that underlying this phenomenon is a particular journalistic lens coloring coverage, one in which journalists manifest a heightened consciousness of being part of the nation, and in the process set skepticism and cynicism aside and adopt a reassuring tone about the well-being of democratic institutions and the dexterity of the country's leaders. While in ordinary times they stand outside and comment on factional conflicts, during crises—particularly ones of great magnitude—journalists incorporate themselves within the nation by using inclusive language, "we" instead of "they."

Although there is little doubt that the national unity that emerged in the wake of the September 11 attacks would have occurred regardless of the choices made by reporters, the media did their part by discussing the events of that day and the months that followed in collective terms. Just as ABC titled its show on the Iranian hostage crisis (which became *Nightline*) *America Held Hostage*, the networks gave titles to their post-9/11 coverage that assigned both victimhood and agency to the nation as a whole. We did not see "World Trade Center Attacked" or "Bush Responds" at the bottom of our screens; rather, it was "America Under Attack," followed by "A Nation Responds" and "America Strikes Back." This is notable particularly because the conflict in Afghanistan was not a collective effort in the same sense as, for instance, World War II. In 2001–2002 the fighting was done by an all-volunteer army, and the President assured Americans that they could do their part by going about their daily lives. When asked if he would be calling on Americans to sacrifice, Bush responded that they were already sacrificing, because they had to wait in longer lines at airports. The collective character of this war was thus for most only psychological.

In statements that in any other circumstance would have seemed unusual, reporters pledged their fealty to the nation's leaders. As CBS's Dan Rather told David Letterman, "George Bush is the president, he makes the decisions, and, you know, as just one American, he wants me to line up, just tell me where." ABC's Cokie Roberts indicated her willingness to believe anything a general told her: "Look, I am, I will just confess to you, a total sucker for the guys who stand up with all the ribbons on and stuff and they say it's true and I'm ready to believe it." On September 11, Tom Brokaw declared, "This is war," and explained, as

Bush later would, that America was a target because of its greatness: "We are so vulnerable because of all those things that make us so great: our freedoms and our sense of security that we have. But America has been changed today by all this."

Reporters were now participating with the government in a common enterprise: unifying the citizenry, reasserting the strength of democracy and America itself, and memorializing the victims.

Journalists turned from cynics to eulogists in the immediate days and weeks following September 11, 2001. *Newsweek* issued a "Commemorative Issue" titled "The Spirit of America." One dollar of the $5.95 price would go to disaster relief, said the cover. "Journalists are accustomed to covering the news from a professional distance," wrote the head of one magazine. "That was impossible, however, on September 11 . . ."[8] Seven months later, Howell Raines, the executive editor of the *New York Times*, said of his paper's seven Pulitzer Prizes, "We are ever mindful of the shattering events it was our task to record in our city, nation, and world community." *Times* publisher Arthur Sulzberger, Jr., noted that the awards signaled "an extraordinary moment in the history of this newspaper," but added, "it is built on the back of a real tragedy." Speaking to hundreds of *Times* staffers, he then called for a moment of silence to remember the attack's victims.[9]

When National Security Adviser Condoleezza Rice went to the networks to ask that they not air videotapes being released by Osama Bin Laden, she found a receptive audience. Rice argued first that the videotapes could contain hidden messages, and second that airing them would serve Bin Laden's propaganda aims. The first claim was somewhat unpersuasive. The tapes, after all, were available on direct satellite around the world and posted on the Internet; any hidden messages could reach their targets regardless of whether the American networks showed the material. By arguing that airing the tapes would be propaganda for Bin Laden, Rice asked the networks to cooperate in the administration's communication strategy. The administration could have taken another approach; for instance, it might have supported airing the Bin Laden tapes, with the sinister figure delivering inflammatory rhetoric, as a way of increasing public anger at "the Evil One." Yet the networks agreed not to air the tapes despite the obvious news value of statements from the man the president had sworn to bring in "dead or alive." CNN issued a statement saying that "in deciding what to air, CNN will consider guidance from appropriate authorities."[10]

News organizations that failed to embrace the new paradigm were sanctioned. After September 11, Reuters, the British-based international news agency, articulated its policy on use of the word "terrorist." Reporters were reminded that "we all know that one man's terrorist is another man's freedom fighter and that Reuters upholds the principle that we do not use the word terrorist." For its policy Reuters was roundly condemned by the press. On Sunday, September 30, conservative columnist George Will used his commentary on *This Week* to respond, "I suggest that Reuters has been corrupting our language by saying 'terrorist' is somehow uniquely judgmental. And I have a suggestion: Throughout this crisis, when you see a story on the crisis by Reuters, skip the story." The *Cleveland Plain Dealer* called the Reuters policy "beyond stunning."[11] The extent to which the public embraced the critique was evident in the laughter elicited when Jay Leno said, "Reuters says that we should stop referring to them as terrorists, because in the minds of these people they are freedom fighters. Shut up! In the mind of a shark, I'm lunch—that still makes it a shark." "You know something," said Leno in another monologue, "here's a story that kind of bothers me. Reuters News Service and CNN [Leno was incorrect about this—CNN's policy was to refer to individuals as "alleged terrorists" unless they were proven to have committed a specific act] are telling their reporters they can no longer refer to Bin Laden and his people as 'terrorists' because in their minds they are freedom fighters. They have to use the term 'alleged hijacker.' This is according to their spokesman—an 'alleged idiot.'" A policy by the *Minneapolis Star-Tribune*, giving preference to more specific terms such as "suicide bomber" or "gunman" over "terrorist" to describe individuals, was also criticized in Web sites, other newspapers, and a full-page ad in the *Star-Tribune*, with a petition signed by numerous Minnesota politicians. When we asked one well-respected reporter covering the political arena about the policy, he discussed the complexity involved in the term that makes its use problematic:

> One part of the problem is that there is not a generally accepted definition of the term that makes clear where the boundaries are. Someone who blows himself up and kills 10 others, innocent civilians, in a pizza parlor, when it was clearly the bomber's intention to kill civilians, probably meets almost everyone's definition of a terrorist. But what are the key elements? Do you have to target civilians? What about those who blew a hole in the U.S.S. Cole? Their target was military, but most people probably view them as terrorists because they aren't soldiers and they did it outside of the context of an ongoing war. What

about the U.S. bombing of Hiroshima and Nagasaki? Almost everyone killed was a civilian and the targets were chosen partly to demonstrate how destructive the bombs could be. Certainly one of the goals, if not the key one, was to terrify the Japanese into surrendering. No mainstream U.S. newspaper ever refers to this as terrorism—at least not in its own voice as an established fact.

But to some readers, officials, and commentators, any reluctance to use any term of condemnation signified an unacceptably incomplete commitment to the war on terrorism.

The rally-round-the-flag impulse also called attention to conventions otherwise unnoticed. So, for example, *New York Post* columnist Neal Travis noted, "I do wish the *New York Times* would stop using the term, 'Mr. Osama Bin Laden.' Yes, the paper's style book stipulates that even criminals are to be given the honorific, but this sick bastard should be the exception to the rule. And, come to think of it, he doesn't use the term 'Mr.' for himself either."[12]

The Picture That Was Selected

The press is the custodian of both the words and the pictures through which we come to understand events. As September 11 unfolded, the nation's newsmagazines scrambled to assemble special issues making sense of what would quickly be reduced to the shorthand of the "terrorist attacks." Among the concerns of the assembled editors was selection of the cover pictures that would digest the meaning of the day. The available choices were visually evocative and conveyed very different meanings: A tower of the World Trade Center enveloped in smoke as a second hijacked plane approached its twin. The implosion of one of the towers. The smoldering gash in the Pentagon. The billowing rubble that earlier in the morning had been a vibrant symbol of global commerce. Or any of a number of pictures that juxtaposed the rubble with the American flag.

A special September 24 issue of *Business Week* showed the second tower at the moment of impact and the first smoldering. The September 24 issue of *People* placed a sepia-toned image of the second plane about to hit the World Trade center with the first tower in flames and the Manhattan skyline a hazy blur under a ceiling of smoke. The *Newsweek* special edition showed the explosion produced on impact by the first plane. Each focused attention on the terrorist act itself. From memory revivified by repeated portrayal, readers filled in what was to follow.

The words affixed to the pictures interpreted the images. "America Under Attack," said the *Newsweek* cover, using the phrase adopted by multiple networks as the headline of their continuing coverage.[13] "September 11, 2001: The Day That Shook America," read *People*. "Act of War," declared *Business Week*. Others focused on the aftermath. On *U.S. News*'s cover, a fireman on a ladder above the rubble secured a torn U.S. flag. "Under Siege," read the words.

But the photo that would recur throughout the following days and weeks was none of these. It was instead some version of the shot carried on the cover of the September 24 *Newsweek*. In it three firemen secure an intact U.S. flag to a pole protruding from the rubble of the World Trade Center, in a moment reminiscent of the one created by the servicemen in Joe Rosenthal's Pulitzer Prize–winning World War II photo of Marines raising the flag at the top of Mount Suribachi, Iwo Jima, in February 1945. That earlier image was, in the words of art historian Karal Ann Marling, the "most dramatic image of war and togetherness and hope for victory ever to emerge from World War II."[14] The analogy between the two photographs invited the conclusion that the United States would defeat the enemy responsible for the ruins just as it had dispatched its enemies in World War II. It would do so because the United States's strength is built on individuals like those in the two photographs. "God Bless America," said the headline on the *Newsweek* cover.

Those on the *Newsweek* cover were surviving rescuers, their clothes covered in ash from the building. Their raising the flag above the ruins of the Trade Center signified hope and resurrection. In the moment captured in the photo, they look up at the flag and at the country's future, not down at the destruction at their feet. This was one of the visuals intercut by ABC News into the speech delivered by President George W. Bush at the National Cathedral memorial service three days after the attack. It was the picture left in a Taliban headquarters raided by U.S. forces the weekend of October 20. Attached to those calling cards was the message "Freedom Endures." Soon thereafter the picture capped a promotional spot for the History Channel that included such memorable moments as JFK's delivery of "Ask not what your country can do for you. Ask what you can do for your country." The image was even available engraved on a coin, hawked on late-night television by opportunistic entrepreneurs. It was the digestive image through which significant news outlets and then the popular culture invited us to see September 11. By selecting this image rather than those of impending destruction or twisted ruins, *Newsweek*, ABC, and then the U.S. government invited audiences to interpret U.S. action and resolve through one iconic moment and not others, through an image transforming tragedy into triumph.

The three firefighters raising the flag remained the iconic image of September 11. The impulse to select an image that carries hope, offering the possibility of redemption while acknowledging tragedy, is a powerful one that can be seen again and again. In the aftermath of the Oklahoma City bombing, the iconic photograph, shown on magazine covers and later awarded a Pulitzer Prize, was of a fireman carrying a wounded infant away from the wreckage of the destroyed building. Although badly hurt, the child has been rescued, just as the nation, symbolized by its flag, transcends the destruction in New York City. These images endorse an account of an event and pronounce the survival of the institutions and nation attacked. By digesting events through them, the press implied that the American nation is both worthy and resilient.

The Story That Wasn't Told

Although the iconic image evoked World War II, another analogy to that war was raised and then suppressed: the story of unpreparedness that made the country vulnerable to the terrorist attacks. The early analogy of September 11 to Pearl Harbor invited a narrative of unpreparedness. The press and pundits initially framed September 11 as akin to December 7 and as such "Our Day of Infamy." So, for example, Richard Brookhiser noted, "The day of infamy was a perfect September day in New York."[15] "The date, like December 7, 1941, will live in infamy," said *Newsweek*. The "thick clouds of smoke and dust billowing up from the spot where the World Trade Center once stood were eerily reminiscent of the photographs from the Japanese attack on Battleship Row in Pearl Harbor—only the clouds were engulfing lower Manhattan."[16]

The analogy to Pearl Harbor evoked a common vulnerability and also lack of preparedness. "There has been much talk about Americans discovering the vulnerability of their heartland in a manner that far exceeds the collective trauma associated with the attack on Pearl Harbor," noted Richard Falk.[17] The analogy served to express horror and surprise but also to differentiate the two events. "Pearl Harbor was, at least, an attack by a military force against a military base," added *Newsweek*.

The analogy to Pearl Harbor also was used to argue that September 11 propelled the United States into war. "The only difference between

Pearl Harbor and the assaults on the Pentagon and World Trade Center is one of magnitude," wrote Victor Davis Hanson in the *National Review*. "Ours now is the far greater loss. No enemy in our past, neither Nazi Germany not Imperial Japan, killed so many American civilians and brought such carnage to our shores . . . Surely, by any fair measure, we should now be at war."[18]

The analogy between September 11 and December 7 is driven by a number of similarities between the two events: the surprise nature of the assault, the way the attacks drew the United States into world conflicts, and the logical question of what the United States could have done to prevent the attacks.

Interviews with survivors of the October 2000 attack in Yemen on the USS *Cole*, an explosion that killed seventeen sailors and injured thirty-seven others, reinforced the unpreparedness narrative. A hull-maintenance technician from the *Cole* noted in an AP interview that "what happened to us was just a test, how they bombed us and got away with it . . . They knew they could get away with it, so they went for a grander scale." Noted the author of the AP article, "Regal also feels angry, wondering whether the Sept. 11 attacks could have been prevented if more aggressive, immediate action had been taken against the terrorists who crippled the Cole."[19]

Unsurprisingly, National Security Adviser Condoleezza Rice moved to quash the Pearl Harbor analogy. "This is not Pearl Harbor," she said. "There are no beaches to storm and islands to take . . . [this will be] a war of will and mind."[20] White House briefings made the same point before Bush's speech to Congress September 20, 2001. On CNBC, reporter David Gregory previewed that speech by noting that "they tend to steer us away from historical comparisons principally to FDR and a Pearl Harbor speech. They say it's important for Americans to understand that the president is going to make clear that this is not Pearl Harbor. This is a much different kind of conflict. It's not going to be resolved with one quick strike."

We surmise that the analogy to Pearl Harbor was also suppressed in the first month after September 11 by both the administration and the press in part because it suggested unpreparedness. Preparedness assumes that the U.S. could have prevented the tragedy. If the country was unprepared, then someone here, presumably the government, is at least partly accountable for the deaths of September 11. And, as Shanto Iyengar demonstrates in *Is Anyone Responsible?*,[21] by imputing responsibility the media describe the political order, detailing who should do what, who gets credit when things go right, and who deserves blame when they go wrong.

News accounts tied September 11 to Pearl Harbor without at the same time raising the question of unpreparedness. Immediately after the attacks, Dan Rather raised the Pearl Harbor analogy, but to emphasize national unity, not unpreparedness: Just as December 7, 1941, is remembered, "so, too, will now September 11, 2001, go down in American history as a day of infamy. At this moment, you may want to recall that Pearl Harbor was a disaster that brought the United States of America together and propelled it to victory. A thought to ponder as we go through this afternoon." On December 2 the *New York Times* ran an extended comparison between September 11 and Pearl Harbor under the title "It's the Same, but Not." The piece compared and contrasted the event, the declarations of war, the declarations of a "new war," the mobilization, the dissent, the enemy, civil liberties, doing your part, comic relief, real-life heroes, villainy, and merchandising—all without mentioning the question of national readiness.[22]

By blunting the analogy of September 11 to Pearl Harbor, the Bush administration sidetracked a narrative of lack of preparedness. They did so with the tacit consent of the press as well as Democrats, who had as much at risk in that telling as did Republicans. Accordingly, in late November 2001 the Democratic chair and ranking Republican on the Senate Select Committee on Intelligence announced that they would put off conducting hearings investigating the causes of the attack until 2002, because "it would not be appropriate to conduct such an investigation at a time when the government's focus is on prosecuting the war against the Taliban and Al Qaeda in Afghanistan."[23] When the hearings were finally scheduled, they were to be held by the intelligence committees (where hearings are usually closed to the public), and members took pains to point out that "this is not a who-shall-we-hang type of investigation," as Congressman Porter Goss said. The hearings would focus on intelligence failures and thus steer clear of questions of past White House policies that might have set the stage for the attacks.

The changed role of the press can also be seen in a narrative line that could have continued after September 11, but didn't. It would have been possible for reporters to renew the caricature of Cheney as puppeteer and Bush as puppet that had been present during the campaign. The events of September 11 lent themselves to this narrative. When the first plane hit the World Trade Center on September 11, Vice President Cheney was in Washington, while President Bush was touting reading at an elementary school in Florida. According to a *New York Times* account, Cheney "effectively ran the government in Mr. Bush's absence." For example, he "told

Bush to stay away from Washington, ordered the Congressional leadership evacuated, dispersed cabinet members to emergency shelters, and urged Mr. Bush to direct fighter jets to shoot down any rogue airliner that threatened the Capitol or White House."[24] It was Cheney who was "coordinating the government response."[25] In the Situation Room in the White House, with the White House, Congress, and the Pentagon evacuated, "Vice President Cheney remained in charge."[26] But the press did not take Cheney's key role as an indication that Bush was ineffectual or not up to the job of the presidency.

Standing In for the President

> He had not looked determined on September 11, or had looked a
> whole bunch of other things as well: tentative, tense, shocked.
>
> Frank Bruni, *Ambling into History*, p. 255.

As word of mouth spread the news that the World Trade Center had been hit by a plane, people turned to television for information. Where Election Night 2000 had been characterized by a network rush to judgment, in the hours after the terrorist attacks on the World Trade Center and Pentagon, the nation's broadcast journalists exhibited an exemplary level of care in transmission of available information. With the country under threat, the anchors sought to unify the people by reiterating democratic values, asserting America's strength, and predicting victory over terrorism. Where President Bush faltered in the opening moments, network anchors spoke the words he failed to say.

At the same time, the coverage of September 11 is illuminating for what was not said. Bush's rhetorically inadequate responses were not subjected to critique. After being informed of the attacks while visiting an elementary school in Florida, President Bush made his first statement to the nation:

> Ladies and gentlemen, this is a difficult moment for America. I, unfortunately, will be going back to Washington after my remarks. Secretary Rod Paige and the Lieutenant Governor will take the podium and discuss education. I do want to thank the folks here at—at the Booker Elementary School for their hospitality.
>
> Today, we've had a national tragedy. Two airplanes have crashed into the World Trade Center in an apparent terrorist attack on our country. I have spoken to the vice president, to the governor of New York, to the director of the FBI, and have ordered that the full resources of the federal government go to help the victims and their families and to con-

duct a full-scale investigation to hunt down and to find those folks who committed this act. Terrorism against our nation will not stand. And now if you'd join me in a moment of silence. May God bless the victims, their families, and America. Thank you very much.

In the language that would all but universally be used by reporters to describe his demeanor, Bush appeared "shaken" as he delivered these remarks. The words did not compensate for the demeanor of the deliverer. Bush's statement was inadequate because among other things it failed to inform the public that Bush had activated U.S. defenses to protect the country. Instead, the president said that the "full resources of the federal government" were going "to help the victims and their families and to conduct a full-scale investigation to hunt down and to find those folks who committed this act." With other planes unaccounted for, this message was less than reassuring.

It was also incomplete. The military had been placed on high alert. And as Vice President Dick Cheney would reveal on *Meet the Press* the following Sunday, Bush had agreed that any aircraft on a path toward D.C. that would not respond to a request to divert would be shot down by U.S. fighter jets.

By using the casual colloquial "folks" to identify the perpetrators, Bush also failed to find a language to describe the perpetrators commensurate with the "tragedy" he described or the horror being experienced by those watching the events unfold that September morning. At the same time, since those who committed the act were presumably dead, hunting them down would be futile. The United States was committed instead to hunt down the instigators. Nor did the statement tell the public what would be done if the instigators were found. Only later would Bush specify bringing them to justice or justice to them as the country's goal.

Finally, Bush's opening sentences are odd. "Ladies and gentlemen, this is a difficult moment for America. I, unfortunately, will be going back to Washington . . ." *Unfortunately?* Moreover, contrary to his statement, Bush was not going back to Washington. The next viewers heard, he had flown to the Barksdale Air Force Base in Louisiana, where he would make another statement. Instead of noting the flaws in Bush's statement, ABC anchor Peter Jennings said that Bush appeared "shaken," but then added that the president said what he had to:

> President clearly shaken, I think, one can say, confirming what we think we all knew, which was that two aircraft in an act of terrorism crashed into the twin trade towers. Nobody was quite certain about the first one at the very outset, but the president absolutely, having talked with

the vice president and the governor of New York, the director of the FBI, now believing and confirming that we have two terrorist attacks on the World Trade Center. And the president saying the two things which a president must say in a moment like this, 'Terrorism will not stand,' which is an important thing for him to say but not always necessarily effective, and "God bless the victims and their families."

Reporters criticized Bush's shaken appearances on September 11 only after he had found the wherewithal to provide the country with reassurance about his rhetorical capacities and leadership. Said an article in the *New York Times*, "As some within his administration acknowledge, Mr. Bush did not project the strongest image on Sept. 11. As Air Force One hopped around the country in the first hours after the attacks, some Americans wondered if he was afraid to return to Washington. Unflattering comparisons were made with the stalwart performance of New York's mayor, Rudolf W. Giuliani. But the president soon overcame that shaky start, and he then ruggedly asserted himself as commander in chief with a speech to Congress on September 20 that dazzled even his critics."[27]

Bush's second statement on the eleventh provided some of what was missing from the first:

> Freedom itself was attacked this morning by a faceless coward, and freedom will be defended. I want to reassure the American people that full—the full resources of the federal government are working to assist local authorities to save lives and to help the victims of these attacks. Make no mistake, the United States will hunt down and punish those responsible for these cowardly acts.
>
> I've been in regular contact with the vice president, secretary of defense, the national security team, and my cabinet. We've taken all appropriate—appropriate security precautions to protect the American people. Our military at home and around the world is on high-alert status, and we have taken the necessary security precautions to continue the functions of your government. We have been in touch with the leaders of Congress and with world leaders to assure them that we will do what is—whatever is necessary to protect America and Americans.
>
> I ask the American people to join me in saying a thanks for all the folks who have been fighting hard to rescue our fellow citizens, and to join me in saying a prayer for the victims and their families. The resolve of our great nation is being tested, but make no mistake, we will show the world that we will pass this test. God bless.

While an improvement over the first, the second statement, too, was flawed. "Faceless coward" suggests a single instigator. Here, the inappropriateness of calling the terrorists "folks" in the earlier statement was heightened by the fact that the same word was now used to describe the rescuers. Yet this statement did what the earlier one failed to do: assure the country that the U.S. military is at high alert, the security of the government protected, and protections in place for the country as a whole. Without criticizing Bush, Jennings expanded on his statement, offering the unifying, hopeful rhetoric the occasion demanded:

> Well, the president could not have spoken more accurately in that fi-
> nal remark there. A great nation is being tested, and the president re-
> assures the nation and anybody else in the world who will hear this
> that the nation will pass the test. And there is no doubt about that, I
> think, in the United States of America. As horrible as this—these inci-
> dents are, and as tragic as Oklahoma City was, the great strength of
> the nation, you know, is always there. I recognize that's one man's opin-
> ion, and doesn't—doesn't account for the individual shock of indi-
> vidual families or the—or intelligence or military establishments,
> which have all suffered a grievous blow today in—in one way or the
> other. But it does say, I think, what most people in parts of the world
> believe, that as horrible as this is for the United States and its citizens,
> the United States continues to be, unquestionably, the leadership of
> the world, and the example in the world of freedom and democracy,
> however much one may criticize it—ourselves included—on any given
> occasion or incident.

Dan Rather also echoed the president's construction, asserting that the attacks were not simply on Americans or even America, but on freedom itself: "In the shadow of the Statue of Liberty, a direct attack on the freedom of every American and, indeed, on the freedom of anyone who has it around the world." In reaching for historical antecedents, Rather quoted Tom Paine: "'These are the times that try men's souls.' And so is this a time to try men's souls. Also, there are times that test the mettle, that test the very character of a nation. Each generation, in one way or the other, faces some kind of maxi-mum test. Who is to say that this is not ours?" asked the CBS anchor. While Bush promised success—that the United States would "hunt down and pun-ish those responsible for these cowardly acts"—Rather went farther to lend the moment grander historical import, describing the "test" America faces as the defining one of our time.

The press tells us what language matters by replaying central mean-ing in the form of sound bites and contextualizing them. The first sign that the statements by the President in Florida and Louisiana had failed rhetorically was the fact that the networks did not locate in either a clip worthy of repetition. The core moment of a great speech is expressed in a synecdochic statement that comes to stand for the entire speech and the moment. These digestive statements and their visual kin are the way in which we remember speeches and with them the meanings speakers have offered in momentous times. From "nothing to fear but fear itself" to "ask not what your country can do for you," they imprint themselves in memory in part because the speeches in which they reside focus our attention on them through internal signals and in part because they are the statements in which the press headlines the speech.

When Bush finally found such words, the press featured them and praised him for the accomplishment. In his speech at the National Cathedral prayer service on September 14, 2001, Bush created such a statement when he said, "War has been waged against us by stealth and deceit and murder. This nation is peaceful, but fierce when stirred to anger. This conflict was begun on the timing and terms of others. It will end in a way and at an hour of our choosing." Of those words, David Broder wrote, "Forty-six words, 35 of them monosyllables and none of the rest longer than two syllables. The message was powerful—and the tone dead right."[28]

Redefining Objectivity

As we discuss elsewhere, reporters' commitment to objectivity, while helpful in many ways, can sometimes leave citizens confused about factual disputes. In wartime, however, evenhandedness stops at the water's edge. In October of 2001, top executives at CNN circulated a pair of memos instructing reporters that if they showed any news unfavorable to the United States (such as footage of civilian casualties from Afghanistan), they should remind viewers of the terrorist attacks on the World Trade Center. A memo from one executive suggested possible language for reporters to use if they felt the need to discuss civilian casualties:

> "We must keep in mind, after seeing reports like this from Taliban-controlled areas, that these U.S. military actions are in response to a terrorist attack that killed close to 5,000 innocent people in the U.S." or, "We must keep in mind, after seeing reports like this, that the Taliban regime in Afghanistan continues to harbor terrorists who have praised the September 11 attacks that killed close to 5,000 innocent people in the U.S.," or "The Pentagon has repeatedly stressed that it is trying to minimize civilian casualties in Afghanistan, even as the Taliban regime continues to harbor terrorists who are connected to the September 11 attacks that claimed thousands of innocent lives in the U.S."[29]

The fact that CNN executives felt the need to remind their correspondents to make sure that all news contained a pro-U.S. tilt at a time when reporting was remarkably uncritical and most networks displayed small American flags in the corner of the screen during news presentations is particularly striking. The instruction was essentially to tie facts to a pro-U.S. perspective.

Some newspaper editors also felt the need to remind their reporters of the proper boundaries of war coverage. On October 31, the copy editor of the *Panama City News-Herald* in Florida sent a memo to the paper's reporters including these instructions:

> Per [executive editor Hal Foster]'s order, DO NOT USE photos on Page 1A showing civilian casualties from the U.S. war on Afghanistan. Our sister paper in Fort Walton Beach has done so and received hundreds and hundreds of threatening e-mails and the like.
>
> Also per Hal's order, DO NOT USE wire stories which lead with civilian casualties from the U.S. war on Afghanistan. They should be mentioned further down in the story. If the story needs rewriting to play down the civilian casualties, DO IT. The only exception is if the U.S. hits an orphanage, school or similar facility and kills scores or hundreds of children.[30]

These memos are notable because they are so unusual. Ordinarily, editors and managers do not have to dictate the frames reporters will use in their stories. Frames take shape in a process influenced by many external and internal factors; seldom are they enforced so explicitly from above. Such extraordinary directives are, of course, temporary. Seven months after the attack, when a reporter suggested on air that criticism of the administration was inappropriate, she was privately reprimanded by her newspaper in an exchange that was later referenced in a column. Appearing on *Fox News Sunday* on April 14, 2002, *Washington Post* reporter Ceci Connolly said of a speech by Al Gore, "If it were October of 2000, that would be a great speech. Solid, substantive, good legitimate domestic issues to be talking about. In the current environment—terrorism, war overseas—it just doesn't quite seem appropriate right now." A week later, the *Post*'s ombudsman wrote, without mentioning Connolly's name, "Well, that is not appropriate, and she has been reminded by a top editor that commentary by reporters is against Post policy."[31]

Accepting the President's Frames

One way to define presidential leadership is as the capacity to develop and disseminate interpretations or frames that are accepted by the press

and the public and as a result become the lenses of which we are unaware but that nonetheless shape how we think about political affairs.
One way to assess the press's role at a given moment is the degree to
which it accepts the frames offered by the president. In the wake of the
attacks on New York City and the Pentagon, the press embraced two
frames offered by the White House: first, that the terrorists attacked because they hate the fundamental principles undergirding the American
system, not what the U.S. government has done; and second, that the
attacks were acts of war, not crimes. The limits of the press's embrace of
the administration's frames is evident in the immediate critique of Bush's
use of the word "crusade" and in the evolving coverage of U.S. bombing
of civilians and its own soldiers.

Terrorists Attacked Because of Who We Are, Not What Our Government Has Done

In his second statement on September 11, President Bush defined the
terrorist attack as an attack on freedom itself, a frame that was quickly
embraced by journalists. There was an alternative frame, that the attacks
were a response to American policies. In his address to a joint session of
Congress on November 20, Bush reiterated: "They hate our freedoms,"
he said. "Our freedom of religion, our freedom of speech, our freedom
to vote and assemble and disagree with each other." By declaring that the
terrorists hate the United States because of who we are, not what we
have done, President Bush framed the attacks of September 11 as an
inexplicable act that had destruction of our civilization as its end. "We
wage a war to save civilization itself," said Bush on November 8.

By contrast, in his statements to the world, Osama Bin Laden focused on the wrongs the United States had in his judgment done the
Middle East and the Muslim world. The first advantage of the Bush frame
is that, if accepted, it ends debate about causes of the attack. If the acts
had been framed as a response to U.S. policy, the frame would have invited debate about the legitimacy of such policies as siding with Israel in
Middle Eastern conflicts, stationing U.S. military personnel on the
ground in Saudi Arabia, imposing an embargo on Iraq, or arming Bin
Laden and the mujahideen in their fight against the Soviet Union. The
second advantage of the frame is that in it nothing that the country could
change is at issue. Freedom is a core democratic value. If the terrorists
hate and want to end the nation's freedom, they are objecting to and
trying to extinguish something that defines the country. Whether the
U.S. should eradicate those who seek to destroy the country is not a

debatable question. Whether the U.S. should eradicate those who seek to change national policies is.

If we assume that the attackers want to destroy the U.S., then the question repeated in articles and broadcasts—Why do they hate us?—makes sense. Alternatively, if the attacks are a misguided way of condemning U.S. policies, then those news accounts might have instead asked, Why do they hate our policies? Reporters asked the first question in dozens of stories; while their analysis was more complex than the president's, it nonetheless fit his frame. Many argued that America was misunderstood in the Third World. "Perhaps a key to deflecting the hatred aimed at the United States is information," said the *New York Times.*[32] At the same time, by asking why they hate "us," reporters indicated that they too were part of this story, part of "us."

Terrorism as an Act of War, Not as a Crime

Before September 11, acts of terrorism against the United States were cast as crimes, not acts of war. Some found this frame controversial. Former Senator Bob Kerrey, a member of the Senate Intelligence Committee while in office, recalls, "Before September 11th, we had three terrorist attacks on America—the Khobar Towers bombing in Saudi Arabia in 1996, the Embassy bombings in Africa in 1998, the attack on the USS *Cole* in 2000—and in each case the lead agency investigating the case was the F.B.I. To my mind, these were acts of war, not just law-enforcement issues."[33] Nonetheless, that past use of language left open the possibility that the September 11 attacks would be treated as a crime, not a war, and thus required a law-enforcement response, not a military one.

However, by labeling the attacks of September 11 "an act of war," President Bush framed them in a way that required a military, not a legal, response. In his televised address on the evening of September 11 viewed by eighty million Americans,[34] Bush defined what was to come as a "war against terrorism." "The enemy has declared war on us," noted Bush in a speech on November 29, 2001. Counteracting crime is a responsibility of law enforcement; responding to an act of war is the prerogative of the military authorized by Congress and led by the commander in chief.

Headline writers accepted Bush's language when an article headlined "War Cabinet" included such statements as "Many officials who had advisory roles during the Persian Gulf War are advising President Bush in the war against terrorism."[35] The language of war also slipped unchallenged into descriptions of the acts and consequences of September 11.

"Wartime Recession?" asked *Time* over a subhead reading, "A war is supposed to throw a life preserver to a floundering economy."[36] Writing of a Chicago businesswoman's first trip to New York after the attacks, a *Chicago Tribune* reporter noted that the trip "took her from her office in the Sears Tower and transported her, with a vague sense of dread, into wartorn Manhattan."[37] "Because we are at war," said Tim Russert, "it demands a different kind of discourse."

Limits to the Acceptance of
Presidential Framing

The role of reporters as rhetorical stand-ins was evident on September 11 when they supplemented Bush's early statements with the words the country needed to hear. The same role was evident when they took exception to Bush's ill-advised analogy of the U.S. effort to a "crusade." On Sunday, September 16, in extemporaneous comments President Bush said of the U.S. response to September 11, "This is a new kind of . . . a new kind of evil. And the American people are beginning to understand. This crusade, this war on terrorism, is going to take a while." "Osama bin Laden has often talked about 'expelling crusaders and Jews,'" noted terrorist expert Jerrold Post. "That sort of language seems calculated to give affirmation to Bin Laden's description of himself. It's going to produce twenty more like him."[38] The term also cast the "war" as one based in religious difference, a direction Bush had diligently disavowed. White House press representative Ari Fleischer apologized two days later, saying, "I think to the degree that that word has any connotations that would upset any of our partners or anybody else in the world, the president would regret [it] . . . But the purpose of his conveying it is in the traditional English sense of the word. It's a broad cause."

Although elite response was almost instantaneous, press comments cast the statement as an innocent error, not a sign of incompetence, historical amnesia, or foreign policy inexperience. "[A] word that has traditionally been used to rally Americans was mistakenly used in the context of opposing a radical Muslim faction, and the White House promptly apologized," wrote wordsmith William Safire.[39] He undoubtedly meant to use the word, noted Safire, the way Eisenhower did when he titled his memoirs *Crusade in Europe*. A word that had the generic meaning of "major sustained noble effort" had for Bush lost its original context.

Active and Passive Frames Reveal the Press's Posture: Errant Bombs and Friendly Fire

Early in the war effort, the press frames cast military blunders in a benign light. "Bin Laden Hunted in Caves; An Errant U.S. Bomb Causes First 3 G.I. Deaths in Action," proclaimed a front-page headline in the *New York Times* on December 6, 2001. The headline invited assumptions about fact, cause and effect, responsibility, and approval or disapproval. By opening with "Bin Laden Hunted," the headline framed the "Errant U.S. Bomb" in the context of a conflict with Bin Laden. The headline assumes that readers know who he is and why and by whom he is being hunted. "Bin Laden Hunted" carries echoes of other uses of the word "hunted." We hunt down criminals or animals. The juxtaposition of "Bin Laden Hunted" and "An Errant Bomb" implies that the two activities occurred, if not simultaneously, then within the same time frame. Those who dropped the errant bomb were presumably hunting Bin Laden or his followers.

No human responsibility is implied in an "Errant U.S. Bomb." Neither an American B-52 nor a U.S. bombardier are the subjects of the sentence. Instead, the bomb takes the blame. "Errant" also implies that U.S. bombing of its own troops is unusual, unintended. Errant says that U.S. bombs are generally more reliable.

The notation that the deaths occurred "in action" separates them from the earlier U.S. casualties killed in "accidents" at sites not proximate to the "enemy." "The cause of the errant bombing," says the article, "remained under investigation tonight. Military officials said it was possible that the spotters on the ground provided the wrong coordinates for the intended target, that the bombardier aboard the B-52 erred in aiming the weapon, or that there was a malfunction in the bomb's guidance system or other equipment."[40]

In the headline the bomb does not "kill G.I.s" but instead "causes" their deaths. "Kill" would suggest intention. Who is dead? The headline says "3 G.I.s". The subhead suggests a tension between G.I.—someone presumed to be fighting—and the role the story actually ascribes to them: "Advisers to Rebels." The United States is not cast here as fighting but rather advising.

Where the "errant bomb" causes the death, the United States becomes the subject of the story when engaged in less controversial activities. "American warplanes continued to attack concentrations of Taliban forces near Kandahar and the cave-pocked mountains . . ." Their bombs are presumably not errant. But note the difference between a headline that reads "American Warplane Kills 3 G.I.s" and the headline that actually ran. Observe as well that the American warplanes are not dropping their bombs on people but on "concentrations of Taliban forces."

The assumptions about causality and responsibility in the headline and story are part of a frame that assumes that the United States is engaged in justifiable action, that its weapons ordinarily work, its military personnel are competent, and that the United States would not deliberately kill its own G.I.s. Hence "Errant U.S. Bomb." Additionally, the story assumes that the United States's might is working in service of a duly appointed head of state and against an enemy whose identity is known. The same assumptions underlie the rhetoric of President Bush, who in the report is quoted as saying, "I want the families to know that they died for a noble and just cause; that the fight against terror is noble and it's just; and they defend freedom. And for that, we're grateful."

In this case, the press frame and the administration frame are aligned. The report does not explore Bush's motives or examine whether those who are the intended targets of the bombing are indeed the enemies of freedom or the proponents of terror. Unchallenged by the article are Bush's assumptions that those who harbor terrorists are terrorists, that the Taliban harbored Bin Laden, and Bin Laden is both a terrorist and responsible for September 11. Unquestioned is the assumption that being killed by a bomb intended for others constitutes death in a noble and just cause defending freedom.

Four months later, the press would discuss a similar event in very different terms. After reporters discovered that an American special forces soldier was killed in an attack on a convoy by an American gunship, newspapers signaled the possibility of agency on the part of the American military. "U.S. May Have Killed Commando," read the headline to a *Philadelphia Inquirer* story.[41] Here the soldier was "killed" not by a piece of machinery but by his own military and his own country. Accountability now rests with the American military, though it is qualified by the "may have" in the article's title. The frame has changed. On July 21, 2002 a *New York Times* front page headline read, "Flaws in U.S. Air War Left Hundreds of Civilians Dead." "The American air campaign," wrote Dexter Filkins, "has produced a pattern of mistakes that has killed hundreds of Afghan civilians." The article also noted that "Often, despite evidence on the ground, [American military commanders] denied that civilians were killed." By contrast, when asked about discussing civilian casualties in Afghanistan a few weeks after September 11, Fox News anchor Brit Hume dismissed the notion that such deaths would be news.

"We know we're at war," Hume said. "The fact that some people are dying, is that really news? And is it news to be treated in a semi-straight-faced way? I think not."[42] The *New York Times*'s report suggested that the press eventually harmonized the roles of patriot, watchdog, and custodian of fact, by placing the civilian casualties in the context of "America's ability to hunt down Taliban and Qaeda forces."

The Effect of September 11: Did Bush Change or Did the Press?

Where during the campaign Bush's garbled rhetoric was often flagged by reporters, after September 11 it was instead overlooked or praised. "In the days since the attacks," wrote Elizabeth Bumiller in the *New York Times* in early January 2002, "historians explain, Americans have projected on to Mr. Bush the qualities they desperately want him to have."[43] So, too, did the press. When Texas Governor George W. Bush said in a campaign speech in late August 2000 that "we cannot let terrorists and rogue nations hold this nation hostile or hold our allies hostile," the *Boston Globe* cited the error and recalled early Bush misstatements. "In Iowa, Candidate Shows Tendency to Trip on Words,"[44] said the headline. The *Los Angeles Times* described the speech as "an evening of verbal quicksand . . . and Tuesday wasn't much better, no matter how much Bush and the campaign tried to fix things."[45]

Why the focus on stumbles, not issue substance? Columnist Lars-Erik Nelson characterized the reporters' perspective by noting, "George W. Bush may be talking about tax cuts or foreign challenges or restoring dignity to the White House. It won't matter. The alert reporters, the TV cameras and the microphones are not trained on him for that. They are waiting for the next gaffe, the stumble, the blunder that will give them another bright story and fulfill the image that Bush is on the losing end of a war with the English language."[46] The focus continued into the post-election period, with reporters commenting that Bush "seemed to grope for several phrases and stumbled over one or two others."[47] Once he took office, the press did not let up: the *New York Times*, for instance, asked, "Could Mr. Bush's ineloquence attain the status of Dan Quayle's potatoe or Ronald Reagan's pollution-causing trees?"[48]

In the wake of the September 11 bombings, the press interpreted Bush's linguistic aptitude very differently. When he coined the phrase "women of cover" in his televised press conference on October 11 to refer to Afghani women forced to wear burkas, proclaimed that "this Thursday, ticket counters and airplanes will fly out of Ronald Reagan Airport,"[49] and in a press conference at a Crawford, Texas, high school said of Russian president Vladimir Putin, "It's one thing for he and me to have a personal relationship,"[50] the press took little notice, where in the campaign it would have been vocal. This change raises some intriguing questions. Was the press wrong when in the campaign it interpreted verbal infelicities as a signal of incompetence? Alternatively, in times of crisis does the press shun a focus on cues that might suggest a lack of command? The timing of such stories both in campaigns and in the presidency of George Herbert Walker Bush suggests a third hypothesis. When a candidate or president is doing well in the polls, inarticulate moments may be seen as inconsequential quirks, where in a leader with unimpressive poll numbers they are taken instead as a sign of faltering leadership or a clouded mind. Since presidents' approval ratings rise in times of crisis, distinguishing the second and third possibilities is all but impossible.

The press repeated over and over that Bush had been "transformed" by September 11. Bush was "transformed by the unimaginable catastrophe of Sept. 11," said the *Dallas Morning News*.[51] "Almost everyone agrees that George W. Bush is a different President than he was two months ago," said *Fortune* magazine.[52] The *New York Times* remarked that "President Bush has seemed transformed from a casually educated son of privilege into a mature leader of a nation at war."[53] Bush was compared to Lincoln, Prince Hal, and even Moses. Bush himself rejected the claim, contending that he was the same person he had always been. In fact, we believe it was the reporters who had been transformed.

To the argument that the events of September 11 altered the operation of press filters, a reader might respond, "Of course!" We argue not simply that press behavior changed but that it changed in ways that raised questions about the accuracy of both the press characterizations during the campaign and those after September 11. The dramatic shift in press assumptions also invited questions about the extent to which press coverage of political campaigns provides a useful forecast of governance.

It was predictable that reporters would change their dispositions in matters related to the conflict itself—challenging the veracity of White House claims on the conduct of the war less vigorously than they would when the subject was domestic policy, or voluntarily withholding information for the purposes of national security. At the same time, however, they altered their reporting on subjects related to talent and temperament, such as President Bush's rhetorical dexterity.

Contrary to the impression that some reporting and much late-night comedy created, candidate Bush did not mangle his messages on a daily basis. Nor did he do so after September 11. The rate at which inelegant phrasing and muddled syntax infiltrated his speeches was much the same before and after the terrorist attack. What changed was press commentary. For example, only the *Washington Post* report added that "Even in the tension of war preparation, Bush gave a clear sign that things were returning to normal, as he employed his favorite malapropism, 'misunderestimate,' three times in as many sentences" to its report on President Bush's September 27, 2001, speech at the CIA;[54] in other outlets, Bush's verbal miscues went unremarked. In that address Bush said, "It's also a war that declares a new declaration that says if you harbor a terrorist, you're just as guilty as the terrorist. . . . And in order to make sure that we're able to conduct a winning victory, we've got to have the best intelligence we can possibly have . . . [We must] . . . make sure that we run down every threat, take serious every incident . . . The folks who conducted the act on our country on September 11 made a big mistake . . . They misunderestimated the fact that we love a neighbor in need. They underestimated the compassion of our country. I think they misunderestimated the will and determination of the commander in chief, too." Reporters abstained from commenting on this succession of verbal slips.

Bush's October 11, 2001, prime-time televised press conference provides evidence for the conclusion that the press was not only at bay but translated what was once considered problematic into evidence of emerging eloquence. In that press conference Bush's facility in constructing sentences was not appreciably different from what it had been during the campaign. Take, for example, this passage: "The greatest generation was used to storming beachheads. Baby boomers such as myself was used to getting caught in a quagmire of Vietnam where politics made decisions more than the military sometimes. Generation X was able to watch technology right in front of their TV screens, you know, burrow into concrete bunkers in Iraq and blow them up."

However, in contrast to the comments characterizing such verbal odysseys in the campaign, the front-page article in the next day's *New York Times*, in a tone unusually complimentary for a news story, observed, "During 45 minutes of questioning, he made no verbal slip of any significance, resorted to humor at times, and otherwise conveyed the seriousness of the moment through a new gravitas—seeming grayer, graver and more comfortable in the role."[55] Bush's verbal slips had now lost "any significance." One might of course question whether they were significant during the campaign; but in any case the *Times*'s editorial page gave the president this note of encouragement: "Mr. Bush should return to this and similar venues to talk to the American people. He's better at it than he and his aides think."[56]

USA Today concurred: "Bush prefers jeans to suits and conversation to public grilling by reporters, but he marched into the historic room on a regal red carpet and seemed comfortable beneath the crystal chandeliers. There was little of the verbal fumbling that often marked his late-in-the-day speeches during the campaign. He spoke with the passion and authority that used to be evident only when he talked of favorite issues such as education."[57] The *Washington Post* acknowledged his verbal stumbles but forgave them: "Without a text, Bush did not exercise the Churchillian phrases that he has invoked in recent speeches, and he stumbled at times. But while losing something in eloquence, Bush presented a homier, commonsense discussion of the war."[58]

Citing the passage above, the *Hartford Courant* focused not on the errors or on the seeming implication that Bush had fought in Vietnam, when in fact he spent the war safely stateside. Instead the article noted that "Bush was alternately conversational and statesmanlike . . . At one point, he spoke about how unconventional this war is, and compared it with those fought by, as he put it, the Greatest Generation (World War II), the baby boomers (Vietnam) and Generation X, which found that technology generally means military might."[59]

Invoking Bush's previous persona, *Today Show* host Matt Lauer said, "I don't want to sound condescending, but he has grown enormously in thirty-one days." Perhaps. Alternatively, Bush was now being seen through a less cynical frame focused by the events of September 11 on how the country would respond, not how well the sentences expressing options diagrammed. Some journalists noted his verbal stumbles but dismissed them, some minimized them, and some denied that they had occurred. By December 23 the *Times*'s reporters' disposition to flag Bush's odd rhetorical moments had returned, but without the indictments that characterized campaign coverage. The *Times* wrote that National Security Adviser Condoleezza Rice's "verbal precision is a sharp counterpoint to Mr. Bush's own tendency to speak in vague and sometimes confusing colloquialisms."[60]

September 11 also eliminated late-night jokes about Bush's intelligence. Jay Leno explained to his audience, "It's hard to do jokes because, as you know, Bush is *smart* now." "When times are good, you make fun of the king. When times are bad, you make fun of the enemy," he told a reporter.[61] The producers of the late-night shows eventually decided that when they would run repeats, they would use only shows originally aired after September 11, to avoid airing anything that included "jabs at the president," which they now considered "tasteless."[62] Between January 1, 2001, and September 11, Bush was the target of 32% of the jokes on late-night television (still fewer than Clinton). In the two months following September 11, he was the target of only 4%.[63] The change from the tone of jokes during the campaign was seismic. These shifts were consistent with alterations in press practices as well.

The explanation? In an interview, television reporter Bruce Morton said about coverage during the Reagan years, "Reagan has brightened the national mood; I don't think there's any question about that. And I think that clearly is reflected in the news coverage. As it should be: we're supposed to be kind of a mirror of what's going on."[64] When asked about his network prominently displaying the American flag on screen after the September 11 attacks, Fox News Senior Vice President John Moody said, "I think that there's some patriotism on camera now, and I think inasmuch as TV news often reflects America's mood at any given moment, that's what it's doing now."[65] The conscious desire to "reflect the national mood" tends to arise when the mood has changed noticeably.

Discerning what prompts the press to shift from one perspective to another is important because it reveals a predictable dynamic that answers the questions we posed in the introduction. The press takes its cue not only from the strategies employed by political combatants, but whether there is a combat at all. For example, press coverage of the war in Vietnam focused on opposition only when that opposition reached the halls of Congress.[66] In the absence of a critique by major U.S. actors, the press carried the consensus of the elites and all but ignored those protesting the Gulf War.[67]

In the same way, after September 11 the passage of time eventually drove reporters to return to viewing domestic events strategically. In April 2002, for example, reporters noted that President Bush imposed steel tariffs and signed campaign finance reform, angering some in his own party; that the Senate defeated his push to open the Arctic National Wildlife Refuge to oil drilling; and that the administration seemed powerless to contain spiraling violence in the Middle East. Critically, the Democratic opposition returned to criticizing the president. Journalists responded by covering politics the way they had before the terrorist attacks. Unlike the stories cast in a patriotic frame, there were now two sides, political strengths and vulnerabilities, and divided public sentiment. Although Bush's approval ratings were still at an extraordinarily high 75%, in April 2002 reporters were writing, as the *Philadelphia Inquirer* did, that "after seven months bestriding the American stage as if he were a political colossus, President Bush is feeling the ground start to shift beneath his feet."[68] Here the public emergence of the opposition on the domestic front invited a switch from the patriotic frame to the strategic one, meaning that press attention could turn from Bush's strengths to his weaknesses, bringing into focus facts that would have seemed irrelevant just weeks before.

When in May 2002 it was revealed that a variety of hints of what was to come on September 11 had been available to the FBI and CIA, the administration came under heavy criticism in ways it hadn't since the attacks occurred. A critical impetus in moving the story forward was not only the information itself but the willingness of prominent Democrats to criticize the administration on matters relating to terrorism, something that had been largely absent up to that point. "The administration's defensiveness suggested America may have entered the post-9/11 period," wrote *Newsweek*, in a description more of the capital than America in general. "Washington politics is back to its partisan snarling, and the media, self-muzzled until now, is yapping at the White House's heels."[69] Typical of the perspective that views any critique across party lines pejoratively, *Newsweek* characterizes disagreements as "partisan snarling."

In contrast to the immediate aftermath of the attacks, here questionable statements by administration officials were refuted by journalists, as when National Security Adviser Condoleezza Rice asserted that "I don't think anybody could have predicted that these people would take an airplane and slam it into the World Trade Center, take another one and slam it into the Pentagon, that they would try to use a hijacked airplane as a missile." In fact, reporters pointed out, security officials had prepared for the use of planes as missiles at the G8 economic summit in Genoa in July 2001, which President Bush had attended. In part because the political landscape now included partisan critique, the accuracy of official statements was scrutinized.

As revelations of missed signals at the FBI and CIA emerged, criticism of the administration's performance in the war on terrorism became first permissible, then common. "In the current climate, it seems," wrote *Washington Post* media writer Howard Kurtz, "everyone's motives are suspect. We now spend almost as much time talking about whether each party is exploiting 9/11 than about terrorism itself."[70] MSNBC anchor Brian Williams noted, "Some are openly questioning the timing of some of the White House announcements on progress in the war against terrorism lately, announcements and leaks about what they have thwarted and who they have stopped. This is happening because, for too many, the White House seems to come up with an announcement precisely when it needs one, when there is trouble on some other front."[71]

But the administration was not the only entity that could be charged with missing signals on terrorism. The press itself could be charged with missing the story, a fact seldom mentioned in post-September 11 analyses. In January 2001, a bipartisan U.S. National Commission on National Security chaired by former Senators Gary Hart and Warren Rudman warned that "the combination of unconventional weapons proliferation with the persistence of international terrorism will end the relative invulnerability of the U.S. homeland to catastrophic attack. A direct attack against American citizens on American soil is likely over the next quarter century." The Commission argued that "security of the American homeland" from terrorism "should be the primary national security mission of the U.S. government."

While the Bush administration paid little attention to the report (which among other recommendations called for the establishment of a cabinet-level department to oversee homeland security, just as Bush later proposed), the press also failed to give it the prominence it warranted. Articles based on wireservice stories about the Commission's report appeared on the inside pages of a few newspapers, while the story was ignored by the country's largest papers, with the exception of the *Los Angeles Times*. Although Hart and Rudman made appearances on CNN and MSNBC, none of the three network news operations did a story about their conclusions. A week later, CIA director George Tenet told the Senate Intelligence Committee that "Osama bin Laden and his global network of lieutenants and associates remain the most immediate and serious threat" to American national security. Tenet's warning did not prompt journalists to explore Bin Laden's network. The day after the attacks, the *New York Times* recalled the report and said that "the alarms have generally gone unheeded," but mentioned only the government's failure to address the warnings, leaving out the press's failure to do so.[72]

Times of national crisis present a dilemma for reporters. The patriotic impulse may suppress the willingness to question officials too aggressively or investigate the possibility of deception too extensively. At the same time, when the country is at war and access to the battlefield is limited, the government's ability to conceal facts from the press is greatly enhanced. The kind of elite consensus that existed after September 11 should not prevent journalists from performing their investigative role. The fact that the opposition is temporarily refraining from criticizing those at the helm does not mean that all of their actions are necessarily beyond reproach.

In the immediate aftermath of the terrorist attacks, the press performed admirably, providing citizens with reporting that was informative, accurate, and compelling. While rumors made their way into the broadcasts—that a second plane was headed for the Pentagon, that a car bomb had exploded at the State Department—on-air reporters were careful to distinguish between what had been confirmed to be true and what had not. Although the initial reporting was less detached than is ordinarily the norm, it was accomplished without sacrificing a commitment to fact. By upholding the standards of their profession, reporters fostered national unity and aided public understanding of what had occurred and what the future might hold.

But as the conflict in Afghanistan began, some in the news media apparently concluded that traditional journalistic standards would lead to coverage insufficiently supportive of the American effort. The consequence was a suppression of scrutiny of the president and the military. When editors issue orders to avoid a focus on civilian casualties or reporters argue that criticism of the president is "inappropriate," they break faith with their audiences. Citizens are thoughtful enough to appreciate that leaders are imperfect and armies make mistakes, even in a just cause.

Journalists' commitment to a factual portrayal of events should be no less strong when the country is threatened. If the government acts appropriately and is honest in describing its actions to the public, the facts will lend support to its cause; if the government deceives, the facts will undercut it. In either case, the press upholds its commitment to the public by not sacrificing accuracy to what it perceives as the national mood. When the press began to examine the official version of events more closely and discuss both the successes and the failures of the government's actions in combating terrorism, support for American institutions did not wane. The lesson is that citizens are best served by a press no less vigilant in times of crisis than in times of peace.

CHAPTER 7

The Press as
Custodian of Fact

J ust as politicians sometimes succeed in deceiving the public, journalists sometimes fail in their task of discovering and describing the knowable, relevant information at play in public discourse. Some cynics believe that politicians always lie. Still, the frequency with which they choose to do so and succeed when they do is in part a function of the vigilance with which reporters discover facts, sort the relevant from the meaningless, and hold those in public life to standards of truthfulness. When reporters carry out these tasks, politicians and those who seek to influence them are deterred from straying from the truth, and informed decision making on the part of the public becomes more likely. In our view, every successful deception or persistent public misconception can be understood in part as a failure on the part of the press in its role as custodian of fact.

New Yorker editor David Remnick captured the notion of the press we have been advocating in the phrase "informed aggressive skepticism."[1] This kind of reporting is informed about the facts that matter, the legislative and political context in which they are situated and by which they are shaped, the points of contest in a campaign, the relationship between these promises and governance, and the history and biography of those who would lead. This kind of reporting is aggressive in ferreting out the truth of a situation as best it can be known, rejecting spin for substance, and holding those who lead accountable. Finally, this kind of reporting is skeptical—neither worshipful nor cynical—toward the institutions and individuals who hold power.

How can reporters assess and contextualize fact in political debate? Before we offer some suggestions to ground reporting in the factual, we should note a number of tendencies in current political reporting that impede the press's ability to perform its role as custodian of fact. The first is political journalists' relentless focus on tactics, particularly in campaigns. For instance, after the 2000 debates, commentary focused on whether Bush had proved that he was up to the job and Gore had established that he was likable. "Was Gore too much of a bully; was Bush too shy?" asked Cokie Roberts on ABC after the October 3 debate. Did either make a fatal gaffe or evince interpersonal characteristics so off-putting that they would drive voters away? On Fox News, Mara Liason observed that Gore "kept some of his bad habits in check, but he had others, like heavy sighing and laughter, that he didn't keep in check."[2]

Even when policy is discussed, it is often channeled through the strategic filter. For instance, this CNN story from October 18, 2000, analyzed a dispute over Social Security by quoting the competing claims and discussing the tactics, but made no attempt to give viewers a guidepost to the truth:

> **Gore:** If you want to see the basic shape of Social Security completely altered in a way that could cause its bankruptcy in a single generation, that is what I'm going to tell you this morning is the likely, expected outcome of the plan that is proposed by my opponent, Governor Bush.
>
> **Jonathan Karl:** The theme is picked up in a new ad put out by the Democratic National Committee.
>
> **Narrator:** (Clip from ad) Bush has promised the same money to pay seniors their current benefit. The *Wall Street Journal* shows he can't keep both promises.
>
> **Karl:** The chairman of the Democratic Party vowed to make Bush pay for touching the third rail of American politics with his plan to partially privatize Social Security.
>
> **Joe Andrew:** Well, he's grabbed that rail. He just didn't realize that we hadn't switched on the electricity yet, and that's what we're going to do with this television ad as well.
>
> **Karl:** The Bush campaign says it is Gore who would bankrupt the program with a status quo approach that would do nothing to ensure it will survive the retirement of the baby boomers.

Will Bush's proposals bankrupt the system? Will Gore's? The viewer relying on this piece hasn't a clue. The central questions of Karl's report are, what are they fighting about, and what's the strategy behind the conflict? It is at moments such as these, when candidates engage in a factual dispute, that reporters have a particular responsibility to sort out the facts for their audience. But from the reporter's perspective, judging the accuracy of the claims not only smacks of bias but subverts the narrative itself. That story line establishes that the candidates are disagreeing and seeks to answer the question Who is gaining the tactical advantage? If the journalist concludes that one side is right, there is no more story, at least not in its current form.[3] What if the tactical advantage is going to the person who is fudging the facts? What if both are selectively using evidence? In fact, contrary to Gore's attack on Bush, the Republican's plan did not affect the benefits paid to current seniors at all. It would, however, affect the baby boomers whose retirement was on the horizon. Nor was Bush's attack fair. Gore had a plan to increase the survivability of Social Security.

Reporters tend to be much more comfortable making evaluative strategic statements than evaluative statements about policy. The statement "Candidate X's Social Security plan is unrealistic" sounds like editorializing; the statement "Candidate X has no realistic chance of winning the New Hampshire primary" sounds like an objective evaluation of a political reality. But if both statements are in fact true, reporters who avoid the first while stating the second are only partially fulfilling their obligations to their audience.

When they cover politics strategically, reporters adopt a variant of the watchdog role. But here it is not government corruption they seek to expose and therefore prevent, but political and rhetorical manipulation. By revealing the strategies behind politicians' rhetoric, journalists may be attempting to make political actors more forthright and citizens more critical. But without an accompanying analysis of issues, strategic coverage leaves voters unable to assess whether politicians' claims should be believed. Voters become, in Todd Gitlin's words, "cognoscenti of their own bamboozlement."[4] If we learn that a candidate appeared at a senior citizen center *in order to make us believe* that he cares about the elderly, we have no evidence that he does or does not in fact care about the elderly, but the implication that he is faking concern is implied. Indeed, in experiments testing the effects of actual political news coverage, Cappella and Jamieson found that strategic coverage elicited cynical interpretations.[5]

If they accept the invitation, citizens may conclude that in politics, motives are always suspect. Political actors rarely admit to the kind of strategic motivations for statements and positions that reporters routinely ascribe to them. The strategic frame by its nature asserts first that real motives are camouflaged by stated motives, and second that the substance of a speech or a policy is less important for citizens to know than the real (strategic) motive behind it. One study comparing network news coverage of the last four presidential elections found that 71% of stories in 2000 were primarily concerned with the "horse race" as opposed to issues, compared to 48% in 1996 and 58% in both 1992 and 1988.[6] Our own content analysis of television news in 2000 showed that fewer than a third of the statements in election stories mentioned any issue at all, no matter how briefly.

The prevalence of strategic coverage can be partly explained by the fact that most political reporters, particularly those who cover campaigns, are greater experts in politics than they are in policy. Since politics is what they know, politics is what they cover. Within that context, coverage gravitates toward the cynical. As Daniel Hallin observed, "Just as TV decries photo-opportunity and sound-bite campaigning yet builds the news around them, so it decries the culture of the campaign consultant, with its emphasis on technique over substance, yet adopts that culture as its own."[7]

This raises the second and third problematic tendencies working against reporters' desire to adjudicate factual disputes: the fear of appearing biased, which leads to a formulaic "he said/she said" reporting style that can stymie citizens in their search for understanding.

Early American newspapers were associated with political parties, catering to the perspectives of their partisan readers. A number of developments in the newspaper industry in the mid–nineteenth century, including the rise of the penny press and the formation of the Associated Press, introduced the idea of journalists reporting events from a neutral standpoint. By the early twentieth century, the norm of "objectivity" had firmly taken hold, and a commitment to "the facts" was an article of faith among reporters.[8] Once this process was complete, "journalists came to think of themselves not as participants in a process of political discussion, even of a nonpartisan character, but as professionals, standing above the political fray."[9] As Fox News claims in its ads, "We report, you decide."

Even after the term objectivity "went out of fashion," as E. J. Dionne notes, "reporters still believed they should not be partisan, should present 'both sides' of a controversy and thereby allow the readers or listeners to make up their own minds . . . Yet journalism was operating under a whole series of contradictory rules and imperatives—to be neutral yet investigatory, to be fair-minded and yet have 'edge,' to be disengaged from politics and yet have 'impact.'"[10]

If respect for fact is one star guiding journalism, respect for balance is the other. If one quotes a critic of the administration, then one must quote a member of the administration. Quote an environmentalist, balance with an industry lobbyist. Although the resulting reporting is balanced, that balance may be a false one. Both sides of a dispute do not necessarily have equally valid claims; indeed, there are often more than two sides. Particularly when placed within a strategic frame, "balanced" coverage implies that all claims have equal merit.

While "liberal bias" in the press has been alleged for many years, the accusation became a commonplace with the explosion of conservative talk radio in the early 1990s. Rush Limbaugh and other, less prominent radio hosts made allegations of press bias a mantra. The primary exhibits in the case for bias were surveys showing that a majority of reporters vote for Democratic presidential candidates, although other polls have shown reporters to be more liberal than the populace on social issues but more conservative on economic issues. Actual evidence of media bias would of course have to be culled from the content of news. Scholarly attempts to identify bias have not borne out the conservative critique; a recent meta-analysis of fifty-nine academic studies found no bias in newspapers, and measurable but insignificant biases in newsmagazines and television news (there were slightly more statements by Republicans in magazines, and slightly more statements by Democrats on television).[11] Perceptions of media bias may be driven in part by assertions that the creature is real: The more discussion there is of media bias, the more people believe that such bias exists, regardless of whether the news at a particular moment is more favorable to Democrats or Republicans.[12]

Recently the charge gained new attention with the publication of *Bias: A CBS Insider Exposes How the Media Distort the News*, by Bernard Goldberg. Goldberg centers his argument that "liberal biases . . . overwhelm straight news reporting" on a CBS news piece, a 1996 analysis of Steve Forbes's flat-tax proposal by reporter Eric Engberg. The report was critical not so much of Forbes's proposal itself, but of the arguments the candidate used to support it: that a flat tax would result in "a Renaissance the likes of which has never been seen before," including a doubling of economic growth, a reduction in the deficit, an end to accountants and tax lawyers enabling the wealthy to avoid paying taxes, and finally, that the flat tax would result in parents spending more time with their children.

Goldberg argued that Engberg's story shows that the media have a liberal bias. But while the report was unusually critical of Forbes, it actually demonstrates not liberal bias but the way the boundaries of debate are constructed out of the positions of the key players in American politics. At the time, Forbes and his flat tax were being criticized not only by Democrats but by most of the Republican establishment as well. Because reporters determine whether a proposal is considered "reasonable" in public debate in large part by whether it is embraced by elite figures, the fact that the flat tax was at the time denounced by the likes of Newt Gingrich (whom Engberg quoted) increased the likelihood that it would be cast as outside the mainstream. To take an example of a liberal idea given similar treatment, a single-payer healthcare system, despite being used by every major industrialized country other than the United States, is dismissed by the press as outside the range of reasonable debate on the future of American health care, because few of those who occupy positions of power publicly advocate it.

In fact, many biases, most of them professional, not political, shape the news. Reporters have a bias toward the use of official sources, a bias toward information that can be obtained quickly, a bias toward conflict, a bias toward focusing on discrete events rather than persistent conditions, and a bias toward the simple over the complex. These biases have a far greater role in determining the content of news than any political preferences a reporter might have.

Furthermore, political preferences can sometimes play a role in reporters' decisions, but not necessarily one that tilts toward their favored candidates and policies. The drumbeat of accusations against the mainstream press as "liberal" has, if nothing else, made reporters particularly wary of living up to the charge. As far back as 1972, Timothy Crouse reported in *The Boys on the Bus* that political reporters, most of whom favored George McGovern over Richard Nixon, were particularly hard on the South Dakota senator in order to avoid the appearance that they had lost their objectivity. Former *Washington Post* ombudsman Geneva Overholser said of charges of liberal bias, "The cumulative effect is the opposite: They're tougher on Democrats."[13] Typical journalists consider themselves trained professionals and see objectivity—however it may be defined—as residing at the core of their professionalism. Consequently, they may bend over backward to present conflicts in even-handed terms.

We suspect that this impulse was at play in the thirty-six days after the 2000 election. Although many reporters produced stories about the limitations of the punch-card balloting system (the *Washington Post* reported that "there is little disagreement among the experts that punch-card machines are not the best way to tabulate votes"[14]), none took the logical next step to test the claim of the Gore camp that, stylus in hand, a voter could fail to punch through the chad and turn in the ballot without being aware of the fact. When asked why not, Leonard Downie, executive editor of the *Washington Post*, said, "I don't see the point in doing a *Consumer Reports* kind of story on ballots."[15] One could hardly argue that the question of whether a voter might unintentionally produce a partially punched chad was inconsequential to the story of the Florida conflict; indeed, there were few questions of greater importance. Answering the question, however, would have produced evidence favorable to either Gore or Bush, something the press seemed eager to avoid.

As citizens, we rely on journalists to sort through competing claims and interpretations and tell us, above all, what is true and what is not. Of late, particularly in stories about political campaigns, that role has become less central to the identity of reporters than it ought to be. We share the belief of *Washington Post* columnist E. J. Dionne that "there is a need to resurrect a concern for what's true—to draw clearer distinctions between fact and opinion, between information and mere assertion, between flip predictions and reasoned analysis. At the same time, there is an urgent requirement . . . to demonstrate that the [public] debate is accessible and that it matters."[16]

While we should assume until we learn otherwise that political leaders are acting in good faith, unless rewards for truth telling and sanctions for dishonesty are in place, the temptation to distort the facts will prove too great for at least some. The custodianship of fact should be the bedrock underlying all the functions journalists perform. The principles we suggest center fact in political reporting and campaigning, tie campaigning more clearly to governance, and reduce audience confusion:

- First, use a "reasonable person standard" to decide when definition is needed and to interpret the accuracy of claims. This standard would sanction statements that are literally true but misleading.
- Second, define terms.
- Third, require those being covered to define their terms and apply the same definitions to claims about themselves and their opponents.

- Fourth, hold leaders accountable to consistently applied standards.
- Fifth, use widely accepted indicators to assess claims. Those who suppress or ignore such indicators should be regarded as violators of the public trust.
- Sixth, when candidates, parties, or others in power offer competing models to project future fact, the assumptions underlying the models should be articulated and explained.
- Seventh, when arguments about policy are illustrated with individual citizens, ask whether the examples offered are typical and thus accurately describe the effects of the policy in question.
- Eighth, fit the story to the facts, not the facts to the story.
- Ninth, tie the facts to a larger context to make sense of current debates.
- Tenth, be skeptical of the frames offered by those with an interest in shaping the news.

The Reasonable-Person Standard

If the end of rhetoric is judgment, then speakers must not only avoid statements that mislead but also provide what is required to guide listeners to accurate inferences. To meet these goals one need only ensure that those seeking high office satisfy the rhetorical needs of a reasonable person. Courts of law utilize this standard in a variety of types of cases, asking juries and judges to assess not what they believe or what they would do, but what a hypothetical reasonable person would believe or do. For instance, in suits alleging negligence, juries are asked whether the behavior of the defendant met the standard of what a reasonable person would have done in a similar situation. The reasonable-person standard is also used in interpreting contracts, to the extent that questions over what contractual language means are settled not by what one party might interpret them to mean (perhaps with fingers crossed), but by their meaning to a reasonable person.[17] Assessing a situation or question from this perspective requires no particular knowledge or training; it is understood to be within the capability of any citizen sitting on a jury. We will illustrate this standard with some recent cases that violated it.

On January 26, 1998, President Bill Clinton stared into the cameras and declared, "I want you to listen to me. I'm going to say this again: I did not have sexual relations with that woman, Miss Lewinsky." The carefully phrased rebuttal set a pattern that Clinton would follow when testifying for a grand jury. The rebuttal misled. In subsequent testimony both Bill Clinton and Monica Lewinsky confirmed sexual contact but not sexual intercourse as the term is usually defined.

If there was sexual contact, then the remaining question about Clinton's declaration about "that woman" before the cameras and before the grand jury is one of definition. If "sexual relations" is defined as intercourse, then Clinton may have been literally accurate when he denied sexual relations. However, in the context of the questions at issue, that move was misleading, a conclusion Clinton accepted when in his plea bargain to avoid post-presidential prosecution, he stated that "I tried to walk a fine line between acting lawfully and testifying falsely, but I now recognize that I did not fully accomplish this goal and that certain of my responses to questions about Ms. Lewinsky were false."[18]

Although he was not in a courtroom, when he made his first statement to the cameras Clinton employed a casuistic interpretation of the words he used in order to deceive his listeners and be able later to claim that his words were factual. When Clinton's grand jury testimony was released to the public, Americans saw their president engaged in a series of linguistic deconstructions, as he attempted to argue that the answers he gave about Lewinsky in his deposition in the Paula Jones case were, if deceptive, nonetheless literally true under some interpretations. As an attorney and former law professor, Clinton understood that if one chooses one's words carefully, one may deceive a judge and jury but escape the charge of perjury. In a political context, however, a reasonable person does not hear a politician's claim and then engage in the kind of linguistic literalism that Clinton's self-defense presupposed. The reasonable person would have understood Clinton's words as he hoped they would be understood, to say that he and Monica Lewinsky had had no sexual contact whatsoever.

Reporters may balk at interpreting the sundry meanings that may be drawn from a particular term, but they are nonetheless able to determine the meaning a reasonable person would find in a statement. Just as a jury in a negligence case can ascertain what a reasonable person would have done in the circumstances in question, reporters can distinguish truth from falsehood without probing motive or intent.

To take an example from Clinton's successor, when the Enron scandal began to break, President Bush was asked by reporters about his ties to that company's chair, Kenneth Lay, who had been a generous contributor to both Bush and the Republican party.[19] "He was a supporter of Ann Richards in my run in 1994," Bush said. "And she named him the head of the Governor's Business Council. And I decided to leave him in place, just for the sake of continuity. And that's when I first got to know Ken, and worked with Ken, and he supported my candidacy."[20]

Putting aside the question of whether Bush "first got to know" Lay after he took office, the part of the statement of interest here is whether Lay "was a supporter of Ann Richards" in the 1994 race. Lay did make a contribution to Richards's campaign, but he and his wife gave three times as much—$12,500—to Bush that year. As with Clinton's denial, how one judges Bush's statement is determined by the meaning attributed to the word "supporter." If by "supporter" Bush meant "made a contribution," then Lay was a supporter of both Richards and Bush, and thus it is accurate to say that Lay was a supporter of Richards. This is not the interpretation most listeners would make, however, because the questioner did not ask about Richards but about Bush himself. By answering the question with a statement about Richards, he made an implicit contrast—Lay supported Richards, not Bush. To make an analogy, if you ask, "Do you have a lawn mower?" and I reply, "My neighbor has one," you probably conclude that I do *not* have a lawn mower. If both my neighbor and I do in fact have mowers, my statement is accurate in a narrow sense but nonetheless misleading in result. The implication contained within the reasonable interpretation of the answer Bush gave—that Lay supported Richards and not Bush—is thus false, even if Lay had supported both candidates equally.

A reasonable-person standard recognizes a truth about human communication known to scholars of rhetoric since Aristotle's time. Rhetoric is enthymematic, meaning that it relies on listeners to participate in making sense of argument by filling in what is unstated. Meaning does not reside in texts—the words themselves—but rather in an intersection of a sender, a receiver, and a context. In the act of constructing meaning, audiences fill in premises left unarticulated by the source and indeed sometimes unintended by the sender. Confronted by ambiguities in language, audiences read in definitions of their own, a tendency that can be exploited by cunning speakers eager to feign surprise that someone heard something that was not actually said.

Although in these illustrations Clinton and Bush used language that invited false inferences to counter a charge made about them, the reasonable-person standard can be applied to any claim whose accuracy is in question. A reasonable person standard assumes that audiences will be told what is necessary to draw the correct inference. So, for example, when former CIA director Richard Helms told reporters in 1975, "As far as I know, the CIA was never responsible for assassinating any foreign leader," he was inviting the inference that the CIA had never attempted assassinations. When asked by reporter Daniel Schorr, "Were there discussions of possible assassinations?" Helms ducked again, responding, "There are always discussions about practically everything under the sun!" Ultimately Senator Frank Church, who led the Senate select committee charged with examining such questions, would report, "When Helms says that the CIA never killed any foreign leader, that statement is correct, but not necessarily complete." Schorr, who had aggressively pursued the story from its inception, closed out the story of the six-month Senate investigation with the line, "In the end it was as Richard Helms said—the CIA never killed anyone. But it wasn't for want of trying."[21] In the language of one of the world's major religions, it is possible to sin by omission as well as commission. It is the job of the press to spot and pursue the omission, as Schorr did in Helms's case.

A dispute over a 2000 presidential primary ad shows how the reasonable-person standard can be applied in campaigns. In his most deceptive ad of the primaries, George Bush's campaign alleged that John McCain opposed funding many women's health projects and breast cancer research. "McCain opposes funding for vital breast cancer programs right here in New York," the ad said. "He opposes funding for the North Shore Long Island Jewish breast cancer program and wants to cut funding for NYU's program in women's cancer. McCain is even against funding for breast cancer mapping, which is essential to breast cancer research." The omission? On the votes the ad referenced, McCain was objecting to the process by which the provisions had been added, not the substance of the bill. The Arizona senator opposed a bill containing more than $13 billion in spending, including some cancer research, because the provisions had not been vetted by Congress.

One doesn't need the details of McCain's intent in opposing the bill to come to a reasonable conclusion about the plausibility of Bush's claim. If you knew that the sister of the Arizona senator was a breast cancer survivor and that he had supported breast cancer research on ten earlier occasions, would you find it plausible that he opposed breast cancer research? Of course, one would have to know those facts to draw that inference. Interestingly, Bush himself applied the reasonable-person standard in assessing the ad. When asked if he personally believed that his opponent opposed breast cancer research, Governor Bush replied, "No, I don't believe that."[22]

The move in the Bush ad is one familiar to campaign watchers. After presenting a statement, vote, or action an opponent has taken, an ad argues inductively that the particular instance proves a general disposition. A single vote to reduce certain prison sentences proves that the candidate is "soft on crime." An inconsistent statement proves that the candidate "can't be trusted." A vote against a pork-barrel bill proves that the candidate "doesn't care about our district." In order to warrant such conclusions, a reasonable person would have to know why the candidate cast the vote and whether the instances cited are representative of the positions the candidate has taken most of the time. In McCain's case the reason for the vote was opposition to the process involved in passage of an omnibus bill and not representative of his position on funding for breast cancer research. Reporters should insist that when candidates move from the specific claim to the general attack on their opponents, the conclusions they draw are warranted by the facts.

Define Terms

Scholars, reporters, and pundits sometimes forget the extent to which they are filling in the premises and definitions that make sense of political exchanges. Because they think about politics and policy every day, they use terms and operate on understandings that are familiar to the knowledgeable but may be unknown to some in their audience. To take one small example, reporters routinely use the term "GOP" without noting what it stands for (Grand Old Party) or explaining that it refers to the Republican party. But do most ordinary citizens understand the term? The problem of definition emerges even in unlikely places. For example, a cautionary article in the *Philadelphia Inquirer* titled "With Statistics, Consider the Source and the Method" included the statement, "Last month, the Census Bureau started releasing figures showing a huge increase in the number of same-sex households from 1990 to 2000. Last week, it reversed course and told reporters not to compare the two sets of data because they had been 'edited' differently."[23] What the reporter assumed is that readers knew what the Census Bureau means by "same-sex household."

Common Definitions and Consistent Standards
of Accountability

In our daily lives, we expect the definitions ordinarily attached to words to hold in our exchanges with others. So, for example, when in congressional hearings about Enron, executive Nancy Temple characterized the results of an assessment of the company as "positive," committee chair Billy Tauzin (R-La.) responded, "We're trying to get to the facts here. But if you will characterize a report that indicates a decline in the value of Enron's stock and the serious risk of adverse publicity and litigation as a positive report from the attorneys, we're going to have trouble with your testimony today."[24]

Those engaged in public deliberation should also be expected to apply consistent definitions and standards of credit and blame. A reasonable person understands that a "cut" in Medicare would mean that less money would go to Medicare than had before; a reasonable person also understands that an "increase" in taxes means that people would pay more taxes than they had before. These definitions seem clear, but both have been the source of contention between the parties. Bill Clinton alleged in 1996 that by proposing a smaller increase in Medicare than Democrats wanted, Republicans were trying to "cut" the program, while George W. Bush declared in 2002 that by suggesting that a round of tax cuts that had yet to take effect be delayed, Democrats were advocating "raising taxes." In both cases, the president in question sought to confuse the public by defining a common term in a completely novel way. By presenting the argument in a balanced way in both cases (the president says this, the opposition disagrees), reporters failed to clarify the confusion.

Although most reporters failed to hold Bush to the common definition of "increase," they did apply a consistency standard to his claim. The *New York Times*, Tim Russert, and Tom Brokaw illustrated the role that journalism can play in clarifying messages and their meanings. "Time out," declared an article in the *Times*. "Didn't Jeb Bush, the governor of Florida and the president's brother, sign into law last month a delay in a scheduled state tax cut . . . ? Therefore is that not, using the White House math, a tax increase?" When asked, President Bush's secretary, Ari Fleischer, offered a nonresponse: "That's a state matter, and the president doesn't weigh in on state matters." When pressed on the inconsistency by Tim Russert on *Meet the Press*, Republican Party chairman Marc Racicot finally conceded, "I think that argument can be made in all fairness, yes."[25] But a few hours later, Racicot issued a press release saying, "I do not believe Gov. Bush supports any sort of tax increase."[26] Trying one last time, Tom Brokaw gently raised the issue with President Bush, who dodged the question:

> Brokaw: Some of your advisers here in the White House are saying to the Democrats on Capitol Hill, "If you defer the tax cuts we'd like to have, that's the same as a tax increase."
> Bush: Yeah.
> Brokaw: Will you say to Jeb, "Hey, if you defer, you're raising taxes in Florida?"
> Bush: No, what I'm going to say to him is that we've got different circumstances. One, I'm not—there's not a balanced-budget amendment that constrains the federal government, and in times of war or national emergency or recession, we might run a deficit, and we will.[27]

Often, it is political cartoonists who best point out the implications of such word games. As the question of delaying tax cuts was being discussed, cartoonist Ted Rall penned a cartoon he titled "Logical Extremes," with a boss telling his underling, "Not firing you is the same as doubling your salary."

The press should also hold officials to common standards of crediting and blaming. Republican nominee Bob Dole, for example, said to Bill Clinton in a 1996 debate, "The record is pretty clear in Arkansas. When you were governor, drug use doubled." If Clinton, as governor, was responsible for the increase in drug use in Arkansas, then presumably we can extrapolate that the Republican governors were responsible for the rise in teen drug use in their states during Clinton's term as president. Similarly, in 2000 George W. Bush tagged the Clinton-Gore administration with an "education recession" while taking credit for improved test scores in Texas. But if Bush deserved credit for improvements in Texas, then wouldn't the governors of other states, and not the federal government, be responsible for the education recession?

Using Accepted Sources and Indicators to Arbitrate Claims

In political debate much of the discussion focuses on individuals taking credit or ascribing blame for the consequences of past action. Alternatively, they forecast positive or negative effects for proposed action. In order to do so, they use accepted concepts and uncontroversial measures. For example, the concept "joblessness" is typically measured by the unemployment rate. In this same basket of tools are such indicators as the Consumer Price Index and Gross Domestic Product. Although these measures are imperfect—the unemployment rate excludes those who have given up and stopped seeking a job, for example—we don't ordinarily debate their legitimacy in campaigns. Instead, we assume that they have been arrived at by trusted individuals, using disclosed, careful methods, and are released on a regular timetable without an eye toward the likely political impact of the report.

Another of our principles holds that thou shalt not deny the public accepted measures. When all parties agree on the way to measure a phenomenon, and a respected group renders the measure, we increase the likelihood that it will be the standard for comparison. The lack of a reliable measure to determine how many people are homeless, for example, makes it difficult to discuss changes across time and hence the effects of efforts to address the problem. Indeed, it makes it less likely that we will discuss it at all, because without numbers it is difficult to assess the extent and significance of the problem.

Denying the public access to measures administered by an institution without a stake in the debate assaults the quality of public discourse. Scholars, pundits, and the press should have called attention to a move made by the Republicans in power early in 2001 that made it more difficult to make the kinds of judgments that facilitate intelligent debate about an important matter. David Rosenbaum of the *New York Times* did this well when he wrote: "Less data is available on the Bush plan than has usually been the case with big tax cuts . . . [T]his year with Republicans in charge of the White House and both houses of Congress for the first time in almost 50 years, neither the Treasury nor Congress has provided distributional tables on President Bush's tax plan."[28]

The reason? "Republicans have never liked that kind of measurement, saying it contributed to class warfare." Distributional tables, which show the impact of a tax plan on people at various income levels, enable one to compare the benefits received by the lower, middle, and upper classes. The other reason the administration was reluctant to offer distribution tables: the existence of such data confirmed the claim made by Gore in the 2000 election about the extent to which the upper 1% benefited disproportionately from the Bush tax cut. Whether the plan had this effect couldn't be as readily assessed when the accepted measure was suppressed.

Assumptions Underlying Alternative Models
Should Be Disclosed and Explained

When respected institutions produce different "factual conclusions" in answering a single question, it is important that they disclose, and the press explains, the variation. If the press fails to explain the underlying assumptions, we risk the public perception either that there is no consensual data, that everything is relative, or, in the worst-case scenario, that everyone is lying. For instance, in late August 2001 the White House projected a larger surplus over the next ten years than did the Congressional Budget Office, and the Democrats believed that there would be even less than the amount projected by the CBO. The difference: The White House assumed higher economic growth than that assumed by CBO and the Democrats. The CBO didn't include any of the projected spending not already passed into law and so failed to include the cost of Bush's plans for the military and prescription drugs.

When various political actors offer differing predictions about the future, it is thus essential not only that they use common measures but that the assumptions built into their predictions be clearly explicated. The nature of prediction allows for plenty of slippery argumentation by manipulating those assumptions. If you don't like the way your numbers turn out, you can simply assume higher or lower growth, more or less future spending.

Because a change in the assumptions underlying a concept can result in radically different interpretations, explaining the differences is an important journalistic task. Reporters often perform this function admirably. For instance, in February 2002 the unemployment rate fell despite the fact that the country had lost 89,000 jobs in the month before. Why would this happen? Was the news good or bad? The *Philadelphia Inquirer* explained in an article's subheading: "Jobless Rate Posts First Drop Since May: It was 5.6 percent nationally in January, down from 5.8. But the reason was not more work—just fewer people seeking it."[29] The article explained that the unemployment rate is a function not of those without work but those without work who are actively seeking work. The decline in the unemployment rate was a result of fewer people seeking work, not more people finding it.

Assessing Typicality

Because humans are inclined to assume that dramatic, visually evocative stories about a specific instance can be generalized to many more, testing the typicality of stories is an important task facing reporters. Just as reporters often interview an individual citizen as a narrative device to illustrate the effects of a trend or policy, candidates commonly use ordinary citizens as illustrations of their or their opponents' plans and records. When they do so, the critical question reporters should ask is not whether the strategy is effective, but whether the story being offered is typical and thus fundamentally accurate. It is the generalization—this citizen represents other citizens—that should be in question.

Judging the larger truth represented in the specific story is an important task for voters and hence for the reporters who bring such stories to them through news. In order to illustrate this principle, we examine the "tax families" used by the Bush campaign in 2000 to argue in favor of Bush's tax plan and against Gore's. Many journalists who covered the "tax families" accepted them as typical illustrations of the impact of both Gore's and Bush's tax plans when they were neither.

In the fall of 2000 the Bush campaign sent out a request to its offices throughout the battleground states, seeking families with a very specific profile. They sought families with incomes between $35,000 and $70,000 and without child-care expenses, college-age children, babies under one year old, or parents in nursing homes. Those who fit the bill might appear with George W. Bush at campaign events. In other words, the campaign was trying to find families who would not benefit from any of Al Gore's "targeted" tax cuts.

The reason was simple. Depending on their income, those with young or college-age children might receive more benefits from Gore than Bush. Wanting to deflect attention from the fact that the wealthy would receive the bulk of Bush's tax reductions, the campaign hoped that these families would invite the inference that those who would benefit most from Bush and more from Bush than Gore were middle-class Americans. The move largely succeeded. Reports mentioning the "tax families" made the atypical seem typical by their focus on the personal evocative stories of these supposedly typical ordinary Americans. Bush in effect made two claims when he presented a "tax family," both of which should have been evaluated: first, that the family in question was typical, and second, that a typical family received more benefits under his plan than Gore's.

Occasional print stories carefully sorted through the two tax plans; for instance, Mike Allen of the *Washington Post* analyzed the "tax family" strategy and offered a careful explanation of the benefits both plans contained for ordinary families,[30] just as there were examples where journalists compared the details and implications of the candidates' plans on other issues.[31] However, these were far outnumbered by stories that accepted the Bush campaign's claims at face value, examining not their content but the intentions behind them. For example, in this story from ABC News on September 17, reporter Ron Claiborne tells us about the "tax family" strategy and quotes print reporters doing the same; none makes an attempt to assess the accuracy of Bush's argument:

> **Claiborne:** At every stop Bush brings out these what he calls "tax families," people who benefit, he says, under his tax plan and would not benefit as much under Gore's tax plan. And it's sort of an odd circumstance that he sort of trots them out almost like human props.
> **Bush:** But I want to share a real-life story with you. The Burkes are here—beautiful family, Tim and Michelle.
> **Deborah Orin** (*New York Post*): It's a stunt. Every campaign does stunts. This is one of Bush's stunts.
> **Frank Bruni** (*New York Times*): These tax families, because they're local people appearing in a local setting, tend to do very well for the Bush campaign on local newscasts. Given how seldom network newscasts do big pieces on the campaign, that's very important.

The story is critical of Bush, but not on any substantive basis; instead, the campaign is said to use the families as "human props" in a "stunt." The question of who benefited from the candidates' tax plans was one in which journalistic refereeing was needed. Making sense of the subject required time to parse the two complex plans and the expertise to evaluate the competing claims. The candidates themselves offered incompatible arguments, each contending that his plan helped ordinary families the most; and the answer was a complex one. But more often than not, reporters quoted the back-and-forth exchanges, commented on the campaigns' strategies, and left it at that, as this story from CBS News did on September 6:

> **Dan Rather:** In the presidential campaign, a new chapter today in the competing claims of Al Gore and George Bush over who has the better plan to keep the American economy healthy. In fact, Gore weighed in with twelve chapters, his detailed blueprint, while Bush ridiculed it. CBS's John Roberts has been sorting the facts on their figures.
> **John Roberts:** Al Gore took a swipe today at what he called George Bush's "cross your fingers" economics and laid out, in exhaustive detail, his economic plan for America.

Al Gore: You don't have to guess at what the specifics are. You can read my plan.

Roberts: Two hundred pages, twelve chapters long, the plan outlines tax cuts and legislation to achieve ten specific goals, including plans to make America debt-free by 2012, raise family incomes by a third, reduce poverty to below 10 percent of the population, and shrink the economic gender gap.

Gore: Let's cut the wage gap between men and women. In fact, let's cut it in half.

Roberts: The strategy was meant to make George W. Bush look vague by comparison, but the Texas governor today had a few details of his own.

George W. Bush: When my opponent talks about tax cuts for the middle class, what he forgets to tell you is that 50 million Americans will not receive any tax relief under his plan.

Roberts: On the campaign trail, the rhetoric has turned white hot. At every stop today, Bush appeared with middle-income families he claimed would benefit from his proposal but not Gore's.

Bush: Under the vice president's plan, they rec—they—they get no savings.

Gore: I will not go along with a huge tax cut for the wealthy at the expense of everyone else.

Roberts: Gore wants to paint the Texas governor as a threat to prosperity. Bush is tarring the vice president as a big spender of historic proportions. Whomever voters believe, experts caution, both sides are making plans based on economists' best guesses.

Todd Buchholz (Financial Analyst): They've proved incapable of predicting this mammoth surplus. They're probably equally unable to predict a decline in the surplus. So you can't trust budget projections.

Roberts: But they certainly let candidates promise the moon. Gore even used Republican surplus projections when he proposed today a $300 billion rainy-day fund in case there's a downturn. It's money his own budget office said isn't there.

While its questioning of the plausibility of the figures for the surplus is useful, the report fails to pair the candidates' plans for spending or taxing. Instead we hear the candidates' charges, are offered a strategic analysis, then hear from a financial analyst who contributes yet more uncertainty. The result is that viewers get the competing claims, but no attempt to decipher the consensual facts at the base of each; the story closes by implying that both candidates are distorting the facts and "promis[ing] the moon."

With the "tax families," Bush offered a concrete narrative where Gore had only numbers. The family was the Republican nominee's protagonist—they struggled, worked hard, had trouble making ends meet; Bush's tax cut would ease their lives. Personal dramatic narrative is the raw stuff of which news accounts are fashioned. Reporters understand well the power of personal stories. They use them every day, describing policies and events through the experiences of individuals who act as exemplars. A contemporary news story on, for instance, the effects of welfare reform is likely to begin and end with a profile of an individual welfare mother; the policy information will be telegraphed in the middle of the story. There is no reason to believe that reporters are incapable of discovering whether what a candidate says about an individual family is accurate.

The core of Bush's argument on taxes was that while under Gore's plan some people received tax breaks and others did not, under his plan everyone received a tax break. However, there was a critical caveat to this argument, which was that because Bush was proposing reductions in *income* tax rates, his plan did not provide any benefits to those Americans whose income is too small to pay income taxes but who nonetheless pay substantial payroll taxes to fund the Social Security and Medicare systems. Because all wage earners pay payroll taxes, but those below a certain level of income pay no income taxes, a quarter of American taxpayers received no benefit from the Bush plan.

In order for Bush to portray his tax plan accurately, he would therefore have had to make the distinction between income taxes and payroll taxes. Much of the time, he did so; his summative statement about his plan was that "if you pay income taxes, you get tax relief." However, Bush occasionally truncated the statement to "If you pay taxes, you get tax relief," a formulation that was false. But reporters seldom corrected Bush when he made this statement and rarely said that it needed explanation. In some cases, journalists mischaracterized Bush's plan in the same way he had. For instance, the *Omaha World Herald*, in endorsing Bush, cited "his proposal for a tax cut for everybody who pays taxes."[32] Bush's omission may or may not have been deliberate, although the fact that he made the incorrect statement dozens of times, including in all three presidential debates, suggests that it was more likely intended.

Reporters also failed to address the intersection of rhetoric and policy represented by the tax families. Whether the figures Bush offered on their tax savings were accurate and the extent to which they were representative were questions requiring answers if citizens were to evaluate the two candidates' plans. The fact that Bush's tax families were not particularly representative, but were carefully chosen as examples of those families who would receive no or minimal benefits under Gore's plan, was highly relevant. The conclusion Bush was encouraging—that Gore's tax plan did little or nothing to help ordinary working families—was untrue. In fact, some families benefited more under Bush's plan and some benefited more under Gore's plan, depending on whether they had children in child care or in college or were caring for elderly relatives.

The contrast between the treatment of the tax families and Gore's statement in their first debate that a girl in Sarasota had to stand in science class because of overcrowding—one of which was often tacitly accepted and the other investigated aggressively—is instructive. Bush's argument about the families was literally true—his figures about each individual family were accurate—but invited a false inference, that ordinary families received nothing from the Gore plan. The story of the girl in Sarasota was literally false—although she had had to stand in class for a time, by the time of the debate she had been given a chair—but invited a true inference, that many American public schools suffer from overcrowding. If a story told by a candidate is literally true but invites a false inference, reporters are far less likely to explore it for deception than a story that contains a literal inaccuracy but whose fundamental argument is true. The former requires the reporter to deal in the uncomfortable ground of implication and inference, in effect reaching inside the mind of the listener.

A good rule of thumb would be that the effort reporters put into investigating the accuracy of a claim and the space devoted to the results of that investigation should correspond to the centrality of the claim to the candidate's argument or character. Gore's example suggested that he trusted a news story, and concerned an issue—overcrowded classrooms—that played a small part in the campaign. Whether Bush's tax families accurately showcased his and Gore's tax plans was of far greater importance; as the centerpiece of Bush's campaign, the tax issue should have been explored in depth, with typicality rewarded and its opposite unmasked.

But the public was ill-served in the case of the tax plans not because reporters didn't spend enough time discussing the issue, but rather because they allowed the strategic narrative to overwhelm a discussion of the facts being contested. If reporters found the "tax families" to be a gimmick, they would have served their audiences better not by discussing the strategy, but by investigating its factual underpinnings. The gimmick either did or did not accurately describe the two candidates' plans; whether it did was the most critical question.

Fit the Story to the Facts,
Not the Facts to the Story

Throughout this book we have observed the ways in which stories organize facts. When they do so in a compelling way, not subject to ready disconfirmation, unless a credible source actively offers a competing account of the facts, reporters are less likely either to search out or see facts that undercut the coherence of the story. That was the case with Tonkin Gulf, the supposed success of the Patriot missiles, and the babies allegedly thrown from incubators. The failure to find or alternatively feature the facts in the cases we have drawn from campaigns—Horton and the Bush tax families—was a function of the fact that the story being told by reporters was one of strategy and tactics, a story that makes its meaning out of asking why. When the focus is strategy, questions of accuracy of the tactically deployed assertions from the campaign do not cohere with the narrative.

The frames that reporters adopt carry with them story lines whose usefulness in the moment should be subject to ongoing review. As we saw in cases such as that of William Horton, what is and is not factually relevant is a function of story line. The story of strategy and tactics features and then accounts for standing in polls and explains how various groups are being targeted to achieve needed votes and turnout. It balances the views of the competing sides seeking office and in the process risks treating all contested fact as a matter of opinion or as evidence of spin and counterspin. The players in this story are cast as self-interested partisans. The underlying tendency in the story line is cynical, with the implication that all who seek office pander and distort. Even when reporters are at their most cynical or appear to be acting as stenographers to government, they attempt to describe events and individuals by giving coherence to the inchoate details of a complex world. That coherence, however, sometimes can be purchased at the price of inaccuracy.

Tie the Facts to a Larger Context

When reporters tie the facts at hand to the larger policy debate in ways that help the public see the connections between specific policies and larger concerns, their successful arbitration of competing claims can enlighten the citizenry. A March 2002 *Washington Post* article exploring the arguments favoring and opposing drilling for oil in the Arctic National Wildlife Refuge shows how reporters can help citizens navigate arguments in which facts, policies, and predictions are contested. In this exemplary piece, Michael Grunwald synopsized the rhetoric, then clarified the factual basis for the major points of contention between the two sides. "The two sides cannot even agree on the terms of the debate: drilling opponents refer to 'the Arctic refuge' or 'the coastal plain,' while proponents tend to call it 'ANWR' or 'the 1002 area,' a legal term," noted Grunwald. His report then went on to answer such questions as "How much oil is out there?" and "Would it [the proposed drilling] reduce the nation's dependence on foreign oil?" His answer to the question "Will drilling sully the refuge's wilderness values?" illustrates the clarifying power of good reporting:

> The simple answer is yes. The coastal plain will have a massive industrial complex on it. The more complicated questions are: How massive? And to what effect?
>
> Oil technology has progressed dramatically beyond the hulking, sprawling infrastructure of Prudhoe Bay; the newer Alpine field nearby sucks oil from an area as big as the District of Columbia on a pad the size of the Capitol grounds. The ANWR bill that passed the House would limit the "footprint" of oil infrastructure that touches the tundra to 2,000 acres. And while those acres could be spread throughout the coastal plain, Alaska would still retain more than half of the United States' designated wilderness—an area the size of Pennsylvania, New Jersey, West Virginia and Maryland combined. Norton has also vowed to limit drilling to winter and to require ice roads and other methods to minimize the environmental impacts.
>
> Still, there will be impacts. Oil infrastructure damages tundra and vegetation even when it doesn't spill; and at Prudhoe Bay, there has been an average of a spill a day, mostly small, but totaling 1.5 million gallons of toxic materials since 1995. In the Kenai National Wildlife Refuge near Anchorage, the Fish and Wildlife Service is studying whether 350 toxic spills from oil fields have contributed to an abnormal number of deformed frogs.[33]

In other words, the issue is more complex than advocates and opponents have made it out to be. Each is telling only part of the story of probable impact. Reporting such as Grunwald's enlightens the citizenry and improves judgment on the issue in three ways. First, it provides readers with information to evaluate the claims and counterclaims. Second, it creates a climate conducive to a more nuanced policy debate. Third, it serves as a resource for other journalists reporting on the same debate. This piece thus makes it more likely that future stories will describe distortions as such, creating a penalty for omission and selective uses of evidence.

Be Skeptical About Frames

Sophisticated political actors attempt to shape the frames reporters adopt
in writing their stories. They understand that by restricting the questions being asked and the answers being offered, they can move debates
to more friendly ground, increasing their chances of success. In response,
reporters need not adopt a cynical posture, assuming all arguments are
disingenuous. What they can do is continually examine not only the
frames they adopt but those being offered to them, as Ted Koppel did in
an interview in March 2001, when an official tried to change the subject
after Koppel raised the question of American politicians being bribed
by drug dealers. While reporters need not go as far as Koppel did when
he said, "That's a bullshit answer,"[34] they should be aware of, and willing
to go beyond, the frames they employ and interested political actors try
to impose.

To take a case in which a number of these principles were needed to
resolve a factual dispute of considerable import, we can apply them to a
question raised during the 2000 campaign: How much did the wealthiest
1% of Americans get from the tax cut George W. Bush proposed? One of
the oldest Democratic arguments is that the Republicans support the rich
and the Democrats everyone else. When politicians debate tax policy, this
general principle translates into often confusing numbers:

> **Gore:** Almost half of all the tax cut benefits, as I said, under
> Governor Bush's plan, go to the wealthiest 1%. I think we have to
> make the right and responsible choices.
> **Bush:** The man's practicing fuzzy math again. The facts are: After
> my plan, the wealthiest of Americans pay more taxes of the
> percentage of the whole than they do today.

Here Bush engaged in what John Stuart Mill called pseudo rebuttal,
a move that pretends to engage the facts of an opposing argument but
instead puts in place alternative evidence that fails to directly take on the
offered data. The evidence itself need not be bad—it may in fact be accurate—but the relevance of the supposed rebuttal to the opposing claim
is not established. Instead the pseudo rebuttal is a tacit concession framed
as a rejection.

But juxtaposing unengaged fact is only the first part of pseudo rebuttal. If one set of facts simply follows another, a discerning viewer
might surmise that one candidate either didn't hear or didn't understand the point being made by the other. Alternatively, those who fail to

ascertain that both claims may indeed be true may instead assume that both are false. Or they may conclude that there is not a clear factual basis for understanding this issue. But in 2000 Bush added another problematic element to such exchanges by rejecting accurate claims by Gore as "fuzzy math," indicating that there was a computational error in Gore's analysis that could be corrected. After doing so, he then offered data that failed to address Gore's evidence. In other words, he signaled that he was going to rebut the false claim or expose the fuzzy math and then failed to do so.

Do the standards we've suggested help us make sense of the exchange? The first problem is definition. Which taxes? Gore meant estate tax plus income tax. Bush meant only income tax. In other words, without saying so, Bush excluded a significant benefit the wealthy would receive as a result of his proposed repeal of the estate tax. What is the measure? Gore meant to say half of all of the *benefits of Bush's tax cut* would go to the wealthiest 1%. Bush didn't dispute this claim directly but instead categorized it as fuzzy math and shifted ground to claim that the wealthiest individuals—note that he did not say 1%—would pay a higher percent of *income taxes* after his proposal was enacted than they did before.

How well did reporters do in making sense of this exchange and the others like it in the debates? Some performed better than others. After a paragraph on income tax cuts, the 2000 *Newsweek* voter guide explained: "Who gains? Gore says that 42 percent of the benefits [of Bush's proposed plan] go to the richest one percent; Bush says the figure is only 21 percent. The truth lies in between; just where, no one knows."[35] No one knows? Define terms clearly and specify the model and we can know quite clearly. Consensual fact does exist on this issue, but it isn't arrived at by a split-the-difference relativism. Gore's 42% is a calculation that includes the proposed elimination of the estate tax; Bush's 21% is a calculation of income tax benefits only. By failing to define terms and implying that Gore was talking about income tax, *Newsweek* mischaracterized his claim. By the reasonable-person standard, the exchange is about all of the benefits of the total tax-cut package. If one hears this meaning, then Bush's claim that Gore was practicing fuzzy math was incorrect.

The *Newsweek* assessment is balanced: Bush says one thing, Gore says another, and we the citizens are left to decide who is right. But in cases where a single standard could resolve the question, accepting the legitimacy—or presuming the falsity—of both sides can stand in the way of clarification.

Did the broadcast media sort out the debate? On NBC Lisa Myers said, "But on one of the most contentious issues of the debate, how much Bush's tax cuts would benefit the wealthy, most experts say Gore is right." By contrast, on Fox News Brit Hume observed that "it now appears that the central charge made by Vice President Gore in Tuesday night's debate is not true under any neutral analysis of George W. Bush's tax plan." Here Myers was accurate.

Of course, if candidates engaged in full disclosure there would be no need for Hume and Myers to step into the void created by the absence of engaged fact. In a world of engaged fact, we envision exchanges that go something like this: "Yes, Mr. Vice President, almost half of my tax cuts in dollars, 42 cents of every dollar to be more exact, go to those in the upper 1%. Before explaining why, let's make sure we're all on the same page. I cut income tax rates and eliminate the estate tax. Since the upper 1% pay roughly a third of the income tax dollars, I think they should get the same percent back. On the estate tax, which is currently applied to individuals with more than $675,000 in assets, I don't think it's fair that those with less than $675,000 don't have to pay any estate tax and those with more do. There's another reason I oppose all estate taxes. I take it as a matter of principle that the same assets should not be taxed twice. That's what the estate tax does."

Gore would say: "Yes, Governor, you're right. I believe people who inherit large sums should have to pay taxes on that income." In response to Bush's charge that Gore's claim that he reduced government was false, Gore would say: "You're right, Governor. A lot of the cut in government personnel was the result of downsizing the military in the post-cold war period, but there was a 100,000-person drop in nonmilitary areas. So I think it's fair to say that we haven't increased the size of government." The first benefit of this level of disclosure is that it would eliminate proposals that won't be accepted by voters if fully explained. The second is that voters will not feel betrayed when the elected official translates the promise into governance.

Why don't those running for the presidency follow these principles? One might suggest that they believe that they are more likely to be elected if the electorate is confused or misled about some of their proposals. But if that is the case, then we have conventionalized a form of campaigning that is all but incapable of predicting governance, a form likely to enhance public cynicism.

A second possibility is that those running for office fear that the concession such engagement entails will be contorted into a killer sound bite in ads. It doesn't take much to imagine the consultants gleefully extracting "Yes the upper 1% do get 40% of the money in my tax plan . . ." in the same way that the Democrats extracted "They want the federal government controlling the Social Security, like it's some kind of federal program" from a speech by Bush or the Republicans extracted what seemed to be a claim that he "invented" the Internet from an answer by Gore. Of course, a reasonable-person standard would penalize those who take statements out of context.

One might also guess that politicians feel licensed to engage in selective omission because they are confident that reporters writing on deadline will not have the time or disposition to parse clarity from the confusion. The result? If the exchange is covered at all, it will probably be cast as a case of he said/he said.

Before wielding these principles like a club over the statements of candidates, it is important to remember that like the rest of us, candidates misspeak occasionally not because they are trying to deceive but because they are tired, distracted, or bored. Therefore, we offer a set of cautions.

First, reporters should presume goodwill and integrity until it is demonstrably clear that our faith in an individual is unwarranted. This notion reduces to *give them the benefit of the doubt*. A single incorrect statement does not deception make. Furthermore, accountability should rise with repetition. What this means in practice is that contrary to the preconceptions of the pundits, misstatements by Gore did not necessarily signal calculation, nor did misstatements by Bush necessarily betray ignorance. Like the rest of us, candidates occasionally misspeak because they are tired, distracted, or focused on their next thought. We would place a number of statements from the second debate in this category, including Gore's claim that his $10,000 college-tuition tax deduction was per child per year (it was per family) and Bush's notion that our allies should put troops into peacekeeping (which they were already doing). He probably meant to say they should do more.

If candidates or their campaigns promptly acknowledge the mistake and don't repeat it in ads or on the stump, we should do unto the candidates what we expect others to do unto us and forgive the lapse. They should therefore be held more accountable for repeatedly aired ads than for a single slip in a debate or on the stump. Both should have pulled their ads saying the other would force seniors into HMOs for their prescription drug benefits, for example, because in both cases participation was voluntary. Were a candidate to become a chronic corrector, the electorate could draw the appropriate conclusion.

We can illustrate this principle with an example from the Iowa caucus period. After Gore asked a farmer named Chris Peterson to stand in the January 8 Iowa debate, the vice president explained that Peterson's farm was flooded in 1993 and Gore and Iowa Senator Tom Harkin "got the extra billion dollars of disaster relief to help Chris and the others who were flooded." To this point Gore was literally accurate. The difference between the final administration position and the position Bill Bradley initially took was one billion dollars. But then Gore got carried away and framed a question to Bradley that assumed that Bradley opposed *any* aid to Peterson. "Why did you vote against the disaster relief for Chris Peterson when he and thousands of other farmers here in Iowa needed it after those '93 floods?" Bradley failed to rebut the claim, which he could easily have done since he supported four billion dollars in aid, opposed an amendment providing an additional billion on the grounds that he didn't think it would benefit the farmers, but when the amendment passed, supported the full five billion. Instead of noting the facts, the local press covered the exchange strategically. As the *Omaha World-Herald* (a paper read by many Iowans) put it the following day, "Many who watched Saturday's Democratic presidential debate gave the nod to Vice President Al Gore because, they said, he was able to show that rival Bill Bradley hasn't always been a friend of the farmer."[36] Our survey data showed that Bradley dropped in favor among Iowans after the debate. The uncorrected inference that Bradley opposed all aid proved consequential. Under a rule that says that relevant facts should be disclosed, Gore had violated a principle and by the reasonable-person standard misled. Bradley hadn't done his job either. Nor did the press.

Gore's phrasing in the debate might have been an inadvertent misstatement. If so, he should have corrected it immediately after the debate. However, instead of doing so his campaign then aired an ad in which Tom Harkin said, "In fact, Al Gore was the only Democratic candidate for president who helped make sure that Iowa got the help we desperately needed after those floods." At that point, the reasonable-person standard says that the campaign had engaged in deliberate deception.

A second caution would be that *all misstatements are not created equal.* Neither misremembering the tune "Look for the Union Label," if in fact that is what Gore did, nor failing a pop quiz on the leaders of small nations as Bush did, is the moral equivalent of repeatedly misrepresenting one's opponent's record or a central policy proposal. When reporters make an inductive argument about a candidate's mistake— for example, that it "raises questions" about his fitness for office—they should articulate for their audiences why the mistake is important and worthy of extended discussion.

In sum, campaign rhetoric as currently practiced too often fractures the audience into enclaves uncritically accepting different sets of facts. This minimizes not only the sense that we are one community, but also our commitment to governance and the ability of citizens to engage each other in debate and discussion about public affairs. It also dulls critical skills by habituating audiences to move to contesting fact or articulating opposing principles, eliminating the need for a facility for using common standards of judgment and assessment. When this occurs, vigilant, knowledgeable reporters are the public's last best hope.

If candidates would see us as reasonable citizens who require the information needed to draw accurate inferences about their positions and who need common definitions and modes of assessment to judge whether one alternative constructs a better future than another, we could be far less concerned that citizens are confused or misled, or that presidents are elected on their strategic skill at manipulating and mobilizing rather than their ability to make a stronger case for their vision of the future than their opponent's. If reporters would grant the candidates occasional lapses when accompanied by acknowledgment and correction, we would not only reduce some of the pressure associated with campaigning but also reward candidates for admitting and correcting mistakes, thus cultivating a useful disposition among those elected to lead. In both cases it is the press that could increase candidate accountability and public understanding.

Conclusion

W hile we chide reporters for their failures we also indict the way politics is practiced and our own shortcomings as citizens. When those communicating to the press provide inadequate definitions, play fast and loose with the facts, and fail to show the trade-offs inherent in governing, the task of reporters is made more complicated. But where the ballot doesn't permit citizens to check a box or punch a chad indicating dissatisfaction with the quality of campaign discourse, reporters must go beyond bemoaning the sad state of political argument. Citizens need journalists to fill in the blanks when definitions are wanting, test evidence when its legitimacy is in question, and concentrate not on who will win or lose but on the ways in which the proposals of candidates and officeholders would affect individual lives.

The proposal we offer is a simple one. Reporters should help the public make sense of competing political arguments by defining terms, filling in needed information, assessing the accuracy of the evidence being offered, and relating the claims and counterclaims to the probable impact of the proposed policies on citizens and the country.

For decades, Walter Cronkite, America's most respected journalist, closed his nightly news program on CBS with the statement "That's the way it is." We have seen that "the way it is" is determined by news frames constructed by journalists. If journalism is, as *Washington Post* publisher Philip Graham described it, "the first rough draft of history," at times the draft is rougher than it might be.

Journalists themselves acknowledge the complexities of navigating, discovering, and relating facts in the political world. As columnist David Broder wrote, "My experience suggests that we often have a hard time finding our way through the maze of facts—visible and concealed—in any story. We often misjudge character, mistake plot lines. And even when the facts seem most evident to our senses, we go astray by our misunderstanding or misjudgment of the context in which they belong."[1] As we have seen, shifting frames and compelling story lines help explain some of the circumstances in which those misjudgments are more likely to occur.

We began by focusing on stories told through the press by those who were either deceived or actively deceiving. We saw cases such as Tonkin Gulf and babies hurled from their incubators, in which the truth eventually emerged, often through the persistence of reporters who concluded that the first draft of history had gotten it wrong. In these cases the first draft appeared in daily papers and broadcasts and a more accurate account emerged later in longer pieces and books. Although in these cases the public was ill served by journalism in the moment, it was well served in the longer term. So we agree with former *Washington Post* executive editor Ben Bradlee when he wrote that "the fact is that the truth does emerge, and its emergence is a normal, and vital, process of democracy."[2]

But in crucial moments, inaccurate stories are often initially believed by the public with consequences for elections and governance. In the case of Tonkin Gulf, the facts were inaccessible at the time the event occurred. Reporters could not have known what happened at Tonkin Gulf until those who were there revealed what they knew. Similarly, reporters would have had difficulty discovering what happened to babies in incubators in Kuwait, because the country was closed to reporters at the time. But in the case of the "Willie Horton" narrative, information that was misreported was readily available. In the first two cases reporters should have reported the stories as alleged versions and in a skeptical frame sought confirming or disconfirming evidence. In the third, reporters could and should have gone to Massachusetts, or made the calls to the custodians of the record—law-enforcement officials and local journalists—to discover the facts. But in nearly every instance in which the press misses parts of the story, there are individual reporters who invest the time and effort to go beyond the dominant frames and ask the questions that reveal the facts on which those controversies rest.

We opened this book with a series of questions about factual disputes that occurred during the period on which we have focused, from mid-2000 to early 2002. We asked why some facts were featured and others ignored, some deceptions punished and others excused, some disagreements settled and others left unresolved. In each case, the answer turned on the interaction between events, the perspectives through which reporters saw events, the narrative themes driving the news, and the frames in which those stories were ultimately cast when presented to the public. The press's focus on strategy overwhelmed factual explication of the effects of the candidates' tax plans and the reasons overseas ballots were or were not counted in Florida. Reporters' impulse to act as amateur psychologists created frames in which some of George W. Bush and Al Gore's words were given outsized importance and others overlooked. A year later, a patriotic lens altered the standards by which Bush was judged and determined journalists' retrospective analyses of the Florida vote. In each case, the public's understanding of the moment was shaped in part by the facts and frames featured in news.

The press serves many functions in a democracy. It informs the public of the world's events; it prepares citizens for democratic participation; it acts as a watchdog to expose government failure and corruption; and it serves as a conduit between government and citizens, informing each of the other's beliefs and intentions. Often, reporters see themselves as stand-ins for the citizenry. In campaigns, they ask the questions the public would ask, explore the weaknesses the public would find important, and celebrate what the public would find compelling. This does not mean that the press should assess public opinion in order to determine its day-to-day coverage, nor that it should examine polls to determine which candidate ought to receive more favorable coverage during a campaign. The stand-in role dictates, to a great extent, giving the public not what it wants but what it needs. At times these are one and the same, and at times not.

The notion of journalism as a tool of participation is one often cited by reporters. Bill Kovach and Tom Rosenstiel of the Committee of Concerned Journalists argue that "the purpose of journalism is to provide people with the information they need to be free and self-governing."[3] Leonard Downie and Robert Kaiser of the *Washington Post* write, "Only great newspapers systematically provide the factual information, interpretation and commentary that make the American system work. The journalism that the great newspapers produce is the basis of the shared knowledge and experiences that make us a relatively self-aware and cohesive society."[4] While we agree that the best in journalism can usually be found in newspapers, and television journalism is more often wanting, we would also add that both media—in addition to magazines, radio, and news sites on the Internet—have the potential to help people refine the tools of citizenship.

We have explored a number of roles the press assumes: historian, storyteller, amateur psychologist, soothsayer, shaper of events, and patriot. Although these roles coexist, some are more prominent at times than others. Throughout the period on which we have focused, the press often acted in what we consider its most important role, the custodian of fact. But when some roles are dominant, verifying fact becomes less central. Stories can shape the selection of facts and dismiss the impulse to search out the data that would undercut the story line. The watchdog role carries with it the assumption that the actions of those in power are suspect, their motives not transparent. In the patriot role, the impulse to challenge the actions of those who lead and probe their motives wanes.

We have made a number of recommendations for better reporting, some specific and some general. But these recommendations can be subsumed under a single overarching principle: The most critical obligation of journalists is to act as the custodians of fact. In order to do so, journalists must not only, in the words of *Washington Post* founder Eugene Meyer, "tell the truth as nearly as the truth can be ascertained,"[5] they must also insist that truth prevail throughout public debate. That means correcting misconceptions, reducing confusion, and punishing deception. In order to do so, reporters have to be cognizant not only of the methods that politicians and other political actors use to bend the truth, but of the lenses through which the reporters themselves see events and the frames that structure the stories they tell about them.

We understand that by subjecting reporters' work to lengthy critique and making the recommendations we do, we set a high standard for journalists, one that could make an already difficult job more challenging. But because the choices reporters make affect what the public knows, understands, and believes about the world, we believe that if democracy is to thrive, holding journalists to the highest standards is not only reasonable but essential. As many of the illustrations we have drawn confirm, journalists are more than capable of meeting those standards. When they do, the nation's government and its citizens are stronger for it.

Notes

Introduction

1. Robert Entman, "Framing: Toward Clarification of a Fractured Paradigm," *Journal of Communication* 43:51–58 (1993).

2. Oscar H. Gandy, Jr., "Epilogue," in Stephen Reese, Oscar H Gandy, Jr., and August Grant, eds., *Framing Public Life*. Mahwah, NJ: Lawrence Erlbaum, 2001, p. 365.

3. Gaye Tuchman, *Making News: A Study in the Construction of Reality*. New York: Free Press, 1978.

4. Herbert Gans, *Deciding What's News*. New York: Random House, 1979.

5. President Clinton vetoed the bill passed by Congress. In 2000, in the case of *Stenberg v. Carhart* the U.S. Supreme Court declared Nebraska's "partial birth abortion ban" unconstitutional, leaving in doubt whether the other bans could be enforced.

Chapter 1

1. The documentation for our account of Bush's 1988 use of the Horton narrative is in Jamieson's *Dirty Politics*. New York: Oxford University Press, 1992.

2. Excerpted on the *McNeil-Lehrer Newshour*, September 16, 1988.

3. This conservative political action committee, not the Bush campaign, paid for what is generally remembered as the "Willie Horton ad," featuring Horton's mug shot. Although Bush ran a well-known ad criticizing Dukakis's furlough program (known as "Revolving Door," it featured supposed menacing convicts traveling in and then out of a turnstile), the Bush campaign itself did not air any ads containing Horton's photo.

4. Tom Raum, "Bush Waiting for Gore Concession," Associated Press, December 13, 2000.

5. "Bush v Gore: The Fateful Ruling" *New York Times*, July 7, 2001, p. A12.

6. The Political Staff of the *Washington Post*, *Deadlock: The Inside Story of America's Closest Election*. New York: Public Affairs, 2001, pp. 234–235.

7. Anthony DePalma, "Cornwall Journal: In Tax Debate, A Hero or a Tobacco Hireling?" *New York Times*, June 27, 1998, p. A4.

8. Saundra Torry, "Tobacco Funds Allocation Adds Settlement Pressure," *Washington Post*, February 3, 1998, p. A8.

9. Kathleen Hall Jamieson, *Everything You Think You Know About Politics and Why You're Wrong*. New York: Basic Books, 2000.

10. Papers of the President, August 4, 1964, p. 627.

11. Michael Beschloss, *Reaching for Glory: Lyndon Johnson's Secret White House Tapes, 1964–1965*. New York: Simon & Schuster, 2001, p. 39.

12. Keith Richburg, "Mission to Hanoi: McNamara Asks Ex-Foes to Join in Search for

War's Lessons," *Washington Post*, November 11, 1995, p. A21.

13. William Safire, "Inside the Bunker," *New York Times*, September 13, 2001, p. A27.

14. Mike Allen, "White House Drops Claim of Threat to Bush," *Washington Post*, September 27, 2001, p. A8.

15. *60 Minutes*, January 19, 1992.

16. David Lauter and John Broder, "Bush Rhetoric Grows but Aides Are Cautious," *Los Angeles Times*, November 6, 1990, p. A4.

17. John R MacArthur, *Second Front: Censorship and Propaganda in the Gulf War*. New York: Hill and Wang, l992, pp. 57–60.

18. Morley Safer, "Iraqi Stealing Incubators From Babies May Have Been a Fraud," *60 Minutes*, January 19, 1992.

19. C. Wright Mills, *The Sociological Imagination*. New York: Oxford University Press, 1959, p. 125.

20. David Chandler, "The Patriot: No Letup in War of Words," *Boston Globe*, April 4, 1994, p. 25.

21. Ibid.

22. Ibid.

23. John Donnelly, "In Anti-Missile Test, Target Signaled Its Location," *Defense Week*, July 30, 2001.

24. Amos Tversky and Daniel Kahneman, "Availability: A Heuristic for Judging Frequency and Probability," *Cognitive Psychology* 5:207–232 (1973).

Chapter 2

1. Leonard Downie Jr. and Robert G. Kaiser, *The News About the News*. New York: Knopf, 2002, p. 8.

2. Meg Greenfield, *Washington*. New York: Public Affairs, 2001, pp. 86–87.

3. Lewis Lapham, *Lights, Camera, Democracy: Collected Essays*. New York: Random House, 2001, p. 82.

4. Dick Polman, "Gore Skewers Bush in Speech," *Philadelphia Inquirer*, April 14, 2002, p. A2.

5. Frank Bruni, *Ambling into History*. New York: HarperCollins, 2002, p. 46.

6. James David Barber, *The Presidential Character: Predicting Performance in the White House* (4th ed.). Englewood Cliffs, NJ: Prentice Hall, p. 1.

7. Leonard Downie Jr. and Robert G. Kaiser, *The News About the News*. New York: Knopf, 2002, p. 58.

8. Erving Goffman, *The Presentation of Self in Everyday Life*. New York: Doubleday, 1959.

9. Ibid., p. 128.

10. Seth Mnookin, "The Charm Offensive," *Brill's Content*, April 2000, p. 129.

11. Frank Bruni, *Ambling Into History: The Unlikely Odyssey of George W. Bush*. New York: HarperCollins, 2002, p. 25.

12. Ibid., p. 187.

13. For an extended discussion of this transformation, see Kathleen Hall Jamieson, *Eloquence in an Electronic Age: The Transformation of Political Speechmaking*. New York: Oxford University Press, 1988.

14. David Sears and Steven Chaffee, "Uses and Effects of the 1976 Debates: An Overview," in Sidney Kraus (ed.), *The Great Debates: Carter vs. Ford, 1976*. Bloomington: Indiana University Press, 1979.

15. Rick Shaughnessy, "Insights Run Second To Foes' Shortcomings," *San Diego Union Tribune*, October 14, 1988, p. A1.

16. Charles Krauthammer, "Why Dukakis is Losing," *Washington Post*, October 21, 1988, p. A23.

17. David Broder, "The Upside-Down Ticket," *Washington Post*, October 16, 1988, p. C7.

18. Clinton, understanding that the power of the town hall format lies in the candidates' ability to be seen connecting one-on-one with individual citizens, walked over to the questioner and said, "Tell me how it's affected you."

19. Jim Hoagland, "Bush's Place In History," *Washington Post*, October 17, 1992, p. A23.

20. *CBS Evening News*, October 17, 1992.

21. *Weekend Edition*, October 17, 1992.

22. *ABC World News Tonight*, October 16, 1992.

23. Samuel Popkin, *The Reasoning Voter*. Chicago: University of Chicago Press, 1991, pp. 76–77.

24. "The Choice For President." *Milwaukee Journal-Sentinel*, November 5, 2000, p. J4.

25. Richard Reeves, "Sometimes, Politics Really Smarts: The Ones Who Leave Lasting Legacies Aren't Always the Ones With the Highest IQs," *Los Angeles Times*, March 14, 2000, p. E1.

26. Clinton responded to reporter Steve Kroft's query about whether he had ever been unfaithful by saying, "I have caused pain in my marriage." A reasonable person would have interpreted this as an affirmative response.

27. David Broder, *Behind the Front Page*. New York: Simon & Schuster, 1987, p. 31.

28. *NBC Nightly News*, January 31, 2000.

29. Katherine Seelye and John Broder, "Questions of Veracity Have Long Dogged Gore," *New York Times*, February 17, 2000, p. A26.

30. Walter Robinson and Ann Scales, "Gore's Record Scrutinized for Veracity," *Boston Globe*, January 28, 2000, p. A1.

Chapter 3

1. Cathleen Decker, "At the Top, Focus Is on Candidates, Not Issues," *Los Angeles Times*, November 5, 2000, p. V1.

2. Judith Trent et al, "Image, Media Bias, and Voter Characteristics," *American Behavioral Scientist* 44:2101–2124 (2001).

3. Francis Wheen, "It's Dumbo v. Pinocchio: George Dubya's Way With Words," *The Guardian*, October 25, 2000, p. 5.

4. Donald Kinder, "Presidential Character Revisited," in *Political Cognition*, Richard Lau and David Sears (eds.). Hillsdale, NJ: Lawrence Erlbaum Associates, 1986.

5. Richard Berke, "Tendency to Embellish Facts Snares Gore," *New York Times*, October 6, 2000, p. A26.

6. Melinda Henneberger, "Tall Tales: Is What We've Got Here a Compulsion to Exaggerate?" *New York Times*, October 15, 2000, section 4, p. 1. Reporters are not the only ones who indulge in psychoanalysis. In April 2000, Jamieson wondered in an interview whether Gore's exaggerations suggested a "personality flaw." Walter Robinson and Michael Crowley, "Record Shows Gore Long Embellishing Truth," *Boston Globe*, April 11, 2000, p. A1.

7. Sissela Bok, *Lying: Moral Choice in Public and Private Life*. New York: Random House, 1978, p. 185.

8. Mike Allen, "Politics a Key Force in Forging Policy," *Washington Post*, March 6, 2002, p. E1.

9. Nicholas Kristof, "The 2000 Campaign: The Decision," *New York Times*, October 29, 2000, p. A1.

10. "Bush Pitches Himself as 'Reformer With Results' in Dig at McCain," *St. Louis Post-Dispatch*, February 8, 2000, p. A9.

11. David Lightman, "A No-Show's Good Showing," *Hartford Courant*, February 9, 2000, p. A7.

12. Kathleen Hall Jamieson and Paul Waldman (eds.), *Electing the President 2000: The Insiders' View*. Philadelphia: University of Pennsylvania Press, 2001, p. 192.

13. Lecture at Annenberg School for Communication, University of Pennsylvania, September 2001.

14. *CNN Saturday Morning News*, March 13, 1999.

15. Robert Parry, "He's No Pinocchio," *Washington Monthly*, April 2000.

16. Katherine Seelye, "Gore Borrows Clinton's Shadow Back to Share a Bow," *New York Times*, December 1, 1999, p. A20; Ceci Connelly, "Gore Paints Himself As No Beltway Baby," *Washington Post*, December 1, 1999, p. A10.

17. Ceci Connelly, "First Love Story, Now Love Canal," *Washington Post*, December 2, 1999, p. A14. Gore had discussed with reporters a newspaper article claiming that he and Tipper had been the models for the couple in *Love Story*. After disputing some of the details in the article Gore had read (including whether Tipper had figured in the book's creation), author Erich Segal confirmed that he modeled the novel's protagonist on Gore and his Harvard roommate, actor Tommy Lee Jones.

18. Elaine Schrader, "Gore Goes to Florida, Leaves Elian Issue Behind," *Los Angeles Times*, April 8, 2000, p. A10.

19. *World News Tonight*, March 30, 2000.

20. *Face the Nation*, April 30, 2000.

21. "Fallout From Elian Raid Will Hurt Gore Most, Analysts Say," *Sarasota Herald-Tribune*, April 30, 2000, p. A12.

22. Kathleen Hall Jamieson and Paul Waldman (eds.), *Electing the President 2000: The Insiders' View*. Philadelphia, PA: University of Pennsylvania Press, 2001, p. 77.

23. Michael Kelly, "Farmer Al," *Washington Post*, March 24, 1999, p. A27.

24. *Inside Politics*, CNN, March 19, 1999.

25. June 16, 1999.

26. "A Question of Character," Project for Excellence in Journalism, 2000.

27. Maria La Ganga, "Bush Portrays Gore As Hypocrite on Hollywood Issue," *Los Angeles Times*, September 21, 2000, p. A1.

28. Clay Robison, "Now Playing: 'Gore the Chameleon,'" *Houston Chronicle*, September 24, 2000, Outlook, p. 2.

29. Laurence McQuillan, "Gore Campaign Faces Questions About Anecdotes," *USA Today*, September 20, 2000, p. A13.

30. Glenn Johnson, "Prescription Story Is a Pill for Gore," *Boston Globe*, September 19, 2000, p. A7.

31. "Social Security Showdown," *Wall Street Journal*, October 26, 2000, p. A26.

32. "Election Year Gimmick," *Atlanta Journal and Constitution*, September 26, 2000, p. 18A.

33. "Swapping Oil for Votes," *Detroit News*, September 26, 2000, p. 8.

34. "Petroleum Pander," *Providence Journal*, September 25, 2000, p. 4B.

35. Kathleen Hall Jamieson and Paul Waldman (eds.), *Electing the President: The Insiders' View*. Philadelphia: University of Pennsylvania Press, 2001, p. 72.

36. Richard Benedetto, "Poll: Bush More Honest, Likable; Gore Losing Ground After First Debate," *USA Today*, October 10, 2000, p. A1.

37. Jackie Calmes and John Harwood, "Course Correction," *Wall Street Journal*, September 15, 2000, p. A1.

38. Kathleen Hall Jamieson and Paul Waldman (eds.), *Electing the President: The Insiders' View*. Philadelphia: University of Pennsylvania Press, 2001, p. 190.

39. Richard Berke, "Bush Is the Man. The Issue Is What He's Made Of," *New York Times*, August 22, 1999, Week in Review, p. 1.

40. "The Test of His Life," *Newsweek*, December 25, 2000/January 1, 2001, p. 36.

41. *Newsweek*, Dec. 25, 2000/Jan. 1, 2001, p. 85.

42. Carla Marinucci, "Bush Gets (Green) Egg On His Face Over Reading List," *San Francisco Chronicle*, November 13, 1999, p. A1.

43. "Books for Christmas," *American Spectator*, December 1998.

44. Arthur Hoppe, "The Very Hungry George W. Bush," *San Francisco Chronicle*, November 17, 1999, p. A27.

45. John Connelly, "Bush Bolsters Texas' Justice System," *Seattle Post-Intelligencer*, June 23, 2000, p. A1.

46. "Hot Spots Put Texan Bush on the Spot," *St. Petersburg Times*, June 23, 1999, p. 3A.

47. Kevin Merida, *Washington Post*, January 19, 2000, p. C1.

48. Dana Milbank, "What's On W's Mind? Hard to Say," *Washington Post*, May 5, 2000, p. C1.

49. Frank Bruni, "Bush's Tune Is the Same Even as the Pitch Varies," *New York Times*, September 16, 2000, p. A10.

50. Frank Bruni, "Bush Stumbles, and Questions Are Raised Anew," *New York Times*, August 24, 2000, p. A23.

51. Edwin Chen, "Campaign 2000: Gore Questions Bush's Qualifications," *Los Angeles Times*, April 30, 2000, p. A1.

52. "Excerpts From a Talk With the Vice President," *New York Times*, March 12, 2000, p. A38; Katherine Seelye, "Gore Challenges Bush Credibility on Policy Speeches," *New York Times*, April 13, 2000, p. A26.

53. Kathleen Hall Jamieson and Paul Waldman (eds.), *Electing the President 2000: The Insiders' View*. Philadelphia: University of Pennsylvania Press, 2001, p. 166.

54. Katherine Seelye, "Attacks Grow Sharp As Time Dwindles," *New York Times*, November 4, 2000, p. A1.

55. David Sears, "Political Behavior," in Gardner Lindsey and Elliot Aronson (eds.), *Handbook of Social Psychology*. Reading, MA: Addison-Wesley, 1969.

56. "Audiences Fragmented and Skeptical: The Tough Job of Communicating With Voters," press release, Pew Research Center for the People and the Press, February 5, 2000.

57. Marshall Sella, "The Stiff Guy vs. The Dumb Guy," *New York Times Magazine*, September 24, 2000, p. 72.

58. According to the Center for Media and Public Affairs, which tracks the target (but not the content) of late-night humor on Leno, Letterman, Conan O'Brien, and *Politically Incorrect*, over the entire year of 2000, George W. Bush was the target of 771 jokes, edging out Bill Clinton (725) and clearly outdistancing Al Gore (494).

59. Hedrick Smith, *The Power Game: How Washington Works*. New York: Random House, 1988.

60. Zaller, John, "The Rule of Product Substitution in Campaign News," in *Election Studies: What's Their Use?* Elihu Katz and Yael Warshel (eds.), Boulder, CO: Westview, 2001, p. 248.

61. Arthur Miller, Martin Wattenberg, and Oksana Malanchuk, "Cognitive Representations of Candidate Assessments," in Keith Sanders et al., *Political Communication Yearbook 1984*. Carbondale, IL: Southern Illinois University Press, 1985; David Glass, "Evaluating Presidential Candidates: Who Focuses on Their Personal Attributes?" *Public Opinion Quarterly* 49:517–534 (1985).

62. Scott Keeter, "The Illusion of Intimacy: Television and the Role of Candidate

Personal Qualities in Voter Choice," *Public Opinion Quarterly* 51:344–358 (1987).

Chapter 4

1. Evan Thomas and Michael Isikoff, "The Truth Behind the Pillars," *Newsweek*, December 25, 2000/January 1, 2001, p. 46.
2. Jonathan Alter, "36 Days: The Fallout," *Newsweek*, Dec. 25, 2000/Jan 1, 2001, p. 56.
3. Richard Benedetto, "Last Dash for Votes: Bush Holds Slight Lead Over Gore as Race Winds Down," *USA Today*, November 6, 2000, p.1A.
4. Tom Brokaw, "Lessons for the Age of 24/7," *Newsweek*, Dec. 25, 2000/Jan. 1, 2001, p. 57.
5. Scott Stossel, "Echo Chamber of Horrors," *American Prospect*, December 18, 2000, p. 19.
6. Thomas Patterson, *Out of Order*. New York: Knopf, 1993.

Chapter 5

1. Douglas Cater, *The Fourth Branch of Government*. Boston: Houghton Mifflin, 1959, p. 7.
2. Timothy Cook, *Governing With the News*. Chicago: University of Chicago Press, 1998, p. 3.
3. Walter Lippman, *Public Opinion*. New York: Macmillan, 1922, p. 229.
4. Data courtesy of Nielsen Media Research.
5. Kathleen Hall Jamieson and Paul Waldman (eds.), *Electing the President 2000: The Insiders' View*. University of Pennsylvania Press, 2001, pp. 116–17.
6. John Bresnahan, "Bush Wants Hill Leaders to Turn Up Heat on Gore," *Roll Call*, November 13, 2000, p.3.
7. "Campaign 2000: The Daily Fix," *Boston Globe*, November 6, 2000, p. A23.
8. "The Last, Frenzied Push for Votes," *Christian Science Monitor*, November 6, 2000, p. A1.
9. Bob Deans, "Electoral Shock: Winning the Most Votes Doesn't Guarantee the White House," *Atlanta Constitution*, November 5, 2000, p. 1F.
10. Michael Kramer, "Bush Set to Fight an Electoral College Loss," *Daily News*, November 1, 2000, p. 6.

11. Kathleen Hall Jamieson and Paul Waldman (eds.), *Electing the President 2000: The Insiders' View*. Philadelphia: University of Pennsylvania Press, 2001, p. 217.
12. Jeff Greenfield, *Oh Waiter! One Order of Crow!* New York: Putnam, 2001, p. 14.
13. "Election 2000: Words From the Two Camps," *Boston Globe*, November 9, 2000, p. D2.
14. *This Week*, November 19, 2000.
15. Somini Sengupta, University of Pennsylvania forum, February 2001.
16. Richard Perez-Peña, "G.O.P. and Democrats Trading Accusations on Military Votes," *New York Times*, November 19, 2000, p. A1.
17. Richard Perez-Peña, "Floridians Abroad Are Counted, Or Not, As Counties Interpret 'Rules' Differently," *New York Times*, November 18, 2000, p. A11.
18. Dana Milbank, "Bush Sues 13 Counties Over Ballots of Military," *Washington Post*, November 23, 2000, p. A28.
19. Campaign representatives never saw the actual ballot on which the votes were indicated. The ballot envelope contained all the information that was used to judge whether the ballot was valid. Once the ballot was judged valid, it was removed from the envelope and counted.
20. Dana Milbank, "Bush Sues 13 Counties Over Ballots of Military," *Washington Post*, November 23, 2000, p. A28.
21. David Barstow and Don Van Natta Jr., "How Bush Took Florida: Mining the Overseas Absentee Vote," *New York Times*, July 15, 2001, p. 1.
22. Susan Schmidt, "Military Ballot Review is Urged," *Washington Post*, November 21, 2000, p. A1.
23. Scott Shepard, "GOP Urges Recount of Military Votes," *Atlanta Journal-Constitution*, November 22, 2001, p. A13.
24. Alicia Caldwell, "Challenges Dog Overseas Ballot Count," *St. Petersburg Times*, November 19, 2000, p. A9.
25. Shailagh Murray, Sarah Lueck, and Trevor Banstetter, "GOP Says Democrats Wrongly Discarded Hundreds of Overseas Absentee Ballots," *Wall Street Journal*, November 21, 2000, p. A28.
26. Quoted by Barstow and Van Natta, *New York Times*, July 15, 2001, p. 17.
27. *Washington Times* reporter Bill Sammon later wrote in his book *At Any Cost: How Al Gore Tried to Steal the Election* that

"some envelopes had been signed by sailors on rolling seas in hostile situations" (excerpted in "Stiffing the Troops Overseas," *Washington Times*, May 8, 2001, p. A1).

28. Raja Mishra, "Bush Suit Eyes Military Votes," *Boston Globe*, November 23, 2000, p. A7.

29. Florida law allowed for absentee ballots with no postmark to count, but only if the voter had signed and dated the ballot envelope.

30. *Inside Politics*, November 20, 2000.

31. Paul Richter and Eric Bailey, "Unanswered Call on Military Ballots," *Los Angeles Times*, November 21, 2000, p. A1.

32. Evan Thomas and Michael Isikoff, "Shootout in the Sun," *Newsweek*, November 27, 2000, pp. 30–32.

33. Michael Cooper, "G.O.P. Drops a Suit," *New York Times*, November 26, 2000, p. A1.

34. David Barstow and Don Van Natta Jr., "How Bush Took Florida: Mining the Overseas Absentee Vote," *New York Times*, July 15, 2001, p.1.

35. *New York Times*, July 15, 2001, p. A16.

36. "Florida's Flawed Ballots," *New York Times*, July 16, 2001, A14.

37. "With Nation Split, Leaders Must Reach Across Party Divide," *Roll Call*, November 9, 2000, p. 6.

38. "Bush, Gore Must Stop Push Toward Constitutional Brink," *Roll Call*, November 13, 2000, p. 5.

39. "Despite the Fuss, Next President and Hill Can Deal," *Roll Call*, November 16, 2000, p. 9.

40. John Bresnahan, "Bush Looks To Democrats," *Roll Call*, November 30, 2000, p. 1.

41. Susan Crabtree, "Impatience with Gore Growing," *Roll Call*, November 30, 2000, p. 1.

42. "GOP Should Stop Pushing Gore to Drop Contest," *Roll Call*, November 30, 2000, p. 5.

43. "After Failing to Deliver for Bush at Polls, GOP Governors Try Again," *Roll Call*, November 30, 2000, p. 6.

44. "Daschle Says He'll Try to Co-operate With Bush, But . . .," *Roll Call*, December 7, 2000, p. 8.

45. Somini Sengupta, University of Pennsylvania forum, February 2001.

46. Jeffrey Toobin, *Too Close to Call*. New York: Random House, 2001.

47. R.W. Apple, "The Limits of Patience," *New York Times*, November 12, 2000, p. A1.

48. 505 U.S. 833 (1992).

49. David Strauss, "Bush v. Gore: What Were They Thinking?" in Cass Sunstein and Richard Epstein (eds.), *The Vote: Bush, Gore & The Supreme Court*. Chicago: University of Chicago Press, 2001.

50. John DiIulio, "Equal Protection Run Amok," *Weekly Standard*, December 25, 2000.

51. *Roll Call*, December 7, 2000, p. 14.

Chapter 6

1. Richard Berke, "It's Not a Time for Party, But for How Long?" *New York Times*, September 23, 2001, section 4, p. 3.

2. Michael Isikoff, "The Final Word?" *Newsweek* Web exclusive, November 19, 2001.

3. Daniel Hallin, *We Keep America on Top of the World*. New York: Routledge, 1994.

4. Howard Kurtz, "George W. Bush, Now More Than Ever," *Washington Post*, November 12, 2001, p. C1.

5. *Today*, NBC, October 12, 2001.

6. Brigitte Lebens Nacos, *The Press, Presidents, and Crises*. New York: Columbia University Press, 1990.

7. Richard Brody, *Assessing the President: The Media, Elite Opinion, and Public Support*. Stanford, CA: Stanford University Press.

8. "Inside People," *People*, October 1, 2001, p. 7.

9. Felicity Barringer, "Pulitzers Focus on Sept. 11, and The Times Wins 7," *New York Times*, April 9, 2002, p. A1.

10. Scott Lindlaw, "Powell Says Terror Network May Be Using Public Statements to Convey Hidden Message," Associated Press, October 10, 2001.

11. "Tell the Bloody Truth," *Cleveland Plain Dealer*, October 5, 2001, p. B8.

12. Neal Travis, "Times Off," *New York Post*, October 8, 2001, p.11.

13. When the United States began its attack on Afghanistan, most switched to some variant of "America Strikes Back."

14. Karal Ann Marling, "Salve for a Wounded People," *New York Times*, October 14, 2001, p. B1.

15. Richard Brookhiser, "Our Day of Infamy," *National Review*, October 1, 2001, p. 17.

16. "A New Date of Infamy," *Newsweek*, Extra Edition, p. 24.

17. Richard Falk, "A Just Response," *The Nation*, October 8, 2001, p. 11.

18. Victor Davis Hanson, "What Are We Made Of?" *National Review*, October 1, 2001, p. 14.

19. Sonja Barisic, "Dedication of Memorial to Cole Victims Planned," *Buffalo News*, October 8, 2001, p. A3.

20. Gar Younge, "Bush Rejects Bin Laden Deal," *The Guardian*, September 21, 2001, p. 1.

21. Chicago: University of Chicago Press, 1991.

22. Greg Ryan, "It's the Same, But Not," *New York Times*, December 2, 2001, p. A5.

23. James Risen and Todd Purdum, "Inquiries Into Failures of Intelligence Community Are Put Off Until Next Year," *New York Times*, November 23, 2001, p. B5.

24. Eric Schmitt, "After the Attacks: The Vice President," *New York Times*, September 17, 2001, p. A2.

25. Serge Schmemann, "U.S. Attacked," *New York Times*, September 12, 2001, p. A1.

26. Ibid.

27. Clyde Haberman, "The Distance Traveled in a Month of War," *New York Times*, October 14, 2001, p. 4.

28. David Broder, "Reasons for Pride," *Washington Post*, September 18, 2001, p. A31.

29. Howard Kurtz, "CNN Chief Orders 'Balance' in War News; Reporters Are Told to Remind Viewers Why U.S. Is Bombing," *Washington Post*, October 31, 2001, p. C1.

30. This memo was posted on Jim Romanesko's Media News (www.poynter.org/medianews).

31. Michael Getler, "Uncivil Wars," *Washington Post*, April 21, 2002, p. B6.

32. Elaine Sciolino, "Who Hates the U.S.? Who Loves It?" *New York Times*, September 23, 2001, section 4, p. 1.

33. Joe Klein, "Closework," *The New Yorker*, October 1, 2001, p. 48.

34. "Enormous TV Audience Peaked with Bush Talk," *New York Times*, September 13, 2001, p. A24.

35. Steven Mufson, "War Cabinet: Veterans on Familiar Ground," *Washington Post*, October 1, 2001, p. A12.

36. Daniel Eisenberg, "Wartime Recession?," *Time*, October 1, 2001, p. 80.

37. Robert L. Kaiser, "Trip to New York Isn't Business as Usual," *Chicago Tribune*, October 2, 2001, p. 1.

38. Joe Klein, "Closework," *New Yorker*, October 1, 2001, p. 49.

39. "On Language: Words at War," *New York Times Magazine*, September 30, 2001, p. 26.

40. James Dao and Eric Schmitt, *New York Times*, December 6, 2001, p. 1.

41. Vernon Loeb, "U.S. May Have Killed Commando," *Philadelphia Inquirer*, March 30, 2002, p. A4.

42. Jim Rutenberg, "Fox Portrays a War of Good and Evil, and Many Applaud," *New York Times*, December 3, 2001, p. C1.

43. "America as Reflected in Its Leader," *New York Times*, January 6, 2002, section 4, p. 1.

44. Glen Johnson, "In Iowa, Candidate Shows Tendency to Trip on Words," *Boston Globe*, August 23, 2000, p. A18.

45. Maria LaGanga, "Bush Tallies Up the Trillions, Trips," *Los Angeles Times*, August 23, 2000, p. A14.

46. Lars-Erik Nelson, "Bush Has a Gaffe Problem: Press Is Lying in Wait for Next Verbal Stumble," *New York Daily News*, August 25, 2000, p. 55.

47. "Details in State of Change Left Bush Struggling," *New York Times*, November 23, 2000, p. A34.

48. Corey Kilgannon, "Keeping an Ear on Bush," *New York Times*, February 4, 2001, Week in Review, p. 2.

49. David Greene and Paul Adams, "Reagan National Set to Reopen Tomorrow," *Baltimore Sun*, October 3, 2001, p. 10A.

50. Sarah Fritz, "Bush, Putin Forge Genuine Alliance," *St. Petersburg Times*, November 18, 2001, p. 2A.

51. David Jackson, "From Florida to Afghanistan, a Year of Making History for Bush," *Dallas Morning News*, December 13, 2001, p. 10A.

52. Jeffrey Birnbaum, "The Making of a President, 2001," *Fortune*, November 12, 2001.

53. Elisabeth Bumiller, "Seeing is Believing: America Reflected in Its Leader," *New York Times*, January 6, 2002, p. A1.

54. Dona Milbank, "Amid War Talk, Bush Aims for 'Normal,'" *Washington Post*, September 27, 2001, p. A4.

55. Patrick Tyler and Elizabeth Bumiller, "Bush Offers Taliban '2nd Chance' to Yield," *New York Times*, October 12, 2001, p. A1.

56. "Mr. Bush's New Gravitas," *New York Times*, October 12, 2001, p. A24.

57. Judy Keen, "President Soothes, Warns in Remarks," *USA Today*, October 12, 2001, p. 3A.

58. Dana Milbank, "For President, Reassuring a Jittery Nation," *Washington Post*, October 12, 2001, p. A19.

59. David Lightman, "Bush: Terrorists on the Run," *Hartford Courant*, October 12, 2001, p. A1.

60. David Sanger and Patrick Tyler, "Wartime Forges a United Front for Bush Aides," *New York Times*, December 23, 2001, p. A1.

61. Andy Seller, "Are We Laughing Yet?" *USA Today*, October 5, 2001, p. 2E.

62. Richard Huff, "A Tale of the Tapes: Reruns Post-September 11," *Daily News*, October 25, 2001, p. 110.

63. Dick Polman, "A President Pardoned," *Philadelphia Inquirer Magazine*, January 6, 2002, p. 13.

64. Daniel Hallin, *We Keep America on Top of the World*. New York: Routledge, 1994, p. 107.

65. Jim Rutenberg and Bill Carter, "Draping Newscasts With the Flag," *New York Times*, September 20, 2001, p. C8.

66. For a theory of how this process works, see W. Lance Bennett, "Toward a Theory of Press-State Relations in the United States," *Journal of Communication* 40 (Spring 1990):103–127.

67. See W. Lance Bennett and David L Paletz (eds.), *Taken by Storm: The Media, Public Opinion, and U.S. Foreign Policy in the Gulf War*. Chicago: University of Chicago Press, 1994.

68. Steven Thomma, "Bush's Popularity Is Still High, But It Has Taken a Few Knocks," *Philadelphia Inquirer*, April 20, 2002, p. A3.

69. Michael Hirsh and Michael Isikoff, "What Went Wrong," *Newsweek*, May 27, 2002, p. 33.

70. Howard Kurtz, "The Second-Guessing Syndrome," washingtonpost.com, June 13, 2002.

71. *The News With Brian Williams*, June 12, 2002.

72. David Rosenbaum, "Years of Unheeded Alarms," *New York Times*, September 12, 2001, p. A25.

Chapter 7

1. David Remnick, "Scoop," *The New Yorker*, January 29, 1996, p. 42.

2. Howard Rosenberg, "Presidential Debate: It's Not What's Said but Media Spin on What's Said," *Los Angeles Times*, October 4, 2000, p. A10.

3. Richard Ericson, "How Journalists Visualize Fact," *Annals of the American Academy of Political and Social Science* 560:83–95 (1998).

4. Todd Gitlin, "Bites and Blips: Chunk News, Savvy Talk, and the Bifurcation of American Politics," in Peter Dahlgren and Colin Sparks (eds.), *Communication and Citizenship: Journalism and the Public Sphere in the New Media Age*. London: Routledge, 1991.

5. Joseph Cappella and Kathleen Hall Jamieson, *Spiral of Cynicism: The Press and the Public Good*. New York: Oxford University Press, 1997.

6. S. Robert Lichter, "A Plague on Both Parties: Substance and Fairness in TV Election News," *Harvard Journal of Press/Politics* 6(3):8–30 (2001).

7. Daniel Hallin, "Sound Bite News: Television Coverage of Elections, 1968–1988," *Journal of Communication* 42:5–24 (1992).

8. For an extended discussion of the rise of objectivity, see Michael Schudson, *Discovering the News*. New York: Basic Books, 1978.

9. Daniel Hallin, *We Keep America on Top of the World: Television Journalism and the Public Sphere*. New York: Routledge, 1994.

10. E. J. Dionne, *They Only Look Dead*. New York: Simon & Schuster, 1996, p. 246.

11. Dave D'Alessio and Mike Allen, "Media Bias in Presidential Elections: A Meta-Analysis," *Journal of Communication* 50:133–156 (2000).

12. Mark Watts et al., "Elite Cues and Media Bias in Presidential Campaigns: Explaining Public Perceptions of a Liberal Press," *Communication Research* 26:144–175 (1999).

13. Eric Boehlert, "The Press vs. Al Gore," *Rolling Stone*, December 6–13, 2001.

14. John Mintz, "It's Not As Easy As 1-2-3; Problems Exist With Both Hand, Machine Counts," *Washington Post*, November 19, 2000, p. A1.

15. Joe Strupp and Greg Mitchell, "Needles and Spin," *Editor and Publisher*, December 11, 2000, p. 21.

16. E. J. Dionne, *They Only Look Dead*. New York: Simon & Schuster, 1996, p. 254.

17. Larry DiMatteo, *Contract Theory: The Evolution of Contractual Intent*. East Lansing: Michigan State University Press, 1998.

18. "I Tried to Walk a Fine Line . . . I Have Paid a High Price," *Washington Post*, January 20, 2001, p. A19.

19. According to *New York Daily News*, Lay and his wife donated over $600,000 to George W. Bush, including a $100,000 donation to the Bush-Cheney inaugural fund. Bob Port, "When Dubya and Lay Were As Closeasthis," *New York Daily News*, February 3, 2002, p. 9.

20. Bennett Roth, "Ken Who? Bush Team Plays Defense," *Houston Chronicle*, January 11, 2002, Business section, p. 1.

21. We are following Schorr's account here. See Daniel Schorr, *Staying Tuned: A Life in Journalism*. New York: Washington Square Press, 2001, p. 270.

22. Terry Neal and Edward Walsh, "Bush Begins N.Y. Swing Talking Breast Cancer," *Washington Post*, March 5, 2000, p. A6.

23. Thomas Ginsberg, "With Statistics, Consider the Source and Method," *Philadelphia Inquirer*, July 8, 2001, p. E3.

24. Excerpts from a House Hearing on Destruction of Enron Documents, *New York Times*, January 25, 2002, p. C9.

25. Elisabeth Bumiller, "If the Math's a Bit Fuzzy, The Politics Are Clear," *New York Times*, January 21, 2002, p. A11.

26. William March, "Republican Rhetoric Deals Sharp Blow to Governor," *Tampa Tribune*, January 24, 2002.

27. *NBC Nightly News*, January 23, 2002.

28. David Rosenbaum, "Doing the Math on Bush's Tax Cut," *New York Times*, March 4, 2001, p. 22.

29. Benjamin Lowe, "Jobless Rate Posts First Drop Since May," *Philadelphia Inquirer*, February 2, 2002, p. A1.

30. "For Bush's 'Typical' Tax Family, Lots of Restrictions," *Washington Post*, September 13, 2000, p. A1.

31. Some examples from early in the general election included Richard Stevenson, "Benefits and Drawbacks to Bush and Gore Proposals for Overhauling Social Security," *New York Times*, May 19, 2000, p. A19; Steven Thomma, "Gore and Bush Budgets Rely on Unreliable Figures," *Philadelphia Inquirer*, May 7, 2000, p. D3.

32. "Prior Endorsements—And Two New Ones," *Omaha World-Herald*, September 5, 2000, p. 8B.

33. Michael Grunwald, "Some Facts Clear in the War of Spin Over Arctic Refuge," *Washington Post*, March 6, 2002, p. A3.

34. *Nightline*, March 23, 2001.

35. David Noonan, "A Voter's Panic Guide," *Newsweek*, November 6, 2000, p. 34.

36. Chris Clayton, "Gore Benefits From Farm Issues," *Omaha World-Herald*, January 9, 2000, p. 14A.

Conclusion

1. David Broder, *Behind the Front Page*. New York: Simon & Schuster, 1987, p. 19.

2. Ben Bradlee, *A Good Life*. New York: Simon & Schuster, 1995, p. 432.

3. Bill Kovach and Tom Rosensteil, *The Elements of Journalism: What Newspeople Should Know and the Public Should Expect*. New York: Crown, 2001, p. 17.

4. Leonard Downie Jr and Robert G. Kaiser, *The News About the News: American Journalism in Peril*. New York: Knopf, 2002, p. 258.

5. Ibid., p. 13.

Index